Crude Reality

Exploring World History

Series Editors
John McNeill, Georgetown University
Jerry Bentley, University of Hawai`i

As the world grows ever more closely linked, students and general readers alike are appreciating the need to become internationally aware. World history offers the crucial connection to understanding past global links and how they influence the present. The series will expand that awareness by offering clear, concise supplemental texts for the undergraduate classroom as well as trade books that advance world history scholarship.

The series will be open to books taking a thematic approach—exploring commodities such as sugar, cotton, and petroleum; technologies; diseases and the like; or regional—for example, Islam in Southeast Asia or east Africa, the Indian Ocean, or the Ottoman Empire. The series sees regions not simply as fixed geographical entities but as evolving spatial frameworks that have reflected and shaped the movement of people, ideas, goods, capital, institutions, and information. Thus, regional books would move beyond traditional borders to consider the flows that have characterized the global system.

Edited by two of the leading historians in the field, this series will work to synthesize world history for students, engage general readers, and expand the boundaries for scholars.

Crude Reality

Petroleum in World History

Brian C. Black

ROWMAN & LITTLEFIELD PUBLISHERS, INC.
Lanham • Boulder • New York • Toronto • Plymouth, UK

Published by Rowman & Littlefield Publishers, Inc.
A wholly owned subsidiary of The Rowman & Littlefield Publishing Group, Inc.
4501 Forbes Boulevard, Suite 200, Lanham, Maryland 20706
www.rowman.com

Estover Road, Plymouth PL6 7PY, United Kingdom

British Library Cataloguing in Publication Information Available

Library of Congress Cataloging-in-Publication Data

Black, Brian, 1966–
  Crude reality : petroleum in world history / Brian C. Black.
     p. cm. — (Exploring world history)
  Includes bibliographical references and index.
  ISBN 978-0-7425-5654-6 (cloth : alk. paper) — ISBN 978-1-4422-1611-2 (electronic)
  1. Petroleum—Economic aspects—History. 2. Petroleum products—History. 3.
Petroleum industry and trade—Social aspects—History. I. Title.
  HD9560.5.B494 2012
  338.2'728209—dc23

2011051805

Printed in the United States of America

For Don and Bev

Contents

Acknowledgments

Many of us in the field of environmental history trace our own efforts to the work of a few select scholars of the past thirty years. I am particularly fortunate that I can claim that my work grows not only from the writing of Donald Worster, but also from his person. For those of us who have benefited from his generosity and intellect, we also owe a debt to his partner, Bev. Together, they have helped to inspire a new generation of historians. I dedicate this book to them because of all that their hard work has made possible for me and for others.

The preparation of this manuscript benefited from my students in courses in global environmental history and the input of a few anonymous reviewers and of colleagues including Adam Rome, John McNeill, Bill Bowman, Ty Priest, Joe Pratt, David Nye, Ed Levri, Joel Tarr, and Marty Melosi. In recent years, many of us have worked hard as a group to broaden the consideration of energy by historians and, in particular, the consideration of energy within a global context. I especially salute the care of Richard Tucker in helping me to bring the manuscript over the finish line.

I wish to acknowledge the hard work of Susan McEachern and everyone at the press, as well as at my home institution of Penn State Altoona. Todd Davis, Ken Womack, Carolyn Mahan, Ian Marshall, and the rest of my good colleagues continue to make it a wonderful place to teach, write, and learn. And, as always, Chris, Ben, and Sam are where it begins and ends. I offer a particular shout-out for Ben's work on the figures contained in these pages.

Finally, though, I will never look at this book without considering Hal Rothman, the UNLV historian who died in 2007. He possessed a knack for providing context and perspective—the "big picture"—as well as for speaking his mind. As we drove near Anchorage, Alaska, in the late 1990s, I had finished writing *Petrolia* and was ready to turn to other, less gritty topics. He turned to me and said: "You're always going to be the oil guy, you know. You gotta keep writing about oil." We all lost Hal entirely too early; however, I feel blessed that I, ultimately, could follow a bit of his sage advice.

Prologue

Dependence, which is tied closely to supply, is the core feature of humans' contemporary relationship with petroleum. Initially, oil flowed so freely that a barrel cost just a few dollars. Oil was so cheap that we used it not just for fuel but also to simplify the manufacture of everyday products, ranging from toothpaste to water bottles. Most often, these were products that we first made without petroleum, but cheap crude made them less expensive. In other words, we looked for ways of making crude more integral in everyday human life!

When for a variety of reasons the price paradigm shifted during the late twentieth century and petroleum's value skyrocketed, nations dependent on oil found themselves at the mercy of a new world order. This current situation is our "crude reality."

The world's voracious demand for consistent supplies of crude propelled its status beyond that of a mere resource to one of a critical actor, capable of shaping an entire way of life—a culture. The following pages tell the story of the construction of our petroleum culture to the point where, today, humans in most developed nations can be said to exist within an "ecology of oil" in which fundamental needs and practices of our species would be impossible without it. An "ecology," however, does not stop with just utility; our ecology of oil also includes the larger implications and issues created by using crude. Recognition of this totality offers the best promise for helping us create a more sensible energy future.

We must understand the history of our life with oil because of the story that plays out all around us in the early twenty-first century. In short, our dependence places us on an inevitable collision course with petroleum's finite supply. Unfortunately, just by reading the daily news, we each have a front-row seat to a dramatic energy transition. It may come in the form of headlines announcing that "China Becomes World Leader in Alternative Energy" or "Oil Prices

1

Rise above $100 per Barrel with No End in Sight" or "BP Found Negligent in 2010 Gulf Spill." Large-scale issues growing out of our ecology of oil, such as climate change, might also define our future in the form of changing weather patterns or rising sea levels. And, finally, the larger lessons of our crude reality might come in accounts of events that seem to have very little relation to oil.

For instance, a news story out of Afghanistan reported that U.S. General Stanley "McChrystal waded through knee-high water to view the blackened NATO tankers, which exploded when a U.S. F-15E Strike Eagle jet dropped two 500-pound (225-kilogram) bombs on them a few miles (kilometers) outside the main town in northern Kunduz province."[1] Essential to the war and occupation in Afghanistan, tankers of petroleum such as these became easy targets for hijacking by Taliban sympathizers hostile to U.S. and NATO forces. Taliban raids on fuel convoys were designed to undermine the American containment effort, which attempted to undercut the Taliban by attacking known gatherings or pockets of its operatives. On this day, the plans of both Taliban and NATO forces went desperately awry. The account continues:

> Reporters traveling with him saw about a dozen small yellow fuel cans had survived the blasts. Several were still full of fuel.
> The NATO investigative team flew over the site on the Kunduz River where the U.S. jet, called in by the German military, bombed the tankers, which reportedly became stuck trying to cross a river. German officials have said the Taliban may have been planning a suicide attack on the military's nearby Kunduz base using the tankers, which were hijacked carrying NATO fuel supplies from neighboring Tajikistan.

Intended for use in armored vehicles known as Humvees, the gasoline was a symbolic extension of military occupation. Now abandoned by the attackers, the wasted crude became the trophy of local residents, who scooped it into small plastic containers. Instead of powering part of the greatest fighting force known to man, a liter or two would be funneled to their homes' heaters, lamps, or stoves. Attempting to keep the fuel from falling into the Taliban's hands, a U.S. bomber mistakenly killed seventy of the scavengers.

A suspended snapshot, this tragedy inadvertently captures the multifaceted human relationship with petroleum and suggests the complexity of our modern world's use of and need for oil. The following pages provide background to help us interpret the complex events that fill our world in 2012. This context will help us better navigate the challenging energy transition away from petroleum.

A critical first step toward participating in this transition is to be aware that humans have known petroleum, an organic creation of the earth's geology, for many generations. For the vast majority of this time, oil was simply a waste mineral that leaked from the earth to interfere with human activities, such as growing the food and obtaining the water that our bodies require for survival.[2] Therefore, it would seem that moving beyond petroleum should not be terribly difficult; however, that's where we run into the complex, multidimensional dependence that defines our current relationship with crude.

Globally, humans now use more than eighty-five thousand barrels per day (85 TBPD). The United States is the single largest consumer of crude oil, consuming more than 19 TBPD, of which nearly 11 TBPD is imported. Of this total, approximately 13 TBPD is used for transportation.[3] In total consumption of petroleum, China is the only other nation to approach 8 TBPD—less than half the U.S. consumption. Table P.1 displays the vast disparity among the top ten petroleum consumers:

Table P.1.   Petroleum Consumption by Nation

Nation	Consumption (in thousands of barrels per day)
United States	19,498
China	7,831
Japan	4,785
India	2,962
Russia	2,916
Germany	2,569
Brazil	2,485
Saudi Arabia	2,376
Canada	2,261
South Korea	2,175

Source: U.S. Energy Information Administration (USEIA).

This is even more evident if the pattern is viewed as a pie graph, as in figure P.1:

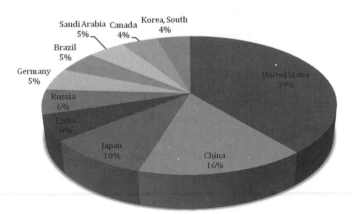

Figure P.1.   Percent of Petroleum Consumption by Nation, 2009 (Data from U.S. Energy Information Administration)

The disparity of nations' reliance on crude grows from an uncomfortable historical reality: for most Western nations and particularly for the United States, dependence on petroleum was optional during the early period of its use. After a century of blissful ignorance, the future of petroleum is now a matter of mathematical calculation. Knowledge of the world reserves (untapped oil supplies) is sufficient—knowable—enough to allow mathematicians to estimate that the high point of the world's production of crude (termed "peak oil") will likely come in our lifetime. It may be an event demarcated by neither pontificating political leaders nor parading school children. It may go entirely unnoticed. In fact, to be honest, it could have already occurred, defined only in retrospect by students of history such as yourselves. Whether the high point occurred in 2004 or has yet to occur in 2021 or 2112, the end of our life with crude has become absolutely obvious.

There is a history to the ironic quandary that faces petroleum-consuming nations. Over the last century, it has been in the best interest of governments, monarchies, and multinational corporations for the public to take supplies of oil for granted. In many developed nations, the blind assumption that petroleum would be available led to great material prosperity. Often, historians have been complicit, as many of their stories overlooked the complex systems that provided the essential lifeblood flowing into developed societies during the twentieth century. Therefore, a revisionary history is needed.

We need to know how we came to face such a crude reality.

Introduction

Beginning as Black Goo

In the early twenty-first century, military leaders in Afghanistan knew that they needed petroleum to win. Realizing this necessity, their enemy carried out a limited military strategy of derailing the supply. The other actors from the preceding pages, local residents, merely appreciated the utility of a resource that they neither possessed nor could acquire. This portrait of petroleum's role in the modern world demonstrates one of the most remarkable achievements of the modern industry: the complete disassociation of petroleum's consumption from the process of making it.

To varying degrees, all consumers of petroleum exist with almost no knowledge of the difficulty of locating, collecting, processing, and dispersing petroleum. Over more than a century and a half, the industry worked hard to insulate consumers from such details. In the process, however, consumers have also become oblivious to the resource's most basic reality: as an organic compound, petroleum happens—it is created naturally—but it "happens" only once. After we use it, oil is gone

In the following pages, *Crude Reality* begins from the certainty that oil, a naturally occurring product of the earth's geology, is finite. This may appear obvious; however, our current culture of petroleum is largely based on the opposite assumption. Since the first well was tapped in 1859, the world's supply of oil has decreased—picture the counter on your gas pump, only see it not ticking up to $30 or more but down from a starting point of nearly three trillion barrels. In this scenario, petroleum has never changed; the variation has been its usage. Particularly over the course of the twentieth century, the numbers on the counter flew by with increasing rapidity as humans' use of crude became defined only by our needs, entirely abstracted from the systems and limits of the earth's geology. To properly comprehend oil's legacy in our lives, we must first get beyond the myths of boom and bust, of war and geopolitics, to begin to understand the natural character and facts of oil.

As a starting point, geologists know that an American gallon of gasoline derives from plant material that decomposed under the earth's surface as it sat tightly packed and pressurized for thousands of years. That gallon of gasoline corresponds roughly to ninety tons of plant matter, which is the equivalent of forty acres of wheat (seeds, stalks, roots, etc.). When the energy in this resource is put to use by consumers, petroleum alters their everyday existence—their culture. The integrality of oil to modern life is so profound that humans in developed nations can be said to live within a petroleum culture, a web of associations formed and informed by crude.

Over the last one hundred years, petroleum has taken on a complex set of roles: becoming the energy to perform tasks, now impossible otherwise; forming the chemical basis of compounds and materials capable of lasting thousands of years or of feeding thousands; and serving as the bartering chip between nations' economic and political well-being. Despite such importance on the macroscopic level, our petroleum culture also functions on the mundane, microscopic level; for instance, that gallon of gasoline, placed in a lawn mower, might be gone in one hour—with only shortened grass to be shown for the earth's centuries-long process.[1] We live at a unique juncture in which we no longer take our petroleum culture for granted while much of our everyday life leaves us largely powerless to dramatically alter it. Reacquainting ourselves with the nature of oil is the best place to begin a new stage in our petroleum culture.

As an organic product, petroleum comes into being simply enough. Over the earth's 4.5-billion-year history, moving tectonic plates and expanding and contracting supplies of water have defined its processes. Creatures of all sorts have populated these water supplies. The most prolific may be the diatoms, half-plant half-animal creatures that reproduce by dividing themselves and that can lay dormant for centuries. Their glasslike shells sink to the bottom of a body of water and gather with the bones and teeth of dead fish and other creatures. Together, over centuries, this organic material forms a substance geologists call "carbonate ooze."[2] As a result of great compression, these pockets of carbon eventually take a variety of forms: fossilizing to form more solid minerals, such as coal; remaining in gaseous form, such as natural gas; or becoming liquid petroleum. Over ten million years, these solid, gaseous, and liquid forms combine with plankton to form a carbon-packed slime that is the ancestor of oil. The crude oil itself is formed when the earth's thirty thousand gigaton supply of carbon slime is joined by other elements spewed from volcanoes and other sources.

In particular, hydrocarbons, including oil, natural gas, and coal, occur when this supply of carbon becomes fused with hydrogen, which repels water. Science writer Sonia Shah explains:

> A single carbon atom with a few hydrogens attached to it is methane, a light gas. A chain of three carbons is propane; four carbons is butane. A chain of eight carbons is octane. As the chains and rings of carbon get longer and longer, they stick to each other better. The hydrocarbon gets thicker. Thirty-carbon chains are waxy; refiners string even longer chains together to make plastics.[3]

When they lived, creatures such as plankton could exist in water because they were surrounded by a membrane composed of hydrocarbon molecules. Over millions of years, the layers of their corpses on the bottom of bodies of water form a dark brown or black rock. Once buried, these piles of debris become heated (rather gently, at approximately 180 degrees Fahrenheit) and slowly split into lighter, more compressed hydrocarbons. As they get buried deeper, the heat alters their composition to form the various types of hydrocarbons. Approximately one-fifth of all of the earth's carbon has been entombed in this fashion.[4] For the supply to remain as oil—black goo—it must have a thick, rock-encased cap to hold it in place.

In this form, petroleum and other fossil fuels exist as one of the earth's great secrets. Satisfying no identifiable need, petroleum was left largely undisturbed by the earth's species. Even humans, as we shall see, lived with petroleum long before they began to unlock its capabilities. Although they were aware of crude where it oozed to the earth's surface, humans were interested in satisfying more immediate needs. For the most part, seeping crude only got in the way.

The following pages tell the story of the shift in the value that humans place on crude—essentially, the construction of our current petroleum culture. Humans' identification of petroleum's usefulness began subtly and with a very limited scope. From this point, however, new uses and their implications radiated outward to create a tidal wave of change in the human condition. Few resources can be said to have similarly affected human living patterns—to have formed an entire culture in which humans live. As these uses for crude grew increasingly significant, their implications reached across political boundaries to change basic characteristics of the human species. In an attempt to group these implications, I use the term "petroleum culture," in which webs of connections spiral outward to form additional associations that begin with the simple, initial human need for crude. Together, this complex spider web–like system of relationships and interrelationships forms a portrait of our life with petroleum.

A dynamic category, petroleum culture—the webs of association emanating between humans and the petroleum that occurs naturally—has expanded its influence on human life during the last 150 years. Although this culture includes the acquisition and extraction of oil, it places particular emphasis on what societies have chosen to do with the petroleum once it is acquired. This culture, therefore, includes politics, consumption, agriculture, ecological impacts, and legal regulation, as well as more vague categories such as ideology and ethics. Many of the outcomes of this culture are intended; however, many others are very clearly unintended and even unwanted. Together, they compose humans' relationship with petroleum in the early twenty-first century. When the implications of this petroleum culture—ranging from air pollution, corrupted streams, and rising global temperatures—are considered, it is clear the dependence on petroleum has impacted the earth's ability to sustain humanity's current living patterns. These costs and implications combine with elements of petroleum culture to shape the larger universe of petroleum use—an "ecology of oil," in which feedback loops bring humans clear consequences of their dependence.

Over the course of the last century in particular, petroleum culture has recalibrated global economics and political power, as well as the basic standards at which different societies live. Of course, petroleum culture has also contributed to massive inequalities between nations and societies. I explore these trends while also providing readers with a template with which to analyze current events. No matter where you sit to read this book, you are each a product and member of this petroleum culture.

EXPANDING HUMAN POSSIBILITIES THROUGH ENERGY

In approximately forty thousand years of existence, humans have developed an increasingly complex relationship to the natural world; basic building blocks, however, have remained consistent from the start. From the start humans have participated in one of the earth's essential and basic processes: the cycles of energy. The story of petroleum, the subject of this volume, is only one segment of what historians will eventually categorize as the "hydrocarbon era" in humanity's story.

For thousands of years prior to this era, which began in the early 1800s, humans harvested energy from the sun in a variety of creative ways. Our own bodies were the first devices used to transform photosynthesis into work. The use of animal labor followed quickly. Falling within the Biological Old Regime, in each case the products of the sun's heat provided working bodies with the energy to perform labor. Certainly, agriculture has moved through a variety of eras and has also grown to have a serious impact on ecological sustainability in parts of the world; however, for the purposes of this book, agriculture has never lost the basic power that it brought the human species: control.

While prime movers—energy sources—such as wind and water offered minimal opportunities for large-scale expansion, they still exponentially enhanced human capabilities. The change was dramatic enough that historians classify the Industrial Revolution as the next great shift in human living; unlike the Agricultural Revolution, however, the Industrial Revolution clearly derives from profoundly new ideas in utilizing energy. Initiated between 1300 and 1500, the early phase of the Industrial Revolution differed markedly from what followed when humans began exploiting what historian Alfred Crosby calls "fossilized sunshine."[5] In fact, most of the early portions of industry dealt with renewable forms of energy and, therefore, would likely be best related to the Biological Old Regime. Therefore, some historians have sectioned off the Industrial Revolution to denote a later era referred to as the Great Transformation that includes a variety of moments of technological "takeoff."

Growing from a similar interest in instrumentalizing natural resources, industry after this Great Transformation was powered by fossil fuels.[6] For instance, although Great Britain had used water power to industrialize, the work of Thomas Newcomen and James Watt in the 1700s carried these undertakings forward with the nearly unlimited capabilities of energy derived from fossil fuels. Starting with the use of coal, the new industry that followed the Great Transformation swept through the cities of Great Britain and much of Europe. By the mid-1800s, the United States shifted to organize its growing economy around this approach to human development and to take advantage of its great reserves of anthracite coal—among the largest in the world. Factories used steam generators powered by coal to carry out countless tasks. The same steam engines were put on wheels and used as the foundation for the transportation system supporting the United States' expanding economy in the late 1800s. And, finally, by the end of the nineteenth century American and European innovators had used this same prime mover to create the most flexible form of energy yet: electricity. Each of these remarkable shifts in human life falls generally within the era of the Industrial Revolution.

Within this era of industrialization, different cultures emphasized different sources of power, creating subcategories. Historian John R. McNeill refers to this structuring characteristic of human life as each society's "energy regime." McNeill defines such a regime as "the collection of arrangements whereby energy is harvested from the sun (or uranium atoms), directed, stored, bought, sold, used for work or wasted, and ultimately dissipated."[7] In each society, then, the ethics with which humans use and manage the natural resources that generate power have broad implications. Very often, these patterns and their implications form characteristics that differentiate one human society from another—possibly even differentiating cultures that are participating in the same energy regime.

Regardless of which prime mover performed the work, the Industrial Revolution was defined by a philosophy of development that infected much of the Western world, particularly Europe. Ultimately, the nation founded by Europeans as an experiment in democratic thought, the United States, marked the most fertile terrain for this new way of controlling and, ultimately, resisting the limitations that nature had placed on humans for generations. The driving ideology of the United States was one of expansion and development, available to all citizens. On a global scale, though, this industrial transition—or fork in the path of human development—propelled some nations to unthinkable advancement and development and left others increasingly far behind. Robert Marks, along with other global historians, describes the fissure separating such societies as "the Gap."[8] Although such a gap of development had occurred by the mid-1800s, new ways of doing things and new energy sources compounded the distinction so that by the early 1900s, nations on each side of the gap might appear entirely unrelated—their human inhabitants perceived as almost different species.

Energy was the key to expanding this separation between humans. McNeill writes that, once deeply into the era of industry, the problem for developed nations was to "get energy in useful form in the right place and the right time for whatever we might wish to do."[9] As some nations mastered this process better than others, their economies and political standing changed. Some societies used this expansive—some might say profligate—use of energy as a defining cultural trait. McNeill argues that during the industrial expansion of the nineteenth century, the worldwide energy harvest increased about fivefold. In the twentieth century, the harvest grew by sixteenfold on top of that![10] He concludes:

> No other century—no millennium—in human history can compare with the twentieth for its growth in energy use. We have probably deployed more energy since 1900 than in all of human history before 1900. My very rough calculation suggests that the world in the twentieth century used 10 times as much energy as in the thousand years before 1900 AD. In the 100 centuries between the dawn of agriculture and 1900, people used only about two-thirds as much energy as in the twentieth century.[11]

Although humans remain the same species as during these earlier eras, many humans have come to use energy in profoundly new ways. What does such massive change look like? As we begin to emphasize this systematic view of human life over the last century, there can be no disputing the clearest public face of humans' high-energy existence: petroleum.

THE NATURE OF CRUDE AND THE PETROLEUM CENTURY

Most of us have neither been oil wildcatters nor students of petroleum geology, yet we know a surprising amount about the nature of crude. Its odor, color, and even its general geographic origin combine with our clearest awareness of crude—its price, which is at least partly a product of the supply's availability. Due to our own—often unappreciated—involvement in the culture of petroleum, we know more basic details about petroleum than we do about most other resources. Some of this information comes to us as consumers of crude, while other lessons come more subtly through petroleum's appearance in the news or its use in popular culture, particularly feature film. Although I draw throughout the book on many specific details to relate the story of how petroleum shaped human life during the twentieth century, I will refer here to films that have helped to form our petroleum culture and also to instill in us some basic lessons about the nature of crude.

Commodification

In every environment, resources exist that have basic value for other constituents in an ecosystem. Commodities possess additional value, which reflects a value derived from markets—other economic entities that place a price on a resource's value within a larger system of trade or exchange. Petroleum has existed as a resource for millennia; it expanded into a commodity during the mid-1800s. Due to variations in its usage and the value that could then be attached to this work, petroleum's status as a commodity has remained dynamic. As these uses have become increasingly essential to some societies, petroleum's value has moved beyond economics. As a critical resource, petroleum now influences the national security of each developed nation, as well as any nations wishing to close the gap and become a member of the developed world.

In his last film, James Dean played Jett Rink in the blockbuster feature film *Giant*. A story of transition in the American West, *Giant* used Rink to personify an era when petroleum grew valuable and replaced better-known endeavors such as cattle ranching. In one seminal scene, Rink stands on the porch of the grand cattle estate that represents the Old West, dripping with the crude that has rained on him following his strike. From being valuable primarily as a source of food for cattle that will become meat, the land has become, simply, a conduit for a resource of much greater value. The moment embodies the act of commodification. It is a vision of wealth and opportunity that reaches across cultures and generations.

"Rule of Capture" and Boom

Why does petroleum develop so differently from other resources? To answer, one need only recall Daniel Plainview, the primary character in the 2008 film *There Will Be Blood*, famously growling: "I drink your milkshake." Much of petroleum's unique story derives from its occurrence as an underground liquid, even though nations handled this legal standing differently. In Plainview's statement, he captures in all its simplicity the fact that as a fluid resource, petroleum neither occurs as other mineral resources nor fits within existing property law. While most nations hold that the state retains jurisdiction over subsoil rights, the United States and a few others (Mexico for a brief period, South Africa, and Galicia, for instance) have allowed this fugacious quality to determine petroleum's legal standing through "rule of capture." By this legal standard, humans have the right to reach into the earth to seize petroleum, and ownership only applies to the crude appearing on the earth's surface. So, when it comes to crude, the race is always on!

Waste, Degradation, and Outcomes of Petroleum

The context for the 2009 film *Avatar* is extractive work on Pandora, an Earth-like moon, to acquire the valuable commodity Unobtanium. Although it could be a number of different commodities, the culture revolving around the mineral sought by the human society bears a strong resemblance to the culture of crude. "Degradation," particularly of the environment, is an inevitable outcome of extraction. In addition, petroleum's 150-year use has bred a significant degree of tolerated waste, both in the extraction and the consumption of crude.

We live in a time of energy transition in which humans are attempting to correct the wastefulness that became an inherent facet of our relationship with crude. Both the era of waste and the conservation reaction are part of the cultural story found in these pages. They are elements of a complex cultural anxiety as we begin to perceive the costs of our dependence on petroleum.

Scarcity

The basic difficulty of locating crude oil, especially in the early twentieth century, led to the cultural and social phenomenon known as the "boom." Scarcity can make humans do extraordinary things, as depicted in the 1940 film *Boom Town*, which portrays the turn-of-the-century rush for oil in eastern Texas. Characters played by Spencer Tracy and Clark Gable grow so engrossed with the possibilities of black gold that when oil is found beneath the community church, their response is merely to construct a derrick in the sanctuary, among the pews that still fill the structure. They proceed with the cultural portions of their life—such as attending church—in the constant shadow of oil production. To residents of the oil patch, this existence becomes normal.

In a world in which petroleum supplies are scarce, complex layers of business and diplomacy must get involved in the acquisition of supplies where they can still be found. In *Syriana*, the CIA works to ensure the political connections for large oil companies in a global network ranging from Iran, to Texas, to Spain, to Washington, to Switzerland. The CIA has become more involved because a competitor nation, China, has acquired drilling rights for crude in a kingdom ruled by the al-Subaai family, which had previously worked only with the United States. In a complex arrangement, actual practices and ethics are entirely disregarded in order to acquire the necessary influence: governments work with large, shadowy corporations to create the simple impression of stable business practices and due diligence. Global influence, which is critical to accessing petroleum supplies, is based less on reality and more on influence and control of the economic system. As scarcity increases, so does the importance of such influence—which is also exerted through military force.

CONCLUSION: ENERGY TRANSITIONING

Human dependence on petroleum caused little discomfort when we enjoyed a century of inexpensive oil. By the start of the twenty-first century, though, we have come to accept that we now exist on the waning end of petroleum-powered civilization. Exploring the history of petroleum means recognizing that it will have a conclusion. We are hooked on an impermanent, limited resource. This is the basic reality of crude, and from it grows the tragedy of humans' reliance on it. This current reality, though, is only part of the story.

Thanks to crude, humans in developed societies have enjoyed a wondrous ride during the last century. The reality of petroleum's finite supply is now often referred to as "peak oil," based on the assumption of "Hubbert's Peak," which is described in detail in chapter 8. In short, modern technology allows us now to know the extent of petroleum reserves—their locations, size, and depth. With this knowledge, a petroleum geologist in Shell's research division during the 1950s computed that U.S. domestic oil production would peak during the 1970s. Proven correct, these calculations have been applied to the global oil supply. Hubbert's Peak for global oil falls between 2004 and 2010. In short, the rest of our lifetime will be spent with a declining supply of crude.

The reality of the "end of oil" offers a new paradigm for organizing our life. In order to properly define the next era in our history, we need to clearly see the paradigm through which we have passed—a glorious episode of energy gluttony that was destined to end. Therefore, in the concluding chapters of this book, readers will also find evidence of an energy transition. The reality of peak oil combines with concepts such as climate change to redefine human existence at its very foundation. Using the nature of oil as well as the remarkable history of humans' relationship with it, this book relates our life with crude and then suggests the difficulties of our future without it.

Part I

CULTURAL EXCHANGE, 1750–1890

INFRASTRUCTURE
Drilling for Saltwater

The predecessor of drilling for oil was drilling for salt. Although historians believe such activity dates back 5,000 years, the first recorded salt well was dug in Sichuan Province, China, around 2,250 years ago. Sichuan developed an entire industry based around tapping brine aquifers, bringing the groundwater to the surface, and then evaporating it with a heat source so that the salt was left behind.

By 2,000 years ago, salt miners in China began the first use of percussive drilling, eventually referred to as "kicking down" a well. Reaching down as much as 459 feet (140 meters) below the earth's surface, rural farmers used a bamboo rig and one or two men on a wooden plank. They stood on either end of the plank and alternated stepping downward. Much like a seesaw, this motion lifted up the drill stem and then allowed it to drop. The drill bit crashed down into the rock, pulverizing it. Later, the solid bamboo pipe was replaced by a thin, light flexible bamboo "cable." This dramatically lowered the weight of the "drill string," which made it easier to lift from the surface. By the 1700s Sichuan wells typically ranged from 984 to 1,312 feet (300 to 400 meters) deep. In 1835 the Shenghai well was the first in the world to exceed a depth of 3,281 feet (1,000 meters). In comparison, the deepest wells in the United States at that time were about 1,641 feet (500 meters) deep. The Sichuan salt-producing industry was centered in the city of Zigong, from which radiated extensive networks of bamboo pipelines to transport brine and natural gas.

This method of drilling for salt and water, referred to as an artesian well, was employed throughout the Western world by the eighteenth century. When the Seneca Rock Oil Company sought methods to acquire another liquid resource from the earth, the kick-down method of drilling was the natural choice.

Chapter One

From Black Goo to Black Gold

Assuming that you wished to gather it—which would have been an odd choice throughout most of human history—how would you collect oil without any equipment?

Eight feet long, four feet wide, and two feet deep, the indents in the earth's surface that one finds in the flat land directly along Oil Creek in northwestern Pennsylvania likely are not the collection tool that leaps to your mind. In fact, for generations local residents entirely overlooked the troughs because no one knew why they existed. As the world's use of oil grew from drilling efforts just a few feet away from the troughs, this valley boomed and busted. Still, no one asked about the troughs. After its bust, this spot where the first well was drilled became the site of the Drake Well Museum, with an outdoor yard teeming with various oil collection hardware used through the ages. Today, the pumping steam engine displaying for visitors to the museum an earlier method of collection releases its pent-up steam with a shrill "toot." Unmarked and unappreciated, these pits remain visible to the naked eye only to those visitors who venture onto the walking trails near the museum.

One reason that the pits remained undisturbed is that locals, asking essentially the question above, hypothesized that humans interested in the oil that seeped naturally out of the earth here might have dug collection troughs and allowed them to fill gradually—naturally. But who had wanted the meddlesome ooze? And why? Over many years, scattered written records demonstrated that many early people throughout the globe found uses for oil or bitumen—a tar-like relative of crude. With this information, trained eyes returned to Titusville, Pennsylvania. Initially investigated in the 1930s and then more carefully studied in the 1970s, the pits in Pennsylvania now mark a crucial beginning for petroleum. Archaeologists established that the pits had originally been lined with logs and designed by early humans to collect the crude coming close to the earth's surface in this remote location.[1] Dating efforts by the archaeologists calibrated the likely time of the pits' usage to between 550 and 600 years ago, approximately 1450 CE. Thus, the archaeological team establishes that the pits were used "well before the time of European contact in 1600."[2]

This is just one example of how piecing together the early history of petroleum requires significant historical conjecture. There is very little certainty, except to say that people all over the world began appreciating the unique capabilities of the earth's natural oil as soon as they came into contact with it. Typically, these uses had little to do with the oil's inherent energy potential, but there are even exceptions to this. As black goo, petroleum was clearly known and identified in early human history. The real revolution was in human society's ability to move it from a relatively worthless state to one of significant value, denoted by the term "black gold" that was popularized beginning in the late nineteenth century. Repackaging crude as "black gold" occurred first in the world's most flexible economy—that of the United States. The American model of development cohered remarkably well with the mysterious, expansive capabilities of petroleum; therefore, the early commercial development of crude emanated from an American source.

This chapter traces the transition of petroleum from its status as a resource, known and even used, to that of a commodity with a clear value—albeit a fraction of what it would become. Commodification, the cultural act of attributing value to a resource based on markets and general applications, is a dynamic part of humans' economic life. This process has created significant distinctions between human eras, such as the Bronze Age or the Age of Sail, in which a society's level of participation in a resource's commodification (metals or wind) distinguished one era from another. Environmental historians and cultural geographers use these associations to shape narratives of human history that transcend political boundaries.

In some sense, these patterns have helped to organize world history since its inception; when the basic paradigm of Western civilization gave way as an organizing device, world and global historians often emphasized the systematic shifts in human existence used by geographers and archaeologists. In a way similar to placing a camera lens on microscopic zoom, the historical view can seize on a specific commodity—without regard to border or era—and thereby clarify certain new continuities while also blurring some well-known facts that become less important. The following pages focus the historical view on petroleum, a transborder and transculture resource, through revealing historical snapshots. These stories of petroleum, strung together into one narrative, demonstrate that artifacts such as the troughs outside Titusville, Pennsylvania, join diverse people and eras in a historical continuity: their awareness of crude oil.

ORGANIC ENERGY AND EARLY HUMANS

Over the last one hundred years, locating the world's oil reserves has helped geologists to better understand the earth's history. Today, scientists know a common story for the earth's development in which the hydrocarbon material described in the introduction gathered in each body of water throughout the globe. Such basic geological understanding helps modern-day geologists map the evolution of earlier land and water forms. In particular, though, the geological sea Tethys, which formed between Cimmeria and Gondwana, gathered significant amounts of this organic material. This is revealed by the large pockets of organic sediments left in newly formed areas of land, including the Middle East, when the sea receded. In the twentieth century, these sedimentary pockets organized entire civilizations. In addition to serving as the center of our "crude world," these areas also hosted what archaeologists agree were the initial ancestors of the human species. Science writer Sonia Shah explains: "It wasn't long before [early humans] found the remains of that ancient rich sea. Its oils were slowly oozing out onto the fertile soils basking in the sun."[3] Although there are scattered records of humans putting petroleum to use, these efforts were extremely limited and involved little effort to expand supply.

In the classical world, few histories included descriptions of any use of petroleum-like materials. The exception was the Near East, where the ancient Mesopotamian traditions included some nominal use of oil collected from seepages. Mention of petroleum became more frequent after the Persian Empire and during the expansion of Islam.[4] As crude oil production became more well-known, Arabic historians, for instance, discussed efforts of Arabic law to consider mining concessions. In these societies, petroleum was included with all "nonexposed" minerals of value that belonged to the sultans, regardless of where they were found. Historian R. J. Forbes writes that "Arab lawyers of the tenth and eleventh centuries after a lengthy discussion, decided that this held also for the 'exposed' minerals such as petroleum and bitumen, gathered at the earth's surface or at shallow depths and that the sultans could allot concessions to other subjects."[5] In these writings, the origin of petroleum was most often derived from classical authors, including Aristotle, who determined petroleum was a type of "coagulate dew." In addition, distillation experiments had been undertaken throughout the region, including in Alexandria and Syria, by approximately two thousand years ago.[6] When the region endured crusades from Arab and Mongol armies, flammable petroleum or naphtha stores often resulted in conflagrations. At times, glass balls filled with the naphtha were used as a weapon. In other incidents, applications were found for the material in medicine, pharmacy, and agriculture. Close proximity to crude that seeped to the earth's surface was a defining characteristic of each of these early civilizations; however, among these disparate societies there was little shared knowledge about petroleum.

In fact, knowledge of the usefulness of oil is most likely traced to the same source that introduced unknown areas of the world to Europe: trader and explorer Marco Polo used his writings of 1298 (based on travels in the 1200s) to familiarize many Europeans with the exotic and active trading world of the eastern portion of the globe. Mixed in with his observations of people and trade goods was one of the earliest written mentions of oil as a resource that could be put to various uses. In Zorzania (modern Georgia), for instance, he observed a geyser infused with oil. He saw locals using the oil to treat wounds and skin irritations. In addition, they burned the oil to provide light. In later generations, these supplies of oil became the well-known reserves of Baku. He also described the applications of a slow-burning stone (coal) and tar used in creating fleets of seaworthy vessels.[7]

As bitumen, this tar was put to use by many early societies. The early Mesopotamians were able to dig up more than fifty thousand kilograms of petroleum sludge that they used primarily to seal the hulls of small vessels. When a lighter liquid oil was found as well, the historian Pliny records that it was found to be combustible and, due to this danger, "quite unfit for use."[8] Pliny, also known as Pliny the Elder, was the primary historian of the Roman Empire, and his work dates to approximately 50 CE. Although petroleum was found in various sites in Europe, he observed only the Germans in Transylvania and Lower Saxony harvesting it to be boiled in iron pots and used as a medicine. This local knowledge about petroleum then spread to a wider audience.

Using Pliny's observations, the German scientist Georgius Agricola published *The Textbook of Minerology* in 1546 in which he called this "unctuous juice" bitumen, which was known to occur in various forms between liquid and solid. Liquid bitumen, which was particularly unctuous, he observed had become known as "petroleum" because it flowed from rocks. Some societies, he observed, referred to the substance as "pitch" and others as "naptha."[9] Its "very powerful fire essence" had led many societies to burn the oil, which occurred in various colors, in lamps. In addition, if spread on copper, the oil was found by Pliny to prevent oxidation. Pliny became a bit of an early clearinghouse for petroleum knowledge, as he also observed that the Babylonians had found many medical uses for the oil as an ointment for wounds and

Figure 1.1. Perpetual fires were known to occur in various parts of the world. By 1932, when this photo was shot of oil wells and a camp of the Iraq Petroleum Company, approximately five miles south of Kirkuk, such constant escapes of natural gas indicated a promising drilling site. (Library of Congress Prints and Photographs Division, LC-M33-14390)

also for treating gout and leprosy. When horses drank from water saturated with oil, though, he observed, they became wild and unmanageable. Without scientific communities to disperse and gather knowledge, historians such as Pliny offer one of the earliest examples of human efforts to shape a larger cultural knowledge about petroleum.

These written accounts are supplemented by archaeological findings that trace the consistent use of oil by native peoples throughout the world. In Egypt and Mesopotamia, for instance, archaeologists have been investigating the use of bitumen during the late Uruk and Chalcolithic periods at the Anatolian site of Hacinebi Tepe in present-day Turkey. In these civilizations, bitumen was used for the construction of buildings and the waterproofing of reed boats. The Olmec civilization, which can be dated more recently between about 1200 and 400 BCE, has attracted archaeologists to the tropical lowlands of the gulf coast in Central America to study the use of bitumen in Mesoamerican cultures. The oldest archaeological bitumen (i.e., mixed with other materials) in Mesoamerica so far was recovered from the Olmec sites of

San Lorenzo and El Manati. Seeps of natural bitumen occur along the coastal floodplains of the Gulf of Mexico; however, archaeological bitumen has been found at sites far into the Mexican highlands. This important discovery suggests petroleum's involvement in very early human trade networks. Researchers Carl Wendt and Shan-Tan Lu established that seeps of petroleum found at a variety of Olmec sites could be connected with bitumen found in other communities without their own local sources.[10]

Finally, sources also suggest that petroleum was known in China as early as 600 BCE. Descriptions from approximately 300 CE presume that petroleum was an impurity struck when Chinese drillers sought salt or water. Crude, however, was never the goal of Chinese drillers, and no known written records discuss its uses in Chinese society (although the salt drillers discussed above inadvertently acquired oil).[11]

As described earlier, petroleum supplies in North America offer a relatively clear record of early uses—even if the written documents are lacking. Deep in the mountains of northwestern Pennsylvania, unique seeps of oil were noted by the earliest humans known to live in this place. Northwestern Pennsylvania had served as a temporary home to the Mound Builder society living centuries prior to the Seneca. Paleoindians of the Woodland period, before 1400, ventured from their original homelands in the Ohio Valley and along the Great Lakes on frequent journeys to Oil Creek, where they collected oil on a fairly large scale for use in their religious rituals. Although no written accounts remain, it was well-known that initial European explorers in the area found long, narrow troughs that had been dug along Oil Creek. Therefore, North America's seeping crude provides us with one of the first instances with which to contrast cultural reactions to petroleum. In the Seneca society, the oil was realized as a resource, and they had learned to collect it from the water's surface using a blanket as a sponge or dipping a container into the water. Their reason for gathering the oil was primarily to use it as an ointment or skin coloring, and they had little interest in trying to trade it to other groups.[12]

European explorers also noticed the oil and designated the Pennsylvania stream Oil Creek beginning in 1755, when the region's oddity was recorded on the Lewis Evans map. Tourists and soldiers passing through the area were known to soak aching joints in the surrounding oil springs and even to imbibe the crude as a castor oil variation. As the oil's reputation grew, settlers sought to use the logic of American capitalist markets on the unique geological feature. On a very small scale, settlers in western Pennsylvania gathered oil from springs on their property by constructing dams of loose stones to confine the floating oil for collection. In the mid-1840s, one entrepreneur noticed the similarity between the oil prescribed to his ill wife and the annoying substance that was invading the salt wells on his family's property outside

Pittsburgh, Pennsylvania. He began bottling the waste substance in 1849 and marketed it as a mysterious cure-all available throughout the northeastern United States. Although he still acquired the oil only by a skimming technique quite similar to that used by previous humans, Samuel Kier's supply quickly exceeded demand because the salt wells produced a constant flow of the oil. With the excess, he began the first organized experiments to use the substance as an illuminant.

Whether in Pennsylvania or Transylvania, this had not been the reaction of other cultures to their largely undesired experience with oil. Kier and others demonstrated that the American model of capitalism offered entrepreneurs in petroleum a particularly dynamic opportunity. The culture of economic expansion and industrial development was beginning to close in on petroleum.[13] Little was actually known about this oil, though. As entrepreneurs learned more, petroleum—particularly with its expansive and flexible supply—grew from this beginning and emerged as a tailor-made commodity for the American economy. Although the resource had been identified in societies throughout the globe, capitalism allowed petroleum to realize the status of a valuable mineral. When it did so, however, supplies of crude would be unlike any other precious mineral because of its fugacious or liquid quality.

THE CHEMISTRY OF MAKING OIL USEFUL

Knowledge about oil grew in each culture in which it was found and put to use. It was not, however, until the early 1800s that this knowledge began to be shared and a science of geology emerged. During this time period, the most aggressive efforts to locate petroleum for development formed in North America, which fueled a more active effort to apply the growing body of scientific knowledge. Efforts to bring entrepreneurial interest in oil together with geology created the moment of historic convergence that produced the first commercial well—the first effort to dig or drill specifically for oil. Fashioning a way that oil could be used for illumination occupied individuals in each of these areas and also created the overlap of commercial chemistry that continues in the petroleum industry today. Particularly in Canada, a few individuals gathered geologic knowledge and then offered their services to financiers who located possible supplies.

During the mid-1800s, Abraham Gesner and others made careers for themselves as public scientists, writing travelogue-style accounts of their field experiences and experiments with new resources, particularly sources of energy. Gesner's work emphasized coal in Nova Scotia and New Brunswick. Most importantly for petroleum culture, though, Gesner became a popularizer of a synthetic product made from coal that became known as kerosene. After becoming involved in the marketing of kerosene gas for lighting in New York City in 1853, Gesner began manufacturing and distributing kerosene oil in New York in 1854.[14] As a respected scientist, Gesner brought credibility to the product and to its viability as an illuminant. Kerosene oil's growing popularity spurred developers to look differently at existing resources, particularly petroleum, which seemed capable of allowing kerosene manufacturers to skip the stage of converting coal into a liquid form.

In his analysis of the emergence of kerosene, historian Paul Lucier stresses the importance of the "Albert Mineral," which in 1858 became the most effective raw material for conversion into kerosene at refineries outside Boston. Derived from coal in Albert, New Brunswick, the "Albert Mineral" very likely involved the influence of Gesner.[15] A kerosene boom swept the American northeast during which, Lucier writes, "coal oil came to control the American market in lamp oils and lubricants. As one observer declared: 'More oils made from coal in one week, in our country than ever was obtained by our whale-fishers in the best year's fishing they ever enjoyed.'"[16] Most important, synthetic oils broke the market open to new competitors. In this queue of potential illuminants, petroleum stood out for its seeming availability—it required neither complex chemical adjustment nor a hunt on the open sea. Therefore, the specific techniques and chemistry that were required to derive useful kerosene from oil forged early bonds between chemists and lawyers. And the stakes were very high.

Legal infighting within the kerosene industry pitted Gesner, inventor of "kerosene," against James Young, holder of the U.S. patent for "Paraffine," which actually covered the energy source referred to as coal oil. These difficult distinctions among kerosene-like products aided the development of petroleum in at least two ways: first, they somewhat limited the expansion of coal-oil production just as it had begun to expand, and second, the legal case that played out demonstrated the new connection between industry and the scientific knowledge of the era. "The Kerosene cases," writes Lucier, "showed that different discoveries (scientific versus practical) and different activities (research versus application) were as arbitrary as the social distinctions. Some men of science, and some inventors, might struggle to demarcate and defend the boundaries that separated the two, but others tried equally hard to erase them."[17]

A clear culture of business and development, therefore, surrounded North American supplies of petroleum, and that simply was not occurring elsewhere in the world. Pennsylvania crude, in particular, emerged as the proving ground for lessons in development, science, and law that would eventually be applied wherever crude seeped from the ground. These were the earliest stages of the process of commodification that would increase the value of crude beyond its status as a somewhat useful resource.

Given the situation related to kerosene in American courts during the 1850s, the well-known oil seeps in Pennsylvania now became a remarkable business opportunity. Although local knowledge of the oil seeps was crucial, development of Pennsylvania's supply of crude required the influence of outsiders, most of whom possessed business acumen from other venues. Dr. Francis Brewer, a resident of New Hampshire, traveled to Titusville in 1851 to work with a lumbering firm of which he was part owner. During the visit, Brewer entered into the first oil lease ever signed with a local resident to collect the oil that seeped to the surface. Instead of drilling, however, the lessee merely dug trenches to convey oil and water to a central basin. Upon his return to New England, Brewer left a small bottle of crude with Dixi Crosby, a chemist at Dartmouth College who then showed it to a young businessman, George Bissell. The culture of petroleum was rapidly changing as its web of associations broadened among people familiar with the illumination oil market.

Petroleum's similarity to coal and whale oil immediately struck Bissell. Marking a critical moment in the commodification of crude, he signed a lease with Brewer to develop the petroleum on the lumber company's land, but first Bissell needed to attract financial backing of $250,000. Petroleum's lack of known utility would make Bissell's task all but impossible. Therefore, he set out to mitigate some of the risk by acquiring scientific knowledge about this odd curiosity. Next to Gesner, one of the world's best-known chemists was the American Benjamin Silliman Jr. of Yale University. Similar to Gesner, Silliman served as a chemist hired by start-up companies to validate their prospective products.

When the Pennsylvania Rock Oil Company of New York hired Silliman, they desired a report that would provide investors with greater confidence in petroleum's future uses. When Silliman's report was released in April 1855, it accomplished this task by reporting: "It appears to me that there is much ground for encouragement in the belief that your Company have in their possession a raw material from which, by simple and not expensive process . . . they may manufacture very valuable products."[18] Silliman estimated that of gathered crude oil, at least 50 percent could be distilled into a satisfactory illuminant for use in camphene lamps and 90 percent of it could be made into distilled products that held commercial promise. On September 18, 1855, Bissell incorporated the Pennsylvania Rock Oil Company of Connecticut, the first organization founded solely to speculate with the potential value of the oil. The company elected Silliman president based on Silliman's professional reputation and the image of stability that it lent to their effort to develop the crude that occurred naturally beneath and around the Oil Creek valley in Pennsylvania.

The next order of business was to establish who would undertake the exploratory trip to Pennsylvania. It was an overwhelming challenge because no one knew how to find oil, nor did anyone know what tools might help them to find it. So, what were the most important criteria for selecting the driller of the first oil well? Free railroad travel was the answer given by James M. Townsend, a New Haven banker and a leading force in the Pennsylvania Rock Oil Company of Connecticut. In 1857, he asked Edwin L. Drake to travel to Titusville to oversee an effort to drill for crude. A former conductor on the New Haven Railroad, Drake had recently left his job for health reasons, but he retained a pass for free rail travel.

During the late summer of 1859, Drake wired to New Haven for more money. They offered only funds for a trip home. The Rock Oil Company would try to begin the era of petroleum somewhere else. However, Drake refused to cease his efforts. With remarkable courage, the former train conductor turned prospector took out a line of credit and stayed on. He wrote Townsend that he could not give up: "You all have your legitimate business. . . . I staked everything I had upon the project and now find myself out of business and out of money."

His courage paid off, but not in a grand gusher of black gold. On August 27, 1859, the drill dropped five feet after one kick. Drake's assitant, Billy Smith, assumed it had broken through an underground crevice. Even he, of course, had no idea how the first well would come in. With no sudden release of pressure to spray the oil upward, this drop by the drill head was the extent of the history-making moment. Ironically, Drake and Smith, assuming they had snapped yet another length of pipe, stopped drilling for the weekend so that Drake could observe the Sabbath. Smith, however, never strayed far from the well since he and his family resided in temporary quarters next to the engine house. Later Saturday, as Smith wandered the site with his son, they found greenish black ooze floating in the well. While not a sky-darkening explosion of crude, the ooze showed Smith that their drilling had reached its goal.

Word spread quickly through northwestern Pennsylvania. When the oil rush swept through Oil Creek and further down the Allegheny River to Franklin, townspeople leapt to recall which of their neighbors' drinking water tasted *most* like oil. Or they struggled to remember which of the region's traditional salt wells had been oil-producing salt wells. With the opening of the first well, Drake and Smith unleashed a period of dramatic changes on society in the region, even though their own well would never be a great producer.

The technological scope began to shift within two years of Drake's discovery. Portable steam engines became the norm for drilling in the Oil Creek

Figure 1.2. Hillside development of wells began near Oil Creek outside Titusville, Pennsylvania, in the 1860s. This nineteenth-century image shows the Shoe & Leather Petroleum Company and the Foster Farm Oil Company on lower Pioneer Run, a tributary of Oil Creek. (Library of Congress Prints and Photographs Division, LC-USZ62-63520)

valley and allowed wells to reach new depths. Natural gas within these deeper wells created the first "flowing" wells, sending a rush of oil upward in a gush of escaping natural gas. Gushers vastly increased the amount of crude on the market. The *Venango Speculator* discussed the effects of the massive increase in the oil supply from twelve hundred barrels a day in 1860 to more than five thousand in 1861 and then to astronomical proportions in 1862.

Although humans all over the world had identified value in crude, American capitalism offered the most flexible system in which to develop it and to link it into larger trade networks. With industry and factory development, expansive markets for goods emerged during the 1800s. Despite the Civil War, technologies such as railroads offered a new era of macroscopic development for entire regions and microscopic development of specific products and resources. Truly, a culture of expansion dominated the United States in the 1860s.

The energy of this national priority could be directed at ideas, such as abolishing slavery, or at technologies, such as the railroad. This same spirit of expansion could be directed at specific resources and, if all the variables were correct, they could take off to remarkable heights. To take advantage of such a moment, though, a resource needed to satisfy two important criteria: demand, which meant that it needed to be useful so that consumers desired it, and supply, so that it could be available in amounts that merited making it more integral to everyday life. In the case of petroleum, events and patterns of the nineteenth-century United States converged to satisfy these criteria most effectively.

WHALING AND PETROLEUM'S FIRST ENERGY TRANSITION

Free enterprise in the United States, of course, did not automatically result in increased value. Entrepreneurs with petroleum, similar to those in any venture, faced immense risk. In the American system, they were free to take an idea and attempt to make it into a profitable business; however, many ideas fizzled at different stages of development. Although a few ideas might succeed and become profitable businesses, most would fail. Petroleum clearly fell into the latter category in the 1850s, particularly due to the lack of a reliable supply.

Increasing supply marked a critical portion of the petroleum puzzle, but chemists still had only modest success finding uses for the crude drawn from Pennsylvania. Lubrication for metal gears in machines, of course, did not require vast amounts of petroleum. For potential investors, the lack of knowledge about petroleum meant that it offered neither stability nor certainty; however, one could certainly see that it possessed a bit of promise.

To create the widespread use for petroleum that would allow the industry to take off, the black goo needed to fit into existing consumptive markets. Making light in the United States proved just the ticket. By the mid-1800s, global markets were ripe for kerosene made from coal. As geological luck would have it, Pennsylvania's oil country overlapped or abutted coal country. According to one 1860 estimate, large coal-oil manufacturers consumed sixty thousand bushels of coal per day. Large firms had set up distilleries of coal-oil products in Pittsburgh, the city nearest the petroleum regions. The *Pittsburgh Post* reported in 1860 that "no better nor cheaper light than good coal-oil can be produced, and the fact that this is the centre of the trade, is an important one for Pittsburgers."[19] The challenge to undercut coal oil was on for developers of petroleum, and the critical component was a lower price supported by sufficient supplies of crude.

As the supplier of each raw material, Pennsylvania marked ground zero for this energy transition; however, refining and shipping technology was advancing elsewhere. Particularly around Baku, technological advancements helped to power petroleum's viability. In addition, pockets such as the Baku supply helped to create a global market to which Pennsylvania petroleum could also ultimately find access. Although in 1860 coal oil appeared to be the next great energy source after whale oil, cheap petroleum kerosene had the capability of usurping its status as heir to whale oil. Kerosene, rent from petroleum, could be burned in lamps similar to those used for all other illuminants. Therefore, consumers needed to do little to accommodate this shift; however, this significant energy transition relied on a number of other factors converging in the 1860s.

Regardless of the source of kerosene, the most widely used illuminating oil in the world remained whale and sperm oil. Each of these oils was harvested from whales and then refined into oil for use in lamps. Once again, available supply and the technological innovation needed to make whale oil into a commodity had, since the late 1700s, focused on the United States. In fact, during the Seven Years' War, France and Great Britain each sought to lure the American whalers to outposts supported by them. Despite these threats, the United States kept its fleet and the industry's hub, New Bedford, Massachusetts. Therefore, once again, the historical convergence of several factors propelled the American illumination market forward. The complex relationship between whale oil and petroleum, though, goes well beyond a transition in existing energy markets for illumination.

Intense strain from a variety of fronts had been placed on the pursuit of whales during the 1860s. Throughout its century or more of industrial-level pursuit, whaling was a culture that tied together global markets and diverse ethnicities. As the whalers' collection area broadened, trading posts and

Figure 1.3. The search for whale oil carried American whalers far afield in the nineteenth century. In this print, the pursuit of right whales brought whalers into the Bering Strait and Arctic Ocean. (Library of Congress Prints and Photographs Division, LC-DIG-pga-00392)

collection stations took shape in distant, exotic locales, ranging from the Ha-waiian Islands to coastal villages in the Arctic. Although it became a global system, all the oil needed to eventually return to refineries in New Bedford. From there, some of the oil was traded abroad, particularly in Europe. There always remained a cap, however, to what was possible: the supply of whale and sperm oil could not expand sufficiently and regularly enough to keep up with the emerging era of industrial expansion. Perfecting the refinement of kerosene from petroleum simply made the situation worse for whalers.

Although the actual techniques for collecting whales had changed little from its earliest years, there were clear shifts in the supply of whales by the 1860s. Some scholars have estimated that the entire population was dwindling; other scholars focus instead on the natural migration of whales that made them less accessible to New England whalers.[20] For American whalers, access to the sea was also complicated by the Civil War.

In 1861, the U.S. government purchased forty older whaling ships, loaded them with stones, and deliberately sank them off the Charleston and Savannah harbors in an effort to make the navigable channels unsafe for blockade runners. The cargoes of stones were intended to prevent the hulks from being raised or washed away after settling into place in the channels. As an experiment in blockading tactics, the enterprise was dubious, but as a drain upon the resources of the whaling industry (which was, of course, not the intention of Union leaders), the "Great Stone Fleet," as it was called, proved eminently successful. Although the government purchased the vessels outright, their destruction left an immediate gap in the ranks of the whaling fleet that was never filled. This was a planned loss, though; in addition, American whalers, forced by their search for whales into distant Pacific and Arctic waters, sailed unprotected as representatives of one of the Union's most critical industries.

For the most part, the war simply forced whalers to stay off the sea and, thereby, disrupted the industry. The only actual attack on the whalers oc-curred on June 28, 1865, more than a month after the surrender by General Robert E. Lee at Appomattox, Virginia. Sailing off the Bering Strait, the whale ship *Brunswick* experienced an unexpected wind surge and crashed onto the ice. Other whale ships had congregated in order to divide up the ship's cargo when one observer espied another steamship approaching on the horizon. A few whalers thought the ship might be a Confederate raider that had been seen rigging out in Australia in February. In moments, their suspicions proved correct when five armed boats arrived from the ship carrying uniformed Confederate soldiers. The soldiers announced to the crews of the becalmed ships that they were the prizes of the CSS *Shenandoah*. The men were ordered to abandon their vessels and come aboard the steamer as prisoners of war or to be blown out of the water. The panicked whalers moved to the steamer, and the soldiers axed open casks of oil and set each whale ship afire.

Two ships were allowed to leave in order to transport the crews. Eight whale ships, however, burned amid the Arctic ice as the prizes of the *Shenandoah* and the defunct Confederacy.

Captives of the *Shenandoah* repeatedly attempted to convince the crew of Lee's surrender. Finally, on June 23 the ship's log verifies that one captured vessel used newspaper accounts to convince the Confederate raider that Lee had surrendered at Appomattox.[21] Eventually, the Confederate crew abandoned its raid and set sail for a safe harbor in Liverpool.[22] During the attack, however, the whale fleet suffered greatly: more than one thousand sailors were taken prisoner, 25 ships destroyed, and cargo valued at about $1.5 million lost. From a New Bedford fleet of 186 whale ships in 1861, this loss of 25, combined with another 21 ships lost in the war and the 40 in the Great Stone Fleet, seriously diminished the industry. Just when it could least afford to lose its lead in the illumination market, whale oil production had been crippled by war and instability in the 1860s.[23]

Although these factors contributed to the transition from whale oil, most historians point directly to the 1870–1871 season when these market pressures forced whalers to linger longer than usual in Arctic waters. Given the context of the illumination market in 1870, the urgency of the whalers' trips deep into the Arctic stemmed from the emergence of competitors: kerosene made from coal and, subsequently, also from petroleum. At this tenuous juncture in the history of American whaling, the whalers stared at the approaching ice, resisted the urge to leave, and then waited for their fate to unfold. Much of the fleet was frozen and eventually crushed in the Arctic ice during the 1871 season. The fate of this fleet represents a moment of historical convergence: the meeting of a variety of factors to create a historically significant moment.

As the whalers remained in the Arctic beyond the limits of their own judgment and the basic facts of the region's seasonal patterns, their panic was an indicator that in the United States, Great Britain, and a few other industrializing nations, the entire energy scene had begun to shift. Historians of industrialization refer to the adoption of energy wrought from fossil fuels as the "takeoff" when boundless energy supplies loosed the limits on industrial capabilities. Thus, part of the transition symbolized by the abandoned whalers of 1871 lay in humanity-wide shifts not just in energy sources but also in the way humans do very basic things—such as making light.

INCREASING AND REGULARIZING
THE PETROLEUM SUPPLY

The illumination market could absorb the quantities of crude that escaped the Oil Creek valley, and soon the area in Pennsylvania became known as

"Petrolia." Similar names were bestowed on a town in Canada, and eventually others in South America. The name in Pennsylvania, however, quickly came to embody much more than a simple location; indeed, "Petrolia" was an industrial sector in which any other consideration for the locale was given over to the individual enterprise that would pry more crude out of the ground and get it to market. Technology supported this rush to harvest crude.

As the value of crude rose, wildcatters' patience with percussive drilling dwindled. New technologies were dreamed up and applied immediately in the oil fields. Particularly during the Pennsylvania boom of the 1860s, knowledge of petroleum geology and the technology to exploit it grew in a vernacular, trial-and-error method. Once the well-known oil seeps had been exploited, finding oil was a growth industry for anyone with composure and audacity. Divining, which was used for locating oil supplies based on hydrology (as water occurred with the petroleum), began in France. Typically, a freshly cut, Y-shaped twig was held by the diviner, who was capable of feeling the tug of the fresh sap in the stick toward the underground water supply. Although there may have been a bit of science behind divining, "oil sniffers," who could offer no scientific credibility, were also popular in the early Pennsylvania boom.[24]

Accessing the oil continued to require drilling and the use of a pump, known as a derrick. The general design for the derrick took shape from the Chinese model; however, the name derived from Thomas Derrick, who used the device in England during the Elizabethan era for a very different purpose: executing more than three thousand criminals. For this gruesome purpose, Derrick devised for his hangings a beam with a topping lift and pulleys instead of the old-fashioned rope over the beam method. The frame used for hangings was adapted to support the devices for drilling for oil, and then the same derrick structure could be used to support the piping and steam engine involved in pumping out the oil once the well had been struck. Since the derrick was on the earth's surface, it became a recognizable icon of oil exploration and development.

The urgency of the search for oil combined with the need to revive dry wells and inspire one of the strangest technologies of the early industry. Although the petroleum landscape was one teeming with the threat of fire, Colonel E. A. L. Roberts proposed that the industry was ripe for the use of the explosives that he had mastered during the Civil War. Following the war, Roberts applied his knowledge of explosives to some of the problematic uncertainties of finding petroleum. On January 28, 1865, Roberts successfully discharged two of his eight-pound torpedoes into a well on Watson Flats, near Titusville. The explosion did not produce a jet of oil. But once Roberts cleared the debris, a well that had been slowly petering out now emitted a steady flow. Roberts quickly set up his company, which was organized around lowering a torpedo—initially an iron flask filled with gunpowder, later with nitroglycerin—deep below the earth's surface and then igniting it by dropping a weight along a suspension wire onto percussion caps in the flask. Normally, Roberts poured water into the hole to hold the explosive force within the oil-bearing sand strata. He charged $100 to $200 per charge and a royalty of one-fifteenth of the increased flow of oil. By 1870, torpedo technology became standard practice even though it often led to accidents.

Little thought was given to the fact that in addition to increasing the likelihood of locating a petroleum well, torpedoes greatly endangered anyone living or working nearby. The use of explosives around the flammable petroleum would seem intolerable to most communities; however, in oil regions all over the world, the priority was not to create a safe living environment for their residents. The priority was to extract oil, and torpedoes simplified one aspect of this process.

With a similar ethic, entrepreneurs quickly identified infrastructure development and control as the portion of the oil industry that was most likely to endure—even if Pennsylvania's supply ultimately diminished. Although the natural occurrence of crude meant that Pennsylvania would follow an aggressive model of development, the industry there identified certain tools that would be used wherever future supplies were found. The boomtown was one of the most important of these.

Figure 1.4. The Spondulix Petroleum Company, like other such companies, used speculation or investment to spread the risk of oil development in Pennsylvania among many different financiers. (Library of Congress Prints and Photographs Division, LC-USZ62-4847)

Following uneven development in the early 1860s caused by the market's inability to absorb an overproduction of oil, new investment arrived in 1864 and 1865 to expand speculation beyond the limits of the slight Oil Creek.[25] This also meant that speculation for oil was leaving the cradle of the methods used for collecting and shipping that had taken shape along the creek. Approximately ten miles from this hub of oil extraction, investors focused on two farms along Pithole Creek that were known by the family name Holmden.[26] The lessees in this area joined efforts and formed the United States Petroleum Company. When the region's first well came in, timing was everything. Similar strikes had been made in the Oil Creek valley during the first five years of the oil boom, and boomtowns took shape around them in order to provide the goods and services that would be needed. However, during the early months of 1865, thousands of soldiers were discharged from the Union Army. These men flocked to the most likely source of jobs. As if staged as an act in a play, the biggest boomtown of all, Pithole, burst onto the scene and represented the greatest possibilities available in the entire nation. Pithole was suddenly poised to boom as no town ever had.

By the end of the summer three thousand teamsters were on hand to drive the oil out of the Pithole area by wagon.[27] The only buildings in the immediate vicinity were the homes of the two Holmden brothers and a log cabin known as Widow Lyon's house. Such a setting left the hordes of visitors and workers with no place to eat or stay. The Holmdens began serving meals to nearly two hundred visitors per day, with workers always eating first. In May 1865, Colonel A. P. Duncan and George C. Prather, two businessmen from Oil City, purchased land adjacent to the oil fields. They were not interested in speculating for oil; their interest lay in creating a town to profit from the tremendous surge in local population.

In this "drawing board city," the first leases for property reflected the predominance of the ethic of transience. Leases for a store or business cost $50 for six months, $100 per year, renewable for three years. This price allowed the leases to move briskly, but with one catch: at the expiration of the three-year agreement, the lessee had the privilege of removing the buildings that he had constructed or selling them to the owners of the land at the landowner's figure. Even if a business owner thought he or she might not be in this place permanently, they may have wished to have a sturdy or nicely kept building; however, with the knowledge that anything they built would basically return to the landowner from whom they rented, few worthwhile improvements would be made. The entire process of town settlement encouraged the tenant to think in short terms and quick profits. Although this model would be used in other industries, Pithole was creating a model of the boomtown that would permeate oil frontiers everywhere.

A critical portion of the boomtown's design was its ability to expand and then collapse like a tent, if needed. Pithole reached its peak production, reportedly between six thousand and eight thousand barrels, in October 1865. On the Thomas Holmden farm there were eighty-one wells on seventy-nine leases, eleven of which were producing and three only marginally. Of the Pithole supply, more than half came from only two wells. In a place where the product had become the rationale for every development, these two wells sustained the largest town in the oil region. Therefore, when their production began to subside, the world had its first example of the other end of oil development: from boom to bust.

Between dwindling oil supplies and the construction of pipelines to replace the workforce served by the town, Pithole, founded on a drawing board in May 1865, had boomed and completely busted in little more than three years. Ironically, the years that Pithole enjoyed success were too short to appear in the census records. In the 1860 Census, Pithole, of course, did not exist; in the 1870 Census, the town's population was down to 281. Falling between the cracks of the decennial census, the story of Pithole's boom was left to be told by those who lived it and observed it. By August 1877, the Court of Quarter Sessions revoked the borough's charter. Pithole was struck from the face of the earth and ceased to exist.

In its disappearance, Pithole embodied a new ideal in the process of extraction: it had performed its role in production and now had no reason to survive. In the production of petroleum, towns had become an important but disposable cog, particularly for a model of development that was committed to allowing the industry—moving synergistically with the supplies—to boom and bust.

AMERICAN EXPANSION MEETS CRUDE TO MATCH IN TEXAS

Even with limited uses for petroleum throughout the late 1800s, oil development spread to other regions. Based on the boomtown model formulated in the Pennsylvania fields, a clear pattern emerged. Contemporary observers mistakenly first associate the state of Texas with American oil development. From Pennsylvania, the U.S. industry actually first expanded to other states, including Arkansas, California, and Ohio. There was even significant oil development internationally by the time that speculators took a hard look at Texas at the end of the 1800s.

In the American model, most regions simply rode with the booms; California, however, presented a bit of a different story. Historian Paul Sabin writes that as oil came to California in the late 1800s, "politics and policy determined how rapidly oil moved onto the market . . . and how avidly it was consumed."[28] These reformers argued that oil's lack of permanence as an industry was primarily "the character of production."[29] The powers behind American petroleum development, though, were not about to allow the industry to alter its pace of boom. Ultimately, this California example was largely an aberration. The American model, in fact, was about to have its defining moment on the Texas oil frontier, which picked up in spirit where Pennsylvania had left off. These Texas wildcatters came to personify an American pattern of petroleum development rooted in individual opportunity.

In particular, during the late 1800s Patillo Higgins saw great promise in the salt domes that created open pockets in the geology beneath eastern portions of the state. Spindletop was the dome that he felt had the best potential for oil, and, much like Drake, Higgins spent years soliciting financial and technical assistance to investigate it. Unlike Drake, Higgins had much more information available to him. He took out a magazine advertisement requesting someone to drill on the Big Hill, the local name for Spindletop. The only response came from Captain Anthony F. Lucas, who had prospected domes in Texas for salt and sulfur. With connections in the petroleum industry, Lucas discussed the site with representatives of Standard Oil in 1898 and was met only by derision. In his report to Lucas, one of the company geologists explained that he had found oil in Russia, Borneo, Sumatra, and Romania, but "there [is] no indication whatever to warrant the expectation of an oilfield on the prairies of south-eastern Texas."[30]

With little industrial support, therefore, Lucas carried out drilling at Sour Spring Mound and other sites in the Beaumont area. From October to January 1901, Lucas's drilling crew, known as "roughnecks" for the hard physical labor of drilling pipe deep into the earth, struggled to penetrate the difficult oil sands that had stymied previous drilling efforts. At this point in the industry's history, roughnecks normally drilled within a casing pipe that they slid into the deepening hole. Driven by steam- or gasoline-powered engines, the drill moved at varying speeds depending on the hardness of the rock encountered at each level. At the turn of 1901, the drilling outside of Beaumont became particularly odd—the stem dropping dramatically and then slowing down considerably. The roughnecks assumed it was caused by layers of sand; however, in hindsight, the bumpiness may have been caused by the natural gas that was pocketed around the immense Texas storehouse of crude.

At Spindletop on January 10, mud began bubbling from the drill hole. The four or five workers at the site struggled to make sense of the mud just as they heard a sound like a cannon. A roar followed and suddenly oil spurted out of the hole with rock, sand, and portions of the drilling rig flying through the air. The Lucas geyser, found at a depth of 1,139 feet, blew a stream of oil more than one hundred feet high until it was capped nine days later. During this period, the well flowed an estimated one hundred thousand barrels a day—well beyond any flows previously witnessed. The event was a symbol for a new age in oil for the nation, but in particular for residents of Beaumont. One of them, Charles Berly, later recalled the view that he took in on that day as he stood on a nearby cupola:

> The [well] was going wild . . . probably spouting 150 feet in the air. . . . Nobody realized the significance of it at the time. We didn't understand oil in those days as a fuel. Oil was axle grease and kerosene for lamps . . . not fuel. . . . In fact, people were pretty disturbed about all that mess that was all over the face of the earth out there. . . . They were worried about the fact that it was going to kill all the fish in the creeks and interfere with agriculture.[31]

When Lucas finally gained control of the geyser on January 19, a huge pool—practically a lake—of oil surrounded it.

The flow from Lucas 1 was unlike anything witnessed before in the petroleum industry: more than seventy-five thousand barrels per day. As news of the gusher reached around the world, the Texas oil boom was on, following the general model of Pithole and other sites. Throngs of oilmen, speculators, and onlookers came and transformed the city of Beaumont into Texas's first oil boomtown. Land sold for wildly erratic prices. After a few months more than two hundred wells had been sunk on the Big Hill. By the end of 1901 an estimated $235 million had been invested in Texas oil.

Just as it had in the 1860s, the American model invited open speculation in 1901. Eager to find similar deposits, investors spent millions of dollars throughout the Lone Star state in search of oil and natural gas. By 1902 there were more than five hundred Texas corporations doing business in Beaumont. Spindletop began Texas's global reputation for oil development. As Texas's leading boomtown, Beaumont took shape around free-flowing whiskey, cash, and crude oil. Temporary homes for oil workers and speculators, boomtowns were designed to last only a few years (as long as the supply of crude held out). Oil developments in the coming decades made boomtowns familiar throughout Texas. This was the "big time" in oil development; however, it also suggested larger cultural patterns at work. The massive quantities of petroleum drove its price downward and forced innovators to search for new uses for petroleum. In particular, Standard's leader Rockefeller and others focused on inventors in France and Germany who had begun to manufacture devices for individual transportation called automobiles, which are discussed in other chapters.

Nearly a half-century after its discovery, petroleum at last was available in quantities that could allow it to become interconnected with human society on an elaborate scale. Although supplies entered the market from all over the globe, the American model of development was most clearly responsible for the expansive supplies that would now define human life in the twentieth century. This emphasis on individual speculation played into the details of the very nature of crude. Petroleum's flexibility made it the perfect commodity for the American model of development.

CONCLUSION: CRUDE AND THE
AMERICAN SYSTEM OF EXTRACTION

The capacity for expansion in oil began along Oil Creek but clearly exploded onto the Texas prairie in 1901. The emergence of oil meant that American illumination was no longer grounded in a limited, maritime version of the hunter-prey relationship, as Pennsylvania oilmen steered the industry through a period of explosive, booming growth. Perfecting the technologies for gathering, storing, transporting, and refining the crude while maintaining profits represented the challenge of the new petroleum industry and the great promise for individual entrepreneurs. Entirely new groups orchestrated this resource harvest: speculators and marketers well-schooled in the nation's energy and illumination needs drove the search for a steady supply of petroleum. Pennsylvania rock oil was a commodity not limited by the amount of fats and oils that could be extracted from a single mammal, however large it might be. Instead, the greatest mystery in rock oil's discovery lay in the amount available beneath the earth's surface. It truly seemed unbounded—if it could first be located and tamed.

To realize such flexibility and opportunity, though, petroleum had to be found. In a manner similar to capturing a whale, a petroleum well needed to be located largely by luck. Although some techniques, including "oil sniffing" and "divining" with fresh saplings, became fairly accepted practices in the Pennsylvania oil fields, there was so little knowledge available about oil's underground occurrence that the only real organization to its pursuit was to follow successful strikes. If a well came in, wildcatters set up additional wells as near as possible. This tendency of oilmen grew out of oil's natural occurrence underground and out of sight. Initially, this led to legal challenges as oilmen sought to restrict the access of followers.

Legal authority was sought to control this reckless and haphazard development; however, oil's nature would not allow it. In British and American courts, surface property law was found not to apply to an underground pocket that reached over surface boundaries. The law of the oil field became, essentially, no law, thus helping to ensure the boom model that predominated the American fields. Known as "the rule of capture," legal ownership was only granted to oil once it had reached the earth's surface. Therefore, the occurrence of crude actually perpetuated the rush of wildcatters following others' successful strikes; early oil institutionalized "boom" development as the primary system for acquiring crude.

The capitalist system of the United States did little to settle the independent nature of crude. In fact, as booms played out in American locales such as Pennsylvania, California, Oklahoma, and Texas, the American model of petroleum development became a vision of disorganized, dangerous, and reckless searching for possible fortune. It was an ugly scene, particularly given the emerging modern business ideas of systemization. By glamorizing the boom of Pennsylvania and Texas oil, in fact, the American model perpetuated this view of the industry and helped to make it part of petroleum's mythology. Another model of development was emerging, though. And its intellectual routes actually grew out of an American mind, even though its greatest impact would be seen in the industry's global development.

Despite the glamour of wild boom, a bit of systemization could take away some of the risk inherent in searching for, harvesting, processing, and delivering crude. Indeed, it could also maximize the profits available in petroleum. This was the feature that caught the interest of a young fruit salesman in Cleveland, Ohio, who personified the emerging new era in business. While cutting waste and systematizing manufacturing had already led some industrialists to great wealth, petroleum seemed industry's wild bronco—unbreakable and untamable. However, John D. Rockefeller Sr. viewed petroleum with an eye toward systematic management, and his dramatic influence on the resource will be discussed in chapter 2.

At the ground level in the United States, however, petroleum resisted this modern sensibility. To an industrialist of the nineteenth century, products such as iron and steel were quite definable—with capital on hand, it was relatively simple to deduce which mines and foundries were required to support one's production. Petroleum, though, remained quite fickle because of its haphazard reliance on speculation and boom. Particularly in the American model of development, the industry's primary response to petroleum's vagaries and inconsistencies was simply to drill more wells.

Order without genuine restraint or control led many to refer to the "rule of capture" as "the rule of the jungle." Ultimately, the boomtown became a tool of this developmental ethic. A distant relative of the whale ship as a device for resource extraction in distant locales, the boomtown's form, initiated in the Pennsylvania oil fields, became a method for oil companies to flexibly access supplies anywhere. If oil was struck, the town grew; if not, the town collapsed and could be gone overnight. The nature of oil created these concrete expressions of the rule of capture; however, Rockefeller remained unimpressed.

With disdain for the unpredictable reality of oil exploration, Rockefeller described the Pennsylvania oil regions as nothing more than a "work camp." In the mindset of the business organizer, petroleum was a failure: as an undertaking, it was disorganized; as a resource, it was inflexible; as a commodity, its supply was unreliable. Therefore, developing crude on a broader scale offered one of the greatest challenges of the new industrial era—requiring much more than simple fortitude, determination, and luck.

Chapter Two

Crossing Borders to Increase Supply

The building material stood out distinctly against the huts of natural materials that predominated the Far East: blue tin stacked, propped, or stuck to other organic matter. Throughout portions of China, India, and areas such as Burma and Sumatra, humans lived very simply into the late 1800s. Obviously, this new building material was an interloper, imported from a far-off land across space and, truly, time. Used only once and then discarded, the cans came from a distant country with manufacturing prowess that took valuable raw materials such as metal and fabricated from them disposable items. The cans had found their way into locales in which most cooking occurred over a fire and education was limited. The presence of so few manufactured goods in such places meant that any waste materials might find new uses, such as serving as building supplies. If one looked closely at the torn tin one might also make out the scripted words: "Standard Oil of California."

The obvious first step to alter human's relationship with crude—whether in Burma or Arkansas—was to increase the supple of petroleum. By the late 1800s, this had at least begun to occur, thanks to Drake's fortitude and wildcatters' technological innovations. Then the 1901 strikes in Texas demonstrated that increased supply also required stabilizing growth in industrial infrastructure. Petroleum's synchronic relationship with the American spirit of expansion would never entirely go away; however, there was clearly an opportunity for another approach. For instance, boomtowns such as Pithole remained part of the petroleum industry because they prioritized the flexibility that allowed entrepreneurs to capitalize on new opportunities. Boom and bust became a necessary part of the industry's development; however, not every region relied so heavily on exploiting individual opportunity in oil. Unlike the predominant American example of the 1800s, petroleum offered great benefit to capital organized around centralized planning and systemization. It is ironic that the primary example for this international model of development sprang from the American experience with crude represented by the tin can.

By reacting against the unpredictable cycle of boom and bust, Rockefeller's Standard was a model for other nations (and was also their competitor) as they devised ways to prosper from their own supplies of crude. In other regions, nations developed the resource themselves or joined with existing petroleum companies (including Standard). Typically, enterprises following the international model relied much less on independent speculators and wildcatters. Often, the large systems around which these international enterprises were organized were constructed from necessity: lacking their own supply of petroleum, a few powerful nations sought the technical and political mechanisms to acquire petroleum wherever it occurred. In doing so, the British, Dutch, and French foreshadowed an era of petroleum scarcity that would befall all nations more than a century and a half after Drake had struck the first commercial well. In the late 1800s, petroleum became simply another resource—albeit an extremely complicated one to harvest and develop—organized into the mercantilist tradition that had become known as colonialism long before the early twentieth century. The international model, therefore, most often was carried out by European oil firms in cooperation with a crown or government that exerted colonial authority in the oil-producing region.

Although little changed in terms of petroleum's usefulness by the late 1800s, new technologies helped to tie together a highly organized, international model of petroleum development by prioritizing methods for dispersing kerosene all over the world—no matter where the petroleum from which it derived had been harvested. Although each aspect of harvesting and dispersing crude required significant economic capital, techniques such as pipelines brought crude to centralized processing and refining locations. And tanker railroad cars allowed refined oil to be moved more easily to points of use or shipment. In these global examples, once supply was reliably established, this expanding infrastructure of dispersal became the next hurdle and the next frontier of great opportunity and profit. It all had to be in place to bring crude from Texas or Pennsylvania to the far stretches of the world. It had very little to do with individual fortitude and fortune; instead, it relied on elaborate, complex corporate organizations. In this model of petroleum development, the construction of an oilcan was not exactly the scale that Rockefeller and the other oil entrepreneurs had in mind as they sought oil's future. Crude's path forward, though, undeniably began with that humble can that served as conduit for the commodity while also bridging lifestyles and civilizations.

STANDARDIZING OIL, ABSTRACTING THE COMMODITY

Petroleum could not grow through any existing business model. With supplies geographically dispersed by geology, oil extraction required that a company possess a scale and scope for collection that allowed tools—in the form of a boomtown, for instance—to be developed wherever it was necessary. Despite all the malice that would eventually be focused on him, John D. Rockefeller Sr. understood this better than any other human; however, he certainly was not alone. Rockefeller's Standard Oil Trust created the model that others would follow and against which they would attempt to compete. His term for his enterprise was "integration," and, on the whole, his organization sought to overcome the vagaries embraced by the American model for developing crude.

Although the *possibility* of fortune drew thousands of speculators into the oil fields, Rockefeller sought the sure thing: ensuring supply. In order to accomplish this goal, he neither denied nor embraced the nature of crude; instead, his corporate system tolerated it. From his specialty in trading and transportation, Rockefeller identified his own method for reining in and systematizing petroleum production so that it would maximize his corporate success and personal fortune. Although he established a framework that would be used all over the world during the next century, Rockefeller's plans were not immediately successful.

Working within the South Improvement Company for much of the late 1860s, Rockefeller laid the groundwork for his effort to control the entire industry at each step in petroleum's production once it had been brought out of the ground. Initially, however, individual producers and businessmen banded together in order to stave off Standard's efforts. This banding together proved successful until petroleum's success leaked out of the Oil Creek valley in Pennsylvania and expanded into other states and nations during the 1870s. Referred to as the "Oil War" in the media, the independents successfully fought Rockefeller in the early 1870s. Through this altercation the corporate financing behind the industry grew separated from the laborers who had defined the early years in Pennsylvania. Refiners in other areas also supported the laborers of Petrolia against Southern, as it was still called. Rockefeller's company planned to make Cleveland and Pittsburgh essentially the only refining points for Pennsylvania crude. Without contracts for transportation, Oil Creek refiners shut down their operations and halted most oil production. After forty days, they had destroyed the monopoly and production began again. Those involved in the industry had learned the positive outcome of banding together. However, the writing that described the future of oil was clearly on the wall. In the transition to using petroleum as a primary energy source, this juncture is crucial. The corporate reaction took a relatively small-scale enterprise and provided it with the capital and organization to enlarge the commodity's scale and scope.

The triumph over Southern could not last. Rockefeller crafted new plans that would make his efforts more permanent. The unity of the teamsters had actually played directly into his plan. In adjusting his strategy, Rockefeller formed the Standard Oil Company of Ohio in 1870. Later, in 1872, Rockefeller laid the groundwork for his effort to control the entire industry (using companies such as Galena-Signal for his own ends). Biographer Ron Chernow writes: "Instead of just tending to his own business, he began to conceive of the industry as a gigantic, interrelated mechanism and thought in terms of strategic alliances and long-term planning."[1] The joint-stock firm of Standard of Ohio, with John D. Rockefeller Sr. as president, William Rockefeller as vice president, and Henry M. Flagler as secretary treasurer, was able to circumvent laws in many states that forbade companies from owning interests outside the state. With its original holdings, Standard controlled about 10 percent of American refining. Rockefeller put his goal simply: "The Standard Oil Company will some day refine all the oil and make all the barrels."[2]

Establishing a shell company known as the South Improvement Company (SIC), Rockefeller implemented his plan to entirely disregard suppliers—who, of course, *had* to sell to someone—and to focus his efforts and capital on playing his refinery competitors off of one another. Railroad companies became the primary tool for doing this. While the railroads would raise their rates, rates for refiners who were members of SIC would be left unchanged and members would even receive rebates. In addition, Standard received "drawbacks" from the railroads on shipments made by nonmember refiners. Railroad companies also agreed to provide information to Standard about the amounts of oil being shipped by competitors. Why would railroads agree to such an arrangement?

The simplest answer is that Rockefeller had done his homework and his business acumen reached well beyond petroleum. In studying large-scale economic developments of the era, Standard's leaders realized that the growth of railroads had left the companies precariously balanced. SIC agreed to act as an "evener" to balance out the flow of oil shipments among different companies and, thereby, benefit and balance the entire railroad business. Functioning almost like a referee or umpire for the transportation sector, Standard calmed the price wars that had begun after the Civil War. Rockefeller wrote in one 1871 letter, "A man who succeeds in life must sometimes go against the current."[3] The public, of course, did not learn about such practices until Henry Flagler disclosed them to the journalist Ida Tarbell. Even then, Rockefeller never admitted illicitly managing the petroleum market. "I knew it as a matter of conscience," he recalled. "It was right before me and my God. If I had to do it tomorrow I would do it again the same way—do it a hundred times." The cycle repeated: refiners who were not members of SIC struggled more and more until, with absolute ruthlessness, Standard swept in and purchased them cheaply. In the thinking of industrialists such as Rockefeller, it was about the efficiency of the system. Exerting such a plan, however, required considerable capital and influence.

By 1879 Standard controlled 90 percent of the U.S. refining capacity, most of the rail lines between urban centers in the Northeast, and many of the leasing companies at the various sites of oil speculation. Throughout the 1870s and early 1880s, Standard Oil would further its dominance over the refining industry, and by 1882 it would form the Standard Oil Trust, a new innovation in business integration that allowed companies to expand and monopolize control of their industries and markets. In each facet of the petroleum industry, the independents were put out of business, unable to compete with Standard's scale and scope. Rockefeller's system of refineries grew so great that at the close of the nineteenth century he could demand lower rates and kickbacks from rail companies. In a manner similar to one individual being in charge of a computer's operating software, Rockefeller controlled the economic infrastructure for American domestic trade and production. It neither was fair nor did it meet the capitalist goal of a competitive marketplace.

However, in terms of oil, this new model of development provided the map for future success. The efficiencies and design of Rockefeller's corporate model could support unbelievable growth in the industry's scale and scope, particularly in exporting petroleum technology and exploiting supplies worldwide. In the case of Standard, control and order had to be aggressively exerted on an existing industry through confrontation and open (at times illicit) competition. Obviously, these efforts were resisted at the grassroots level of the petroleum industry and then again at the level of federal law. These were lessons from which other corporations could learn. In addition, regions developing their oil resource for the first time might insert corporate structure and control from the start.

The modern-day oil company became a version of the joint-stock companies that had been created by European royalty to explore the world during the mercantilism of the 1600s. Now, though, behemoth oil companies were transnational corporations, largely unregulated and seeking one thing: crude oil. As in the mercantilist model, oil development required that business interests extend far from home to take on unfamiliar tasks. The early phases of development might require individuals to explore primitive communities and then to negotiate access with local authorities. If supplies of crude were found, though, the negotiations often moved to the highest level of national, diplomatic discourse. Although its primary use remained illumination, wherever "black gold" occurred, oil tycoons set the wheels of development in motion. Boomtowns modeled after those in the Pennsylvania oil fields could suddenly pop up in Azerbaijan, Borneo, or Sumatra.[4] Typically, though, these were not organic developments such as Pithole; instead, they were part of the resource development strategy of a corporation funded from a far-off nation.

In the early twentieth century, the competition in global crude would be among corporate entities drawing on Standard's model to divide up the world's known oil reserves. Using the model of horizontal integration in the late 1800s, Standard controlled the means by which the oil would move and be processed. Although this model worked masterfully on the domestic level, there were many additional challenges to developing global supplies. In addition, when Standard ran into legal limitations deriving from the American ideal of free enterprise, international entities were poised to step into the breach. The international model was based on intense competition between these very large corporate players and the colonial powers who supported them.

Therefore, even prior to its legal disputes during the first decade of the twentieth century, Standard found that it could not match one attribute brought by many of its competitors: governmental or royal support. From 1880 to 1910, with such support, massive oil corporations—reaching into jungle and frozen tundra—transformed the entire globe into a game board on which these massive, flexible corporate entities competed with one another.

BAKU AND THE FORMATION OF A GLOBAL COMMODITY

Resembling a drop in a large pool, the American commodification of oil radiated outward and created ripples of development throughout the world. The first shipment of kerosene made from crude left Philadelphia for London in 1861.[5] Although there was great fear on board about the cargo's safety, once the trip proved uneventful and the kerosene remarkably useful, Europeans clamored for more and word spread to Russia and elsewhere of the "new light." Through the 1860s and 1870s, most kerosene would come through the hands—and tin cans—of Standard Oil and originate from the fields of Pennsylvania. Rapidly, though, activity stirred around the ancient world where humans had found oil for generations. The quest to tie these scattered supplies into a global market involved the names of businessmen that still resonate with significance today, including Rothschild and Nobel. Their efforts originated with the best-known supply outside of Pennsylvania.

In the Baku area, where the Caucasus Mountains extended into the Caspian Sea, the supply of oil fell within an independent duchy that was annexed to Russia during the early 1800s. With primitive efforts to collect oil already going on, by 1829 there were nearly one hundred hand-dug pits operating to collect oil seepage. In the 1870s, Russia's Czarist administration opened the area to competitive, private enterprise.[6] The first oil wells were sunk in 1871, and Robert Nobel emigrated from Sweden to eventually catapult the region to oil supremacy. He did so, however, in a Baku that was entrenched in Asian traditions, including minarets and old mosques of Persian shahs. Populated by Tatars, Armenians, and Persians, Baku soon became the focus of the joint efforts of the Nobels and Russia's imperial system.

The Nobels' innovations built on Pennsylvania's oil experience and, for a time, allowed Russian oil to surpass U.S. production. In particular, they followed Rockefeller's model and focused on transportation to get the oil out of this remote area. It was the railroad portion of this trek that involved another great business family, the Rothschilds of France. Ultimately, their Caspian and Black Sea Petroleum Company, known as "Bnito," competed directly with the Nobels. In addition, the rise of Russian oil demanded the attention of Standard Oil, which began activities in the region around 1885. By the late 1880s, Standard had become a true multinational enterprise in order to compete with these entities based in Europe. Transporting Russia's oil became their primary battlefield.[7]

On the side of the Rothschilds was the considerable influence of Marcus Samuel, a London merchant with shipping connections throughout the Far East. It was his mastery of this network and his integration of the new telegraph that provided the Rothschilds with a distinct advantage over Standard. This, he hoped, would prevent his price on oil from being undercut by Standard—the hallmark of the Rockefeller's successes by the 1890s. In addition, Samuel committed to dealing oil in bulk and shipping it by tankers, thereby cutting down on costs to pack the oil in tin. It was a remarkable innovation in the trade of oil that clearly put Standard on its heels in the Far East; however, the risk to this new market was a lack of the cans themselves. Initially, Samuel sent none, instead relying on recycling by consumers.

In short, when he unleashed a fleet of oil tankers to pass through the Suez Canal in 1891, Marcus Samuel assumed that consumers would have their own cans to fill. Almost exclusively, these cans would be the empties that had previously been filled with Standard's imported crude. Samuel did not realize that Standard's tin cans had in their own right become prizes of people throughout the Far East.[8] Adjusting quickly to maintain the competitive advantage that he had earned for the Rothschilds, Samuel immediately sent ships laden with raw tin to be fabricated into vessels. His red cans were also soon being used in home construction and other activities completely unrelated to the oil that they had once carried. Clearly, it was a moment of worlds meeting across time and space.

GLOBAL CORPORATIONS DEVELOP PERSIAN CRUDE

With their gaze fixed permanently on one specific commodity—what historian Daniel Yergin made famous as "the Prize"—transnational petroleum companies could not necessarily choose their political partners. Very quickly in the early twentieth century, such far-flung enterprises proved difficult in some of the politically unstable locales in which oil was found. The Boxer Rebellion in China and the Boer War in South Africa contributed to difficulties in expanding the oil operations into these areas. In some cases, Shell's facilities were destroyed or pillaged. Additionally, when the Sumatra wells began producing saltwater instead of oil, Royal Dutch nearly collapsed. Company geologists feverishly sought out new supplies—and found them. Royal Dutch, however, found competing with Standard more difficult than ever. The competition forced Royal Dutch to ask the basic question of the international model of development: should oil corporations become even larger in order to conduct similar enterprises in different regions?

Responding in the affirmative, Royal Dutch and Shell began to consider forming an amalgamation that would control most of the oil in Russia and the Far East. However, arranging such a union of great powers would prove challenging. The difficulty came when the companies' leaders had to decide which one would take the lead. Although Samuel also carried out possible negotiations with Standard, the Royal Dutch/Shell Group combined and in 1902–1903 became known as Royal Dutch. Negotiations did not end there; ultimately, in 1907 they officially formed the Royal Dutch/Shell Group, which was most often simply called "the Group."[9] The goal, of course, was to create a corporate oil conglomerate large enough to compete with Standard on a global scale. By 1910 the Group's stability allowed it to make a frontal assault on Rockefeller's Standard by expanding operations into the western United States.

Therefore, as the twentieth century began, the petroleum market reorganized the globe based on available supplies of crude. Each national power—particularly those with no oil of their own—sought its own reserve. Entering the game relatively late, Great Britain sought to catch up by using a government-associated corporation to find crude and facilitate its delivery from a locale not yet exploited. The company that would become known as British Petroleum (BP) grew out of the efforts of William Knox D'Arcy, an adventurer who had made a fortune in Australian mining. Following the great tales of oil seeps in today's Middle East, in 1901 D'Arcy secured a concession from the Grand Vizier of Persia (now known as Iran) to explore for petroleum throughout most of his empire. In need of additional capital, D'Arcy accepted assistance from members of the British Admiralty and formed a Concessionary Oil Syndicate in 1905. The first large discovery came in May 1908 in southwest Persia at Masjid-i-Suleiman. Historian Arash Khazeni observes the cultural impact of this development when he writes:

> The tribes whose winter pastures lay in the vicinity of the fields were soon forced to adapt to a radically transformed environment. Oil derricks and pipelines appeared on the landscape and roads were paved through the mountains. Where flocks and black goat-hair tents had once quietly dotted the hills, houses with running water, schools, and hospitals were built . . . [t]he local tribal population, many of whom became employed as workers earning wages in the oil fields, remaining in the lowlands instead of making the seasonal migration to the summer pastures.[10]

Forming the Anglo-Persian Oil Company, D'Arcy and others proceeded from this one strike to explore for oil throughout the Middle East.

Formed in 1909, the Anglo-Persian Oil Company sought to "prove out" these fields and to validate the long-held suspicion that a great amount of crude lay beneath the cradle of human civilization. Although Anglo-Persian Oil had located a prolific oil field, it encountered major problems in other aspects of the undertaking, particularly in refining the crude oil. The company also lacked a tanker fleet and a distribution network to sell its product. Risking possible acquisition by one of the more stable global oil companies, Anglo-Persian Oil instead formed an association with one; in 1912, the company signed a ten-year marketing agreement with the Royal Dutch/Shell Group. Focusing on the portion of Persia that is primarily modern-day Iraq, Britain led the industry from an era of backroom political deals with national leaders to one of full-blown petroleum colonialism. Locating and developing known supplies were already a priority; however, the determined commitment behind this new expansion grew from an important new application of petroleum: fuel for shipping, which will be discussed below. When it took on the specific authority of the crown, Anglo-Persian also took a new name: British Petroleum, or BP.

The expansion of petroleum supplies from 1900 to 1920 shaped a new aggressiveness toward wildcatting as well as an increasingly active corporate culture. As impressive as the United States' domestic production was during this era, however, the real revolution occurred on the international scene, as British, Dutch, and French powers used corporations such as Shell, British Petroleum, and others to begin developing oil wherever it occurred. These entities became the mechanism for oil's great expansion in supply and usefulness through a remarkable connection to governments around the world. As imperial European powers focused on a multifaceted era of colonialism, securing petroleum supplies became a priority. Obviously, the power wielded by such well-connected companies soon gave a new, international scale to corporations more generally.[11]

Developing oil wherever it occurred demanded cooperation between government and capital. By the end of the 1800s, this relationship had grown into many examples of colonialism. Possibly the best known was Royal Dutch, which was formed in 1890 in the Dutch West Indies. Nearly a decade earlier a manager for the East Sumatra Tobacco Company had stumbled upon locals gathering oil from ponds on a Dutch plantation. Working with the support of Holland's King William III and various banks, the company built a pipeline to bring the oil out of the jungle and to a refinery on the Balaban River. The output was called Crown Oil.

Transportation was the key to the success of emerging network for accessing crude. By 1895, Samuel, through his experience in shipping, had steered petroleum development into the even-more-remote East Indies, in particular the region of Kutei in east Borneo. With the nearest depot more than one thousand miles away, workers cut a four-mile path into the jungle in order to access the area that natives called "Black Spot." Chinese workers carried out much of the labor, with many dying from disease. After oil was struck in 1897, Samuel set up a new company specifically tasked with shipping the oil out of the Far East. Known as the Shell Transport and Trading Company, this foreign-owned corporation was created to conduct its business abroad and was prepared to initiate new efforts wherever they might be needed. In this growing, competitive business environment, Samuel's Shell also advanced its relationship with the Rothschilds' Russian oil supply.

Recalibrating the global geography of human life based on resource supply was not a new idea; doing so specifically for supplies of petroleum, however, was a revolutionary development. In each case, nation-states noted the obvious: a secure supply had to precede the nation's full-blown reliance on this useful substance. In another era, trading companies created plantations and colonial settlements using capital from European nation-states; by the late nineteenth century, the same logic was being applied to the harvest of crude wherever it occurred. Often, this international model increased the industry's efficiency. Clearly, though, the cost was a complete severing of nations from controlling the development of their own resources. Particularly in the case of oil, realizing the resource's value demanded that a nation sign on with one of the international corporations that could develop it. Behind companies such as Shell, British Petroleum, and to some extent Standard came the influence of colonizing nations.[12]

AT THE GROUND LEVEL OF GLOBAL OIL EXPLORATION

As the global effort by Standard and other corporations remade petroleum as a tradable commodity, the limited number of nations with existing supplies of seeping oil assessed the extent of their own supplies and how best to fashion a method for them to profit from its development. Although their desire for profit compelled them to action, any degree of urgency grew from the nature of oil itself. The freewheeling idea of the "rule of capture" respected no international boundaries; therefore, imperial capitals sought knowledge or control of their supplies before they were confronted with offers or onslaughts from international corporations. Although some nations did so in order to negotiate the best deal possible, others sought to gather knowledge and control in order to hold off outside developers.

In the latter cases, petroleum often became an extremely complicating factor in internal political shifts. This was not an era of dictators drawing on the political power gained by controlling petroleum resources (later called "petrodictators"); instead, as nations struggled to transition from royal traditions or to integrate modern political philosophies, petroleum emerged as a significant consideration. Often, each empire's system of property law became a vehicle for resisting or facilitating development by external corporate entities. Most likely, however, there was no resisting these external pressures and opportunities. The global effort to develop crude brought with it exploitation and degradation of local people and environments. Indigenous people, who were rarely users of petroleum, became a temporary labor force and often reaped little or no profit for themselves. Particularly in these early years of development, most deals were unfair and involved simple payments or royalties directed only to the political leader with whom the oil companies negotiated.

Azerbaijan, Baku

Discussed earlier as one of the first great examples of international corporate development, Baku's great oil supply existed under Russian control throughout the nineteenth century. Development came in the 1870s when state authorities liberalized licensing by allowing longer lease terms.[13] When the Nobels, Rothschilds, and other European corporate entities developed kerosene, Russia protected the industry through tariffs that were designed to suppress American companies, particularly Standard. European companies supported regional oil magnates, including Musa Nagiyev, Murtuza Mukhtarov, Shamsi Asadullayev, and Seid Mirbabeyev. Established respectively in 1887 and 1893, Nagiyev's and Asadullayev's companies were the largest of Baku's oil producers. The companies owned oil fields, refineries, and tankers. By the beginning of the next century, more than a hundred oil firms operated in Baku. Between 1856 and 1910 Baku's population grew at a faster rate than that of London, Paris, or New York.

Known as the "Black City," this polluted industrial center stood out from all around it. Internally, the society also was distinct. Through the influence of the Nobels and the Russian government, Baku became a world hub for the developing field of petroleum chemistry. The refinery district that took shape was referred to as "Black Town" and was separated from shipping ports by approximately eight miles.[14] After examining the pipelines in use in Pennsylvania, Ludvig Nobel constructed one in Glasgow and installed it in Baku in the late 1870s. Due particularly to the strong ethnic divisions among the existing laborers—primarily divided between local Azerbaijani Turks and Armenians who despised each other—the pipeline became the focus of saboteurs who were focused on preserving their jobs as wagon drivers and barrel coopers. This ethnic fault line defined much of the difficulty in developing Baku's crude potential.

Most of the Armenians were members of the wealthy or merchant population. In addition, they would ultimately serve as the leadership for Lenin's Bolshevik revolutionaries. Predominantly laborers, the native Azeris were far less prosperous and educated. "Unlike Nobel," writes historian Steve LeVine, "other industrialists treated the Azeri-dominated labor force with deplorable disregard."[15] With the oil industry as its backdrop, this age-old ethnic conflict mushroomed in the early twentieth century, particularly through strikes organized by a young Georgian labor organizer who would later become known to the world as Joseph Stalin.

Beginning in 1903, the Bolsheviks used the vast oil shipping network to distribute Lenin's revolutionary newspaper *Iskra*. Baku was soon host to a secret army of counter-revolutionaries, referred to as "the Black Hundreds," who carried out various assaults on pipelines and refineries. As revolutionaries led uprisings in St. Petersburg in 1905, the ethnic division in the Baku oil fields intensified. Muslim Azeris proceeded to massacre their Armenian neighbors and to set the oil fields afire. To most Western oilmen, this instability made the Baku oil reserves too volatile to be of interest.

Austrian Galicia

In Europe, the best-known supply of petroleum bubbled up to the surface naturally in parts of Austrian Galicia, which composed a large portion of modern-day Ukraine. Its commercial use actually predated that of petroleum's use in the United States, because it had long been used as a lubricant.

The work of two pharmacists, Jan Zeh and Ignacy Lukasiewicz, allowed Galicians to refine their petroleum into kerosene and put it to use in lamps. In fact, in 1853 the Lviv General Hospital became the world's first public building lit solely by petroleum lamps. Although the refining industry became big business during this era, petroleum extraction in Galicia did not really take off until Stanislaw Szczepanowski introduced steam-powered drilling in 1880. Focused in central Galicia, particularly around the small cities of Boryslaw and Drohobycz, the deeper wells powered new undertakings that became further modernized in the 1890s when a Canadian engineer, William Henry MacGarvey, imported cutting-edge drilling technology and quadrupled production. By 1909, Galicia was the third-largest producer of crude oil.[16]

Historian Alison Frank describes the late nineteenth-century Galician industry as a particularly ripe one for wildcatters. Galician autonomy, especially after 1867, allowed landowners from both the noble and peasant classes to prevent government from monopolizing oil rights—even though the central government monopolized other mineral rights in the province. During this era, Frank describes an oil-producing region very similar to that seen in the earliest years of Pennsylvania's oil development. Often described as a "Galician hell," the absence of centralized control often fueled waste of a resource that seemed unlimited at first. The independent efforts to seize oil led to improper extraction and storage that proved ruinous to human health and the environment. While most fires were extinguished quickly, others burned for months and even became tourist attractions, including one in which "the fire and column smoke resembled a volcano."[17] Water sources were polluted by oil that escaped from storage lagoons and flowed into streams and rivers, killing fish and poisoning soil. The result, she writes, was overproduction and inefficiency. In summary of these early decades, Frank writes:

> Every person with access to enough capital to secure a lease of mineral rights to a diminutive plot of land had the chance to be an oilman. This fragmentation may have given local peasants a feeling of empowerment and made large landowners feel more secure about their own property rights, but it also cost oil producers for decades all the advantages associated with coordinated production—in marked contrast to their competitors elsewhere.[18]

In general, Frank finds that Galicians were suspicious of foreign capital, including capital from other parts of the Austro-Hungarian Empire. Despite these suspicions, the Galician industry of this era combined entrepreneurs of different ethnicities and immigrant laborers from abroad who often worked well together. In a foreshadowing of future difficulties, Poles filled out the ranks of the skilled workers and some Jewish workers found it hard to cooperate with their class equals. Anti-Semitism in the oil fields led some Christians to attack Jewish workers and capitalists.

Centralization finally occurred for the Galician supply of oil in 1909 when one cartel successfully achieved domination over production and refining. This arrangement was made with an agreement with the Austro-Hungarian government to buy large quantities of oil to modernize the railways and military. The impact of this potentially beneficial development was limited, however, because the oil fields' reserves were running down quickly at a time when the outbreak of World War I put new demands on it.

During Austria-Hungary's war effort, Galician oil offered a terrific resource—approximately 60 percent of the Central Powers' petroleum supply. However, the supply did not come without difficulty because it was found in very remote locations. Leading up to the war, though, Frank writes that the problem was overproduction, which kept the price low. One outcome of this situation positioned the empire well for the world that emerged after World War I. "Overproduction," Frank writes, "had inspired a relatively early conversion to petroleum use in the empire, enabling oil to compete with coal in industry, the railroads, and the navy."[19] As the needs increased, though, Galician production steadily decreased between 1909 and 1918. Even during the conflict, argues Frank, the grassroots feeling that centralization would prove politically fatal "led to the complete failure to control oil extraction and distribution effectively."[20]

Through the war theaters in and around Galicia and Eastern Europe's oil supply, World War I forecast the resource's strategic significance. Under Field Marshal von Mackensen, the German campaign in Romania reorganized Steaua Romana, which was the English, Dutch, French, and Romanian oil refiner, to operate solely as a German concern. During World War I, Romanian crude was the only secure petroleum supply for Germany's air and tank forces as well as its U-boat fleet.[21]

Mexico and the Americas

In the case of Mexico, petroleum development rode the waves of political and social revolution. Although oil was used by both Aztecs and Mayans during the pre-Columbian era, the first exploratory wells were drilled in 1869. Marking the initial presence of foreign oil companies, this effort was carried out by the Gulf of Mexico Exploration Company in the state of Veracruz. Development, however, did not follow. In 1884, laws granted ownership of oil resources to those owning the surface land. This attracted the interest of American and British oil firms, and when wells became productive around 1901, most of the financial benefits went to the foreign interests that had bought up the land during the prior decades. One example was Henry Clay Pierce, who owned an affiliate of Standard Oil, which monopolized the importing of oil into Mexico to be refined into kerosene in his factories. Pierce attracted the involvement of the U.S. oilman Edward L. Doheny, who established the Mexican Petroleum Company. Over the next twenty years, Doheny's company took a commanding position over Mexico's expanding oil production, including the world's largest well in 1916 at Cerro Azul.

British and American efforts to develop Mexican oil were stabilized by two important Mexican laws: the Petroleum Law (1901) allowed the granting of concessions on public lands, and the Mining Law of 1909 reaffirmed the rights of landowners to develop their subterranean assets. In addition, the government removed import taxes on drilling equipment and exempted oil-company capital stock from taxes. All of this legislation helped keep the Mexican oil industry in the hands of foreigners and allowed those foreigners who already had control to get a tighter grip. By 1910, prospectors had identified the Panuco-Ebano and Faja de Oro fields located near the central Gulf of Mexico coast town of Tuxpán. Systematic explorations by foreign companies (mainly American) came to supersede the uncoordinated efforts of speculative prospectors. Mexico became an oil-exporting nation in 1911.

The oil industry continued to expand through 1921, as the industrialized countries kept demanding more and more oil due to wars and an increasing volume of motorized transportation. Also during this time, foreign ownership increased to the point that almost all of the productive oil land in Mexico was owned by foreigners. However, prior to 1921, there were hints that Mexicans wanted their oil back. In 1917, article 27 of the constitution basically said that any oil or energy-related substances found underground belonged to the state. Foreigners could lease the underground privileges but never actually own them. By 1921, Mexico was second to the United States in petroleum output; with this supply, however, Mexico became the leading exporter of oil in the world.

Historian Myrna Santiago uses this history of oil development to explain political and social patterns during the era of the Mexican Revolution, which extended from 1910 to 1938. The new state apparatus that emerged in 1920, Santiago writes, "brought new pressures to bear on oil companies. They sought to wrestle control over nature from the oilmen as part of a nationalist development program based on a platform of conservation of natural resources. The result was the intensification of the conflict between the revolutionary government and the companies."[22] A force precipitating the social and political revolution, oil workers, argues Santiago, resisted the dominance of foreign companies in the 1910s. "They deserve credit for the nationalization of the industry," she explains.[23] Such was the economic power of oil supplies by the first decades of the twentieth century.

In the case of Mexican oil, nationalization initially resulted in a drop in production. Political instability combined with the emergence of reserves in Venezuela to reduce Mexican oil production by 1930 to just 20 percent of its 1921 level. Production began to recover with the 1932 discovery of the Poza Rica field near Veracruz, which would become Mexico's main source of petroleum for the next several decades. This would cause conflicts between the Mexican government and foreign companies—especially American oil companies—until the matter was resolved in the 1930s.

Similarly, oil companies moved swiftly into Venezuela during the early twentieth century. They came at the behest of Juan Vicente Gomez, the dictator who became president in 1908 and then granted oil concessions to his close associates. Passed along to foreign oil companies, these concessions were developed by Caribbean Petroleum (owned by Royal Dutch/Shell) through the 1910s so that by 1935 the amount of its oil that Venezuela exported had risen from 2 percent to more than 90 percent. In particular, the 1922 Maracaibo strike allowed Venezuela to become one of the world's great oil exporters, second only to the United States in 1929. Under Gomez's guidance, though, Venezuela did little to develop its infrastructure and economy beyond the oil industry. To explain such lopsided development, economists coined the term "Dutch Disease" based on the Venezuelan experience before 1950.

The foreign control of Venezuela's oil began to be reined in when a new president enacted Venezuela's Hydrocarbons Act in 1943. This law did not yet nationalize Venezuela's resource; instead, it introduced the concept of a fifty-fifty split in profits between government and the oil industry. This growing stake set the foundation for Venezuela to nationalize its supply later in the century.

BRITAIN MAKES OIL ESSENTIAL

Throughout Europe and into the Americas, the new international model of developing crude significantly increased supply. This boom worked in tandem with the emergence of new uses for crude to greatly expand transnational oil companies. In scale and scope, the new uses of crude introduced a new era in petroleum's centrality to human life in developed nations. Such a moment, created partly by technical and corporate innovation and partly by new roles for the nation-state and ideas of individual autonomy, ushered in the first period in which we see clearly the formation of a culture of petroleum.

Although the popularity of kerosene had increased petroleum's value, illumination appeared a fleeting application of crude by the late 1800s. Tinkerers and scientists in Europe and the United States began to apply electricity for a variety of purposes. Most important, American inventor Thomas Edison joined with others to make electricity made from coal or fossil fuels the most likely illuminant of the future. By the 1890s, therefore, the primary use of petroleum was for lubrication and manufacturing. Ironically, at this same moment, international efforts to develop and acquire petroleum intensified. In the first decade of the twentieth century, therefore, resourceful political leaders sought ways to make petroleum useful and even integral in ways that extended beyond lubrication. In both the United States and Great Britain, the energy transition was openly manipulated by the political and military establishment. As early as 1910, petroleum emerged as a strategic tool for ensuring global power. Petroleum was first used in this regard to ensure naval supremacy for these powers.

Mastery of shipping since the 1500s had largely been about technology and the design of sailing ships. Building on models from China and elsewhere, Portugal and Spain defined an era of interconnection over the seas. By the late 1800s, coal-fired engines emerged but continued to share the seas with sailing vessels. Shipping was the essential method for moving goods all over the world, and therefore it marked an important opportunity for petroleum's expansion. When utilized to power vehicles and ships, petroleum brought flexible capabilities for expansion that proved a new type of weapon. The ability to use petroleum in various aspects of warfare became a strategic advantage for any nation.

Within a few decades of this realization, the pursuit of petroleum had become similar to an international arms race. Even more significantly, the international corporations that harvested oil throughout the world acquired a level of significance unknown to other producers. By the 1920s, the nearly useless product had become the lifeblood of national security to the United States and Great Britain. For the British, Dutch, and French, petroleum also functioned as a new component of colonialism—both acquiring supplies and utilizing it to administer their empires.

This era was introduced in July 1903, when the crew aboard Britain's HMS *Hannibal* attempted a critical watershed. After using coal to steam out from Portsmouth Harbor, the ship shifted to oil power. Historian Yergin writes: "Moments later, the ship was completely enveloped in a dense black cloud. A faulty burner had turned the test into a disaster."[24] Control of the sea remained the preeminent expression of European power. From the 1890s forward, Germany made open mention of its effort to power a new navy with petroleum. This effort was a barely disguised attempt to threaten the stability of Britain's naval dominance. Because petroleum is a more flexible fuel that was much simpler to transport, its adoption in ships reflected a great strategic advantage. The pursuit of the technology to do so and the construction of such a fleet quickly grew into a turn-of-the-century arms race among the European powers and the United States.

Although the 1903 experiment may have been unsuccessful, it marked an ongoing commitment to crude. The British effort at naval conversion was eventually led politically by young Winston Churchill, who began as a member of Parliament and by 1910 had become the president of the Board of Trade. The early 1910s brought Churchill, who did not begin on the side of naval expansion, a clear education on the advantages of oil (speed capabilities, flexibility of storage and supply, permitted refueling at sea, etc.). He later wrote:

> As a coal ship used up her coal, increasingly large number of men had to be taken, if necessary from the guns, to shovel the coal from remote and inconvenient bunkers to bunkers nearer to the furnaces or to the furnaces themselves, thus weakening the fighting efficiency of the ship perhaps at the most critical moment in the battle. . . . The use of oil made it possible in every type of vessel to have more gun-power and more speed for less size or less cost.[25]

By 1912, the policies had been put in place, and, as Churchill recorded, in the world's greatest navy, "the supreme ships of the Navy, on which our life depended, were fed by oil and could only be fed by oil." Churchill and Britain's military strategists emphasized the great benefits for their naval superiority; however, their decision also marked a defining moment in a new culture of petroleum. By association, committing their fleet to petroleum meant that a consistent and reliable supply of petroleum had just become one of the most important commodities on the earth—nations' security depended on it. Also by association, any nation wishing to compete with them had to follow suit.

As described earlier, the British government went into the oil business in order to ensure this supply. In his 1913 report, "Oil Fuel Supply for His Majesty's Navy," Churchill left no doubt that the future of the Anglo-Persian Oil Company and its undertaking in Persia was directly tied to national security. Agreements were signed in 1914 that gave the British government a ruling interest in the company for a price of £2 million (it would retain this role for many years). By mid-June 1914, Parliament had approved Churchill's proposal. Thus, writes Yergin, "Oil, for the first time, but certainly not the last, had become an instrument of national policy, a strategic commodity second to none."[26] The impetus was the perceived growth in the strength of Germany and its navy. Therefore, Britain's navy set a bar for any nation aspiring to global power on the sea. The moves were seen as preventative and precautionary; within weeks of the proposal's passage, though, global affairs took on an immediacy that was previously unimaginable. On June 28, Archduke Franz Ferdinand of Austria was assassinated at Sarajevo. The world spiraled toward the First World War, with Great Britain declaring war on August 4. Interestingly, the Anglo-Persian Oil Convention received royal assent on August 10. Clearly, the war only made petroleum supplies more critical.

By declaring this new energy era, Britain forced any competing nations to also consider oil with this new logic. At the highest levels, U.S. leaders debated the implications of converting their military, particularly the navy, to petroleum. Their conversations had begun in the late 1800s but took on greater urgency as British reconversion altered global affairs. The United States had one significant strategic advantage in the area of naval conversion: in the early 1900s, American oil fields produced approximately one-third of the world's oil. Indeed, the United States approached all such strategic decisions from the basic realization that it was the only nation in the world that could power its military with petroleum and largely be able to supply it from its own reserves—it possessed energy autonomy, which would later become known as energy independence. Although this was an obvious advantage over other nations, the American situation also required a new type of relationship between business and government. Given such critical importance, petroleum's supply demanded federal oversight or management. In times of an overabundance of supply, this control was often referred to as conservation.

In truth, the shift in the U.S. administration of petroleum was more problematic than simply creating mechanisms for government oversight. The conservation ethic grated against the existing culture of petroleum. In fact, conserving and even managing supplies of petroleum went contrary to the general rules of capitalism. In addition, the right of others to "drink your milkshake," otherwise known as the rule of capture, placed petroleum as one of the resources least able to be regulated in the American economy. Indeed, an important portion of the growing image of petroleum in popular culture was its inability to be limited by borders and laws. These circumstances created unique problems as the status of petroleum supplies changed from superfluous to integral during the 1910s.

In the case of the U.S. Navy, fuel management and conservation had been carried out over coal supplies during the late 1800s. Therefore, the conversion to oil already had a regulatory or managerial mechanism in place to facilitate it. With massive amounts of petroleum available in the United States after 1901, the navy set up a "Liquid Fuel" Board to investigate its use. Similar to the efforts in Britain, this investigation showed that conversion to petroleum had definite advantages. Over the next few years, the navy focused on how to distribute the supply to ships throughout the world and how to lock up reserves in the United States to secure the navy's supply. In terms of reserves, the focus fell on western lands that were contained in the public domain. They held a great deal of the nation's mineral reserves and, in addition, were free of the difficulties of private ownership.

On September 27, 1909, President William H. Taft authorized more than three million acres to be taken out of the public lands and designated as Naval Petroleum Reserves. As was the case for President Theodore Roosevelt's coal withdrawals, Taft's act garnered a great amount of debate—particularly in the West. Congress then passed the Pickett Act in 1910 to allow presidents to withdraw public lands for examination and reclassification for various "public purposes." During the 1910s, this act enabled the president to withdraw nearly all of the known oil lands. In California, Reserves Nos. 1 and 2, commonly known as Elk Hills and Buena Vista Hills, were designated in 1912, and in 1915 Reserve No. 3 was added at Wyoming's Teapot Dome.[27] In 1916, Naval Secretary Josephus Daniels wrote to President Woodrow Wilson: "In view of the great advantage of oil fuel, and in view of the fact that this country produces annually two-thirds of the world's supply of petroleum and upon assurance of the Department of the Interior as to the oil contents of the naval petroleum reserve, in 1913 the Navy definitely adopted the policy of building oil-burning vessels only."[28] In 1911, U.S. Navy ships burned 5.8 million gallons of fuel oil at a cost of $131,000; in 1912 this usage increased to 14.1 million gallons at a cost of $340,000.[29] Designating the reserves and keeping them secure—not from foreign terrorists but from industrial development—were two separate matters.

Historian Peter Shulman describes a scene of transition that took three basic forms in the United States: confused legal status of property, oil producers willing to ignore the new reservation designation, and a lack of administration for the reserves on the navy's part. Even the very strategic idea behind the reserves had not been fully considered: were they to be kept untouched until absolutely necessary or were they only to be used in a time of war? These answers were largely left unresolved. Of this period in the mid-1910s, Shulman writes: "A fuel shortage would have been disastrous. By 1917 the Navy was thoroughly dependent on fuel oil consumption." Daniels did not mince his words as the United States neared involvement in World War I when he wrote: "No other power is in sight and we can not assume that other power suitable for ship propulsion will be discovered."[30] Although petroleum became even more critical to national security by the 1920s, the reserve questions remained largely unanswered. Many observers grew frustrated by the inaction on the existing U.S. Navy Reserves.[31]

Figure 2.1. **"Old King Coal's Crown in Danger," by J. S. Pughe, was a 1902 cover from *Puck* magazine. It depicted the transition of factories from energy generated by burning coal to that generated by burning oil. In the shape of a hand, the smoke from oil burning looks to snatch the crown from a royal figure labeled "Old King Coal." (Library of Congress Prints and Photographs Division, LC-DIG-ppmsca-25671)**

In the end, though, it was Churchill who seems to have most clearly formed the necessary new vision of the twentieth-century world when he proclaimed to the House of Commons on June 17, 1914:

This afternoon we have to deal, not with the policy of building oil-driven ships or of using oil as an ancillary fuel in coal-driven ships. . . . Look out upon the wide expanse of the oil regions of the world. Two gigantic corporations—one in either hemisphere—stand out predominantly. In the New World there is the Standard Oil. . . . In the Old World the great combination of the Shell and the Royal Dutch. . . .

For many years, it has been the policy of the Foreign Office, the Admiralty, and the Indian Government to preserve the independent British oil interests of the Persian oil-field, to help that field to develop as well as we could and, above all, to prevent it being swallowed by [others]. . . .

[Over] . . . the last two or three years, in consequence of these new uses which have been found for this oil . . . [t]here is a world shortage of an article which the world has only lately begun to see is required for certain special purposes. That is the reason why prices have gone up, and not because [of] evilly-disposed gentlemen of the Hebraic persuasion.[32]

CONCLUSION: CHANGING VALUE FORCES NEW MODELS OF DEVELOPMENT

The international model for petroleum development allowed the search for and development of crude to expand incredibly during the first decades of the twentieth century. Starting with the oilcan and extending to the first oil tankers, global trade of crude became a worldwide system. By utilizing the economic form of colonialism in particular, Western nations seized petroleum wherever it occurred and then tied it into their quasi-corporate infrastructure in order to convert it into the commodity that they needed. With the industry so powerful and the commodity increasing in its usefulness, petroleum was now poised for unparalleled expansion, and much of this preparation was made possible—even necessary—by the systems and growth of the international approach to development. In particular, the necessity of petroleum for military purposes had dramatically altered the world's power structure. In Britain, petroleum added new fuel to its system of colonization and promised to perpetuate it for another generation.

In hindsight, these complex enterprises helped to prepare European powers for the growing scarcity that emerged by the end of the twentieth century. By contrast, vast domestic supplies proved to be a crutch for Americans, who organized a culture of petroleum development and consumption based on gluttonous use and overreliance throughout the middle decades of the twentieth century—some would argue through the end of the twentieth century. During the second half of the twentieth century, though, the American model of expansive, largely unregulated development fluctuated somewhat as petroleum became essential for matters of national security; however, vast domestic supplies belied any ideas of scarcity and the conservation ethic that it might inspire. In addition, the U.S. system of government and economic development reacted awkwardly to the international model of centralized, systematic development of petroleum as early as the 1920s.

The system of free enterprise and opportunity in the United States had been tailor-made for the boom-bust pursuit of petroleum; as the industry gained systematic structure, federal oversight emerged as a necessary control. However, due to the focus in the United States on free enterprise, such government involvement and strictures were viewed with great scrutiny. This sentiment was demonstrated, for instance, during the initial effort to implement efficiencies such as conservation to manage supplies of crude, now that it was essential for purposes such as national security. Grating against the laissez-faire, wildcatter, American model of petroleum development, these concerns present in the international model for petroleum development would not be accepted easily in the United States. While Britain's government worked with corporate suppliers to ensure supplies for national security purposes, the United States tried and failed to do so.

For Americans interested in implementing such controls, supply became a key issue in the second decade of the twentieth century. Historian John Ise was one of the first observers to emphasize the fleeting supply of petroleum and the need for better management of it—the concept most often referred to in the United States as "conservation." In 1926, he focused attention on the ownership of resources such as petroleum when they were found on public lands: "During this time there was always overproduction of oil from privately owned lands and there was never any need or justification for opening any public lands."[33] As petroleum became more integral to the society in the 1920s, new attention centered on public land development. Lawmakers in the western United States, where most reserves were located, focused on setting this crude aside from development and, much like a forest reserve, designating the oil for use by the federal government (particularly the navy). In the Mineral Leasing Act of 1920, otherwise known as the Smoot Bill, for instance, Congress attempted to bring relief to some of these issues and to offer more equal treatment to the interests of those in the western United States. In the naval reserves, leases were given only on producing wells, unless the president chose to lease the remainder for federal use. Within six months of the passage of the Mineral Leasing Act, the U.S. secretary of the navy was granted extensive jurisdiction over the U.S. Naval Reserves.

Although ensuring national security would seem a common good, the American culture of petroleum was in transition: although it was clearly essential for naval use, supplies truly seemed endless and any ideas of "conservation" struck some as antidevelopment. Many observers, particularly residents of the American West, asked whether it was sensible for the United States to take possession of such a valuable resource and to restrict its development. While some observers criticized the policy openly, others continued the less formal American model of petroleum development and moved behind the scenes to contradict the policy from inside the government. In other words, they sought to use their political and economic power to subvert the law that ensured domestic reserves would be set aside for military use.

In 1921, the most famous moment of conflict occurred when President Warren G. Harding appointed Albert B. Fall, a senator from New Mexico, the new secretary of the interior. In short order, Fall convinced Secretary of the Navy Edwin Denby to relinquish control of the reserves and had Harding sign a secret presidential order to this effect. Within a few months, word leaked to the public that Fall had leased government reserves in California and Wyoming to his friends in the oil business. Although the episode is most recalled by historians for the breach of executive stewardship that it represents, in fact "Teapot Dome" is more revealing for what it says about the corporate and political culture of petroleum that had emerged in the United States. First, it suggests the radically different value that was placed on petroleum once it had become militarily essential. Second, in one of the first instances of federal conservation and resource management we see the intellectual struggle of leaders attempting to define and weigh the common good as it related to petroleum. Primarily, though, the Teapot Dome incident shows the difficulty of developing the commodity within the modern parameters of the American model of development predicated on laissez-faire and the rights of individual speculation.

Although the need to manage the petroleum supply became obvious in the United States by the end of the twentieth century, there was little public support for the idea of conservation early in the century. With oil seemingly gushing all over the American West, it appeared ridiculous to many industrial leaders to open any discussion about oil's finite supply. Such an approach might be tenable while domestic supplies lasted; however, the nation made no preparations for when most crude needed to be imported to the United States.

Chapter Three

Modeling Big Oil

On the Texas plains, the oil exploded from the earth like a freight train, streaking black straight upward into the sky. At first, the spectacle was similar to those seen elsewhere. One observer wrote that the field "was almost impassable. . . . Teams are dragging wagons . . . with the wheels buried to the hubs in the mud, while the men are wading about in the marshy ground knee deep in water and slush." The amount of oil, though, quickly changed the scene into something otherworldly. "Salt water and thick black scum crept over the pastures and contaminated the bayous. Escaping gas was insidious and was flared for safety's sake, lighting the woods and driving off game." Another observer summed up the scene: "To get the oil out of the earth and get it converted into money was the sole thought of the acreage owners."[1]

Starting near Spindletop in 1901 and continuing through the decade, massive supplies of unexpected crude oil spewed out of gusher oil strikes to create a petroleum landscape unbelievable even to those in the industry: lakes of oil collected on the flatlands, teeming with mud and seeping natural gas. Even in such a bizarre scene, energy can be tied to larger social processes.

A terribly irrational resource, petroleum endured serious scrutiny and efforts to make it function rationally. The oil pools on the Texas plain awaited organization and infrastructure, and they also loomed as a complication in the global effort to establish and maintain a system for using and pricing crude. After huge tanks had been added to hold the crude, the scene symbolized even more clearly the new scale thrust upon the industry by escalating supply worldwide. The reaction to this new abundance as well as the unintended consequences of efforts to systematize crude extraction created an entirely unique corporate culture. As a primary part of this culture, the effort to rationalize the irrational actually—and quite ironically—made petroleum's public face permanently irrational. In short, as a flood of crude erupted in Texas,

Figure 3.1.   Located near Beaumont, Texas, the Heywood #2 gusher helped make the 1901 Spindletop oil discoveries a revolution in the global supply of crude. (Library of Congress Prints and Photographs Division, LC-USZ62-4723)

Russia, and elsewhere during the first decades of the 1900s, oil's price—the way that almost every consumer knows crude—became a fiction.

In fact, price was only one portion of the realities and exaggerations that merged into a new culture of crude. The oil fields had always possessed mythological elements that helped fuel a larger-than-life image of boom and bust; now, the significant value of the commodity—its increasing essential-ness—allowed it to function on an unparalleled plane of power and politics. However, this new stature did not prevent the mythical aspects of the industry from continuing to serve a valuable purpose. The new culture of oil that took shape maintained elements of the oil myth that, now, relative to the com-modity's increased stature, often helped to ground the industry in vernacular traditions—to give it a homespun feeling. Simultaneously, the industry could be viewed as an increasingly dominant force in global politics and markets.

The international model of development had created a scale and scope for petroleum that placed it in a very unique, separate category in the early 1900s. No other commodity possessed similar status in Western societies; therefore, the public began to use a uniquely inclusive term to describe it: "Big Oil." This term expresses the all-encompassing nature of petroleum's influence, reaching over national borders, past political revolution, and even beyond the pricing patterns of the global marketplace—at times, appearing as if in a parallel universe to other commodities. During the interwar years, having been stoked by the massive discoveries starting in 1901, petroleum became exceptional.

THE BIG OIL CONTINUUM

In describing the emergence of petroleum as a transborder commodity, the term Big Oil, first and foremost, captures the new scale within the industry. It is oversimplification—but just barely—to say that big amounts of crude created Big Oil. Massive quantities of crude in the United States, Russia, and Mexico compelled new organization both within and outside of the industry. The need to increase scale grew from the nature of crude itself and

Figure 3.2.   During the 1940s, coastal oil development grew significantly in areas such as the California coast. Some of these wharfs extended to drilling sites offshore, albeit still in very shallow seas. (Library of Congress Prints and Photographs Division, LC-DIG-ppmsca-13480)

the industry's desire to better manage it and, thereby, to divorce oil from its natural vagaries. The industrial apparatus to accomplish this involved technology, organization, and political will; however, the emergence of petroleum at the start of the twentieth century also required a general mindset that would permeate corporations and connect them across borders with political agencies and nation-states. A corporate swagger of sorts took shape that distinguished the oil industry from all others.

Organization, which was a major principle of the international model of development, formed the core of Big Oil. Symbolized by the lakes of crude on the Texas plains that began the century, massive supplies of petroleum in the early decades of the twentieth century initially overwhelmed any efforts at structure and organization that had been previously established. For those involved in petroleum, Big Oil was the necessary product of their odd resource's growing integrality to human life. Building on the essential concepts espoused by Rockefeller, corporations took shape to control crude. Ironically, for the United States to pursue such measures, it had to first vilify the originator of the concept: what began with the breakup of the Standard Oil Trust in the first decade of the twentieth century quickly bred mechanisms within the United States that would essentially formalize Big Oil and create a permanent role for the federal government in the commodity's future.

Although this movement involved regulation and the use of the term "conservation," Big Oil did not express concerns about managing supply; instead, their control was required to stabilize price and, therein, their profits. This last aspect of Big Oil drove a permanent wedge between producers and consumers that continues into the twenty-first century. In the Big Oil paradigm, price provided the primary mechanism for control. By World War II, particularly in the United States, the price of oil had become a government- and industry-managed device for stimulating consumption.

However, to see Big Oil only as a corporate strategy misses some of its most dynamic aspects. While the entire industry became more streamlined and independent producers merged into a few massive corporations, Big Oil also maintained cultural and social holdovers from the earliest days of oil: namely, petroleum's presence in popular culture. The personal stories of success and failure in oil speculation had always entranced the public. Over just a few decades, these stories formed a mythic history of the business. By exploiting these mythic components, the idea of Big Oil became much more than business; in the minds of consumers, taming crude became a heroic endeavor. Instead of occurring in the mountains of Pennsylvania or the flatlands of Texas, though, the search for oil now might go on in distant jungles or exotic deserts. Through the imagery of the oil business, however, it maintained a familiar continuity.

A product of this mixing of the mythic stories of boom and bust with the standardized corporate reality, Big Oil also garnered a public image that placed it outside of the control of consumers and even regulators. Inevitably, this meant that starting in the early 1900s, the term Big Oil also endured severe demonization, particularly as it affected smaller competitors or interests, ranging from Native populations to laborers in the oil fields. The corporate ideology of Big Oil emerged as an entity larger than nations and with a mandate to acquire crude regardless of any social or environmental costs. The unintended consequence of organizing the industry more than ever before was that these mythic elements were also perpetuated. Therefore, Big Oil included large-scale corporate infrastructure that spanned the globe without ever releasing the basic elements that titillated the public: fortune, danger, and bust.

Today, the term Big Oil most likely evokes a negative visceral reaction from most consumers. In fact, this negative connotation extends back to the same period that found Higgins begging for help in his search for oil; the reasons for it, though, concerned neither Texas's rate of production nor unregulated development among indigenous populations. Although the public had been enthralled with stories of petroleum exploration since the 1860s, during the late 1890s its unique corporate culture also made it one of the nation's best-known industries. Much of this publicity revolved around the ethics with which some oilmen carried out their business. In a place such as Texas, for instance, the culture of Big Oil was reason for celebration; however, in the reform-minded United States of the early 1900s, the large oil companies became the single best representative of illicit business practices. A few decades later, a similar sentiment added fuel to the people's revolution in Mexico, which helped to ban foreign companies within that nation.

The story of Big Oil forms a continuum that is perpetuated into the twenty-first century. This ongoing narrative suggests the other end of the legacy in which Spindletop participated: the formation of a larger consumer culture in the twentieth century that was defined by low-priced energy made from petroleum—energy that was enabled by a massive increase in supply. Efficiency and effectiveness created corporate profitability by the early 1900s, and this helped to make petroleum one of the cheapest sources of energy in human history. Roger Olien and Diana Davids Olien, historians of the Texas oil business, describe this unique, turn-of-the-century industrial culture:

> When Americans began to talk about the new petroleum industry from an economic or political perspective, they already had a way to look at it. They commonly used venerable rhetoric, replete with themes predating the industry's emergence by well over a century. They used that rhetoric to vent moral indignation. Once Americans put certain themes and ideas together in their understandings of the petroleum industry, they constructed a specific ideology relating to

it. Thereafter they repeated those constructions about industry again and again, often with little apparent regard for particular circumstances. Repetition of what was said about the industry, especially when what was said contained elements of moral discourse, reinforced the ideology and made it common knowledge.[2]

This uniquely expansive industrial culture—with its concepts of rush, boom, and bust—begins within the corporations harvesting oil as early as the 1860s. The "moral indignation" referenced by the Oliens, of course, stems primarily from the person and practices of John D. Rockefeller Sr., introduced earlier. Over time, an ideology formed to manage petroleum's present and future. This approach to resource development is encompassed by the term Big Oil.

Unique among nearly all other resources, this expansive culture and its ethic of extraction never has gone away. In fact, the culture and ethic remain as vibrant within Big Oil today as in Rockefeller's petroleum empire, particularly the Standard Oil Trust, and consumers today, as then, grumble about its effects. Although the expansive possibilities of oil were evident when Drake and Smith's well arrived in 1859, they were magnified many times when Higgins and the other wildcatters watched the crude spray out of the salt dome beneath the Texas thicket in proportions never dreamed of. Though it was initiated within the United States, this crude reality became part of the industry and would follow wherever petroleum was pursued. As a transborder corporate culture, this American creation helped to dictate the relationship all humans had with crude during the twentieth century.

Rationalizing the petroleum industry, of course, was intended to create stable, predictable profits. Very likely, these great corporate leaders would have rationalized whichever resource they were harvesting. Petroleum, though, belied such efforts. Partly for this reason, the greatest success was reserved for a company such as Standard Oil, which accepted the vagaries of oil exploration and, instead, emphasized the parts of the process that concerned preparing and distributing the product for consumption around the world. This emphasis, of course, also maximized Standard's profit and minimized its risk. Expanding the search for oil around the entire globe diminished the role of small, independent oil companies and expanded the dominance of the large, monolithic corporations that shape our idea of Big Oil today. Using the international model of development, European oil firms established relationships not with independent nations possessing oil reserves but with the European governments under whose colonial authority the oil would be gotten.

In short, Big Oil blends the American and international trends to define petroleum development as a unique undertaking in the twentieth century. This international trend also created a transient, global population, primarily of male workers. Very few people called the oil business their home from birth. In active oil towns, men far outnumbered women and most of the men left their families far behind. It follows, then, that those who were raised in the midst of the oil industry and matured while watching its unique details could claim to know the industry best. It was just such a discerning eye that brought consumers their first unfiltered view of the ethics that guided petroleum's development and shaped the idea of Big Oil from its infancy.

DEMONIZING BIG OIL

American journalist Ida Tarbell, who would later be identified with the re-form-minded group known as "muckrakers," knew oil, and, starting in 1902, she chose to expose its unique culture to every consumer.

The tales told by Tarbell grew from the Pennsylvania oil fields and included her own upbringing of moderate privilege—at least for her early years. She was born in 1857 in Titusville and grew up playing among the derricks, storage tanks, and other tools of the nascent petroleum trade. The ironies of the business took physical reality in her life: Tarbell spent her upbringing residing in a splendid home that her father built from materials that he acquired at auction when the oil boomtown Pithole was abandoned. He purchased the materials that had been used to build one of the boomtown's most exquisite hotels and used them to make the family home. His business of manufacturing barrels was part of petroleum's stable infrastructure in the 1860s. Later in the century, though, his independent storage barrel and tank manufacturing business was absorbed by corporations such as Standard that tried to organize the process of petroleum.

Although petroleum reached the turn of the century without a large-scale application, its relevance in the popular culture reached new heights with the emergence of Big Oil, the perceived villain to American progress. Despite the fact that the priorities of corporate management had won over petroleum development, many individuals never forgave Rockefeller for his ruthless ethics. Watching from the family home in Titusville, Ida Tarbell saw her father lose his barrel and tank business because of the dominance of Standard. Just as petroleum offered a great symbol of the Gilded Age through the efforts of Standard and Rockefeller, Tarbell worked assiduously to make it also exemplify a new era of industrial reform. She formed her own reputation as a journalist while others, such as Henry Demarest Lloyd, used critical writing to attempt to rein in Rockefeller's empire. Lloyd used Standard as the subject of a series of antimonopoly articles in the 1880s.[3] However, Lloyd's exposé was written too early for American society to fully accept and act upon.

Throughout the 1890s, though, Lloyd did not let up. His accusations were repeated by many more people and helped to result in the Sherman Antitrust

Act. As an indication of the times, though, the act went largely unenforced, and Standard continued its phenomenal growth. Standard, however, began to combat some of the disdain of Big Oil by hiring its own literary bureau, a type of public relations firm.[4] Tarbell, who had reached literary fame with biographies of Napoleon and Lincoln that were first excerpted in *McClure's*, began corresponding with Lloyd in 1894. Hired on as a staff writer for the magazine, she focused all of her energies on preparing an exposé of trusts (complex business organizations, similar to today's corporations) in the United States at the turn of the century. She looked into the steel and sugar trusts, but when the discovery of oil in California exploded on the public consciousness, Tarbell decided that Standard Oil Trust's business practices presented the best model of them all. From the start, of course, Tarbell's perspective was not an objective one: she had seen Standard's impact on her father and others firsthand. In more recent years, Tarbell's brother William Walter Tarbell had helped to establish the Pure Oil Company, which was one of the most serious domestic challengers to Standard. In addition, during the writing, Ida's father, Franklin, was dying of stomach cancer. Therefore, Ida Tarbell had a variety of reasons to feel highly critical of Rockefeller. More important, though, was the reading public's reaction to the manuscript that she placed before them. They seemed already to be deeply suspicious of this example of Big Oil.

Figure 3.3. "Next!" was the title of this famous 1904 illustration from *Puck*. Standard Oil is depicted as the octopus with tentacles wrapped around other industries and nations. The dominance of Standard Oil shaped the "international model" of oil development and moved petroleum into a position of significant international influence. (Library of Congress Prints and Photographs Division, LC-DIG-ppmsca-25884)

The very early 1900s marked a unique upheaval for Americans, with threats of socialism and many public strikes and uprisings. On guard when in public, Rockefeller became fearful for his safety in September 1901. After President William McKinley, a great friend to big business, was assassinated in Buffalo, New York, Rockefeller and other tycoons feared they would be the next targets. The real threat, though, was not to the safety of Rockefeller's person but to his empire. Threats to Rockefeller emerged from outside cultural attitudes as well as from shifts in the attitudes of some of his closest internal confidants. Henry Rogers, Flagler, and other industry insiders had talked with Tarbell and provided her with crucial information.[5] Combined with general social unrest, growing distrust of big business, and the ascendancy of Progressive leaders, a fateful moment of historical convergence was upon Rockefeller and the image of Big Oil for which he had become a symbol.

In 1902, *McClure's* published the first installment of what became Tarbell's *History of the Standard Oil Company.* An alarming picture of Big Oil took shape in the form of Standard's ruthless business practices, including rollbacks and insider pricing, to squeeze out its competitors. Across the nation, readers awaited each of the nineteen installments of the story published by *McClure's* from 1902 to 1904. By early 1903, the magazine's circulation had skyrocketed to 375,000. Although Tarbell teemed with bitterness for what Rockefeller had done to the private businessmen of Pennsylvania's oil industry, she allowed the details of the practices to express her point of view. The articles were compiled into book form as the *History of the Standard Oil Company*, which was released in 1904. After at first not taking Tarbell's efforts seriously, Rockefeller was now openly struggling to present the best public face. His rare public appearances during the summer came on Sundays as he attended church and taught Sunday School at the Euclid Avenue Baptist Church in the Cleveland suburb of Forest Hill. His biographer Ron Chernow writes: "It probably hurt his image that he appeared in public only at church, for it played to the stereotype of a hypocrite cloaking himself in sanctity."[6]

Tarbell found him there in 1905 for her only public observation of him. She published her reaction as a character study of the man: "My two hours' study of Mr. Rockefeller aroused a feeling I had not expected. . . . I was sorry for him. I know no companion so terrible as fear. Mr. Rockefeller, for all the conscious power written in face and voice and figure, was afraid, I told myself, afraid of his own kind." She went on to report to Americans that "Mr. Rockefeller may have made himself the richest man in the world, but he has paid. Nothing but paying ever ploughs such lines in a man's face, ever sets his lips to such a melancholy angle." Fair or not, Tarbell made Rockefeller into the personification of Big Oil as well as the embodiment of other treacherous ethics common among many successful businessmen. Partly because of her moralistic spin of the Standard story, political leaders focused more than ever on Rockefeller and Big Oil as a symbol of the ills of the era. Any effort to better social and ethical shortcomings in the United States and elsewhere had to include petroleum.

In the United States, the business-friendly McKinley was replaced as president by the virile reformer Theodore Roosevelt. Inspired to use the presidency as a "bully pulpit," Roosevelt listened to and read intently the accounts of reform-minded journalists. The oil historians the Oliens write:

> When it attracted the attention of . . . Roosevelt, Standard Oil came up against a truly daunting adversary, expert in manipulation of discourse, the most successful manipulator of the press to occupy the White House to that time. Roosevelt recognized a useful target when he saw one, and, beginning in 1902 and continuing through the rest of his administration, he used moralistic attacks on Standard Oil to advance his personal political agenda and to effect resolution of inconsistent elements of Progressive economic policy.[7]

Spurred by the muckrakers, Roosevelt helped to create federal legislation that concerned the welfare of "common" people. With the justification of reform, Roosevelt's administration entered into open confrontation with big business. Roosevelt's reputation as a progressive grew in 1902 when Pennsylvania coal miners went on strike for higher wages and better working conditions. Roosevelt threatened to send in the army to operate mines unless the owners agreed to arbitration. Some people said that this governmental interference went against the U.S. Constitution. They argued that the government had no right to take command of private property. Roosevelt replied that the Constitution was intended to serve the people, not vice versa. In the move that would garner him the designation "trust buster," Roosevelt followed the findings of the muckraking journalists and attacked a few giant business trusts. His primary weapon in doing battle with such massive organizations was the Sherman Antitrust Act, which had been enacted in 1890 but largely left unused.

Roosevelt's trust-busting efforts tapped into a spirit of the times. He perceived the impact of reformers and journalists and appropriated it as part of his progressive initiatives. Progressives argued for an activist government that foresaw problems and acted aggressively to prevent calamities before they occurred rather than reacting to damage already done. Thus, Progressives in Congress demanded safety legislation, closer regulation of public health issues, and better management of things such as public utilities. Even in business, argued reformers, certain ethics needed to be respected. Regulating such business practices, they reasoned, was a job so large and so significant that it could only be trusted to the federal government.

In the case of petroleum and Big Oil, Tarbell's investigation inspired new efforts to enforce antitrust laws. In 1909, the U.S. attorney general brought suit against Standard for violating the Sherman Antitrust Act. The suit argued that Standard and its directors had "conspired and confederated for the purpose of combining all the said companies in restraint of trade . . . for the purpose of monopolizing commerce."[8] After adverse rulings, the case reached the U.S. Supreme Court. In 1911 the Supreme Court ordered the dissolution of Standard Oil. Tarbell's "muckraking" exposé of Standard and Rockefeller's business ethics led to stricter enforcement of antitrust laws and in 1911 to the breakup of Standard into eleven companies. In basic terminology, however, the concept of Big Oil had permanently been added to the national lexicon, linking petroleum with corporate efforts to control the commodity without any input from the general consumer.

The outcome of this demonization of Big Oil, therefore, was not really what it might have seemed. Initially, the influence of the U.S. government shattered at least one dominant corporation to spawn twenty large, vertically integrated corporations. Around these larger companies grew hundreds of smaller ones focused on just one portion of the industry but beholden or related to one of the larger entities. Known as "independents," these companies significantly expanded the industry and the applications of petroleum.[9] As the industrial shifts continued into the 1920s, the fracturing American industry found new ways to rebind itself, including trade organizations such as the American Petroleum Institute (API) founded in 1919. Historian David Painter argues that the "associationalism" of this era helped the petroleum industry to form some habits and procedures of self-regulation and coordination in a climate of individualism; the API and other ideas, however, also helped to perpetuate the idea of Big Oil in a post-Standard era.[10]

As the essentialness of crude grew, so did the status of Big Oil. The authority needed to develop petroleum wherever it occurred brought great power to these large corporations but developing petroleum also demanded power— particularly political power, which varied globally in its exact organization. In the United States, government initially became a tool for reining in the industry; around the world, though, government and industry operated oil development as a joint venture. In the international sphere, Big Oil needed to function on the level of national leaders as well as royalty. In fact, in the modern era, the industry even became a player in the politics of certain nations.

THE BOLSHEVIKS: WHO OWNS THE OIL IN A REVOLUTION?

The political revolutions of the early twentieth century influenced many societies, but what became known as the Bolshevik Revolution rocked Russia to its core by 1917. In such a situation of social transition and political turmoil, who could claim ownership of one of the world's oldest known supplies of crude? Was petroleum, in this era of Big Oil, larger than such shifts in national leadership? In particular, how did this commodity relate to the revolutionary new philosophies of Communism?

In the case of the Bolshevik Revolution, the situation was preceded by the Rothschilds' sale of their significant interests in Russian oil to Royal Dutch/ Shell just prior to World War I. By contrast, the Nobels maintained their interests in Russian oil even after they fled. As the country fell into revolution, the Nobels—some of whom disguised themselves as peasants—crossed into Finland and ultimately set up the family's new headquarters in the Hotel Meurice in Paris, France. From there, the family sought to reap any possible value from their oil interests, which now were at best inaccessible and at worst, very possibly, seized interests of a new nation. As the Nobels sought to find a purchaser for their interests in Russian oil, few suitors could tolerate the uncertainty of the revolution and how the victor would observe outside ownership resources such as petroleum. The primary suitor, Henry Wilhelm August Deterding, sought assurances of assistance from the British government and others, but each refused. From the ashes of the U.S. government's breakup of Rockefeller's empire, one suitor stepped forward and appeared ready to take the risk: Standard Oil of New Jersey (Standard/Jersey).

Yergin writes that Standard/Jersey "remembered all too well the impact Russian oil had once had on the old Standard Oil Trust, frustrating its efforts to create a universal petroleum order." The revolution marked their chance to overcome this age-old rift in the industry and also to supply the Mediterranean markets much more cheaply than their current efforts to ship American crude there.[11] Negotiations with the Nobels grew more intense, even in April 1920 when the Bolsheviks recaptured Baku and nationalized the oil fields. Despite such uncertainty, in July 1920 Standard/Jersey bought from the Nobels control of approximately 35 percent of all Russian oil output, 40 percent of its refining, and 60 percent of the internal Russian market for a down payment of $6.5 million and up to $7.5 million in eventual additional payments. Big Oil, in the form of Standard/Jersey, had decided to take the risk that petroleum's value would transcend political revolution. No matter how the political turmoil turned out, the governing authority would need a friend to help make Russia's oil industry functional and profitable. And, if the revolution succeeded and the Bolsheviks sought to stabilize a new nation, the certainty of petrodollars would be even more essential.

The new government had already demonstrated the importance of Russian oil to the nation's future. In 1920, the Bolshevik government sent its first foreign representative to meet with the British prime minister about Russian oil. Throughout the year, the Bolsheviks and their leader, Vladimir Lenin, debated how to proceed. As the severe limits of the Soviet's internal industrial infrastructure became more and more pronounced, Lenin offered concessions to foreign investors and opened the Soviet Union to foreign trade. "We cannot by our own strength restore our shattered economy without equipment and technical assistance from abroad," he explained in unveiling the New Economic Policy.[12] Although idealists such as Joseph Stalin and others protested such external involvement in the new nation, Lenin believed that the future of the Soviet Union required that the nation take advantage of oil's international value. As the grand experiment in Communism advanced, the vast majority of its oil was harvested and managed by companies based abroad, either Royal Dutch/Shell or Standard/Jersey.

After its collapse during the revolution, production from the Russian oil fields stabilized somewhat during the 1920s, which had a dramatic influence on oil's global price. In fact, when Soviet-owned production revived and grew after 1923, it undercut the global price, which drew a furious reaction from the other interests involved in the Russian fields. Observing this growing threat, Standard/Jersey, Royal Dutch/Shell, and the Nobels joined forces as the Front Uni to ensure each other's interests against Soviet encroachment and to help stabilize the price that would be paid for any of their crude. In fact, during the mid-1920s, the Front Uni took to purchasing Soviet oil on the market at the low price that the Kremlin charged and then selling it at the going rate. Price control was their main goal, as well as ensuring the value of their own investments in Russian oil. By the late 1920s, though, Big Oil interests, such as the Front Uni, found a much more expansive and flexible option in Middle Eastern oil and largely left the development of Russian oil to the Soviets.

PRICE, STRATIGRAPHY, AND MANAGING "HOT OIL"

Control was the operative term for the new petroleum business, whether focused in central Asia or central Arkansas. In the first decades of the 1900s, the system and order of the international model of development were swiftly squeezing out the true independents as each developed nation scurried to establish access to reserves and also to maintain stable pricing. As the commodity was mastered and its production streamlined and systematized, Big Oil clearly emerged as an entity more powerful than single nations.

In Great Britain, when Churchill committed the Royal Navy to petroleum in 1913, he forever compromised the nation's energy autonomy: Britain had neither domestic sources of oil nor existing supplies in its colonies. Anglo-Persian/BP, with its access to oil in central Asia (particularly Persia, the future Iran), quickly became the most sensible option to ensure Britain's energy future. Large capital expenditures, such as pipeline construction, had left Anglo-Persian/BP in deep debt and near bankruptcy by 1914. To convince Parliament to help the company, Churchill argued: "If we cannot get oil, we cannot get corn, we cannot get cotton and we cannot get a thousand and one commodities necessary for the preservation of the economic energies of Great Britain."[13] Parliament approved his plan to purchase a 51 percent stake in BP for £2.2 million in June 1914. Maintaining and developing oil supplies soon became a critical aspect of the British colonial efforts.

Global use of petroleum grew by 50 percent during World War I, which exacerbated the difficulty of managing the global supply. These difficulties grew more acute in 1919 when one of the world's significant producing regions, Russia, destabilized. The United States, however, still dominated oil production in 1919: producing one million barrels annually, approximately 70 percent of the global output. But the culture of oil was changing. Most important, the U.S. Senate's special report predicted coming shortages. It estimated that the nation's oil supply would last only twenty-five more years. The head of the U.S. Geological Survey was even more dour, predicting depletion in nine years.[14] As the world's other great oil consumer, the United States quickly responded to the forecast in a way similar to Churchill's actions in 1914; however, unlike Churchill, those in the United States also approached forecasts of petroleum depletion as the world's greatest producer of crude. It was clearly a position of strength for the Americans who had mastered crude; however, developing petroleum in this international competition would require the involvement of the public sector with Big Oil in an unprecedented fashion.

The effort to control American oil production began when U.S. President Calvin Coolidge established the Federal Oil Conservation Board in 1924. In doing so, Coolidge, only a decade after Churchill had retrofitted the British Navy, spoke for a new era of air warfare in which it was "probable that the supremacy of nations may be determined by the possession of available petroleum and its products."[15] In addition to the federal effort to protect some domestic reserves, including those involved in Teapot Dome, U.S. authorities urged diplomacy that would look abroad before other global powers swept up the known reserves. This marked a direct about-face from previous refusals by the American government to become involved in the overseas operations of Standard, its largest player in the global enterprise. However, such initiatives did not reach fruition until the end of the 1920s. In the American industry's increasing awareness of scarcity and intricacy, overproduction became a major preoccupation. In fact, federal efforts at conservation did not gain traction when the primary motive was ensuring supply and national security; instead, the greatest fear became collapsing prices.

A severe drop in oil prices, went this thinking, would destabilize the entire industry, and the ripple effects would affect the patterns of consumption that were beginning to take shape on the ground level of everyday American life. Big Oil, behind the scenes, had vulnerabilities, the possible implications of which merited federal action.

One reason for what experts referred to as an "oil glut" was an increased understanding of oil geophysics, which began with the U.S. Geological Survey in 1908 and industrial publications such as the *Oil and Gas Journal*, which began publication in 1902. Particularly in the United States, the changing culture of petroleum in the 1920s moved serious science into the petroleum industry. New understanding allowed regulations to begin to place limits on the rule of capture that made oil fields fair game to any wildcatter. The unity of oil fields—meaning the connectivity of underground wells—was substantiated by theories including the anticline theory, which demonstrated the underground occurrence of natural gas, oil, and water and tied them to surface features such as domes, and also by subsurface mapping, which grew into stratigraphy after World War I. Using stratigraphic features of geology, drilling exploratory fields became much less a leap of faith and much more a technical, scientific certainty administered by corporate managers. This also contributed to the development of secondary recovery, which involved flushing out existing wells with natural gas to acquire previously inaccessible reserves.[16] Big Oil was able to acquire the oil that it pursued at a higher rate than ever before.

In addition, chemical science applied to refining led to the breakthrough of thermal cracking that was introduced in 1913 by William Burton and allowed crude to be systematically separated into a variety of products. Most importantly, gasoline acquired from each barrel of crude grew from 15 percent of American production in 1900 to 39 percent in 1929.[17] In the emerging era of Big Oil, corporate entities such as Shell and BP integrated each of these new sciences to gain a mixed profile, while others specialized. For instance, Texaco, Chevron, and Gulf specialized in locating and harvesting crude while Exxon focused on refining. As gasoline emerged as a primary output, each corporation also gained a public face through which, in the form of gas stations, it interacted with consumers. Overall, writes industry veteran Leonardo Maugeri, "This transformation of the industry into its modern shape involved a vast process of mergers and acquisitions, favored by its growing capital intensity. . . . Mergers and acquisitions proved a quicker and more profitable way to achieve integration, scale, and market presence than building them step-by-step."[18] By the late 1920s, Big Oil was an adjective to describe diversified corporate goliaths that controlled the availability of crude for nations that required it.

Such efforts at corporate and scientific efficiency combined with the sta-
bilization of Soviet supplies in the 1920s to produce a bona fide oil glut that
drove the global price dangerously low. Initially, some of the corporations
secretly implemented selected practices from Rockefeller's repertoire to fix
prices, particularly regarding oil produced outside the United States. When
the economic crash hit in 1929, crude prices in the United States, which had
dropped from $3 per barrel in 1919 to $2 per barrel in 1925, plummeted to
only a few cents per barrel by 1931. As chaos reigned in the large oil fields of
Texas and Arkansas, a state agency created to oversee rail shipments in Texas
became the first global regulative authority in the industry. To perform this
duty, however, it required new cooperation between Big Oil and government
in the United States.

When it was created in 1891, the Texas Railroad Commission was tasked
to regulate the trade of various commodities. In 1918 and 1919, this duty was
focused on crude and natural gas, and the commission tasked to monitor output with a system of mandatory quotas it enforced for each producer. Without
authority to enforce these regulations, the effort failed; however, the agency
remained in place. When the pricing crisis took shape in the early 1930s,
President Franklin Delano Roosevelt's New Deal empowered Secretary of
the Interior Harold Ickes to use federal authority to back up a similar system
of quotas. Before it could be fully enacted, the U.S. Supreme Court ruled
that the National Industrial Recovery Act (NIRA) efforts in this regard were
unconstitutional. The U.S. Congress then passed laws banning "hot oil," as
the glut came to be called, and worked with states by the late 1930s to implement a complex regulatory architecture on domestic supplies and duties on
imported oil. The outcome of these policies was to buoy the price to near $1
per barrel by 1940. Thus, in a formulation very different from that seen in
Britain and elsewhere, Big Oil joined industry and government in a new oil
economy. Due to the overwhelming leadership of Texas in domestic production by 1930, the Texas Railroad Commission stepped into the coordinating
role that would guide these diverse quota systems forward. Although unof-
ficial, the commission became the primary enforcer of control over the price
of all oil in the United States.[19] In this position, the agency became a primary
author of the fiction of oil pricing when it was permanently divorced from
any real connection to supply and demand.

More massive oil discoveries in Texas made price management even more
important as the Great Depression wore on. Dwarfing everything before it—
even Spindletop in 1901—East Texas exploded in unimaginable amounts of
oil. Just as the industry at large pursued standardization, the independents and
their boomtowns and shantytowns had another resurgence in Texas through
the early 1930s. As hundreds of thousands of barrels of new oil flooded onto

the market from East Texas, the task of righting the industry fell to the previously existing Texas Railroad Commission. A convergence of forces had come to make oil too important to be left to its own devices by the 1930s. As Maugeri writes simply: "Paradoxically, it was not the purported scarcity of 'black gold' but its ruinous overabundance that was the threat to this civilization, and that risked destroying its irrational producers as well."[20] The informal infrastructure of Big Oil made the United States the global industry leader through the 1970s; however, it was the model of regulation inspired by this difficult earlier era that inspired cartels of the later twentieth century, including OPEC.

The new oil economy that began in the 1930s created a reality of crude that was organizationally restrained and systematized. The concept of Big Oil that took shape, of course, subsumed many of the ground-level realities of extracting crude. Leading the list of these glossed-over details were the workers and local residents impacted by the development of this global commodity.

WORKING THE OIL FIELDS

Behind the facade of the new industrial order, the development of the world's petroleum supply continued to carry a serious human toll. Wherever Big Oil pursued new supplies, it also brought similar burdens upon local communities. The ethic of flexibility driving most of the industry led to this reality, particularly in the international sector. At its core, the industry relied on a transient workforce of knowledgeable, well-trained specialists who could be moved to the new hot spots all over the world, yet in each region the local populations saw their existence changed by oil. More often than not, Big Oil served as a mechanism for enforcing industrial priorities and, when pressed, mitigating— or squelching—complaints about the industry's impact on local populations.

Historian Myrna Santiago traced how oil companies in Mexico's early oil industry, for instance, remade the region's entire labor structure. "The tycoons," she writes of oilmen such as Edward Doheny of Pan American, "had to confront the reality that the object of their desire was buried in what they considered inaccessible areas with no workers."[21] The basic pattern in Mexico's oil industry during the first decades of the 1900s placed men from abroad in supervisory positions while the more menial labor was performed by locals. Often, entirely new populations, such as Chinese, were brought in to function as household employees. Because none of the jobs were needed if oil was not found first, expediency of development fueled these basic patterns.

To get oil flowing in Mexico, American geologists and drillers flocked in by the early 1910s and established camps. Often, Santiago notes, teams arrived intact from the United States. If a team had a particularly well-known reputation, they might be hired as contractors or even given a percentage of the well's flow. "Prizes for gusher wells were also common," writes Santiago, "either expensive watches . . . or bonuses worth 50% of their total wages."[22] In the Mexican fields, other specialists—particularly in the mechanical trades— arrived from Europe (Germany, France, and Britain).

In the stage preliminary to oil development, access had to be established to the remote jungle locations sought for development. Therefore, companies recruited Mexican nationals as "machete men" to prepare passage for men and equipment and to set up the camps. Through the 1910s, local men, regardless of their skills or qualifications, provided unskilled labor. Boys as young as ten years of age joined these labor forces. Similarly, women and children were hired to support the labor force, though a few literate women in Tampico and Tuxpan worked as secretaries in company offices.[23] In each category of labor, recruiters used a process of "el enganche" (the hooking) in which agents combed the Mexican countryside offering contracts to laborers for a specific length of time. Often they made such offers at a staged party in which they combined free music and alcohol to help attract potential workers. "They offered the moon and stars," recalled one worker. "We would have houses, good wages, payment in gold!" From these rural excursions, agents delivered lots of six hundred to seven hundred persons to Tampico through 1920.[24]

In the Mexican oil fields, indigenous employment, particularly of men, was temporary by design. The boom of development offered financial opportunity, but in most cases indigenous workers did not remain in oil. Despite high wages, many indigenous workers rejected ongoing opportunities in oil because of the realities of the work. Members of the industry, such as Doheny, explained this tendency of Mexicans in this fashion: "natives . . . [were] not accustomed to the continuous application which was necessary in the opening of a field."[25] Santiago, however, places the blame on the exploitative tendencies of the companies and the destructive tendencies of extraction.

Neither the oil nor the industry needed to process and distribute it left the native Huasteca people. Santiago's research suggests an overall trajectory of acculturation in the industry. By 1938, these patterns subsided and Mexicans nationalized their industry. Therefore, the social impacts from oil only increased and, writes Santiago,

> as they lived and worked in the tropical forest, the social groups affiliated with the oil industry experienced and interacted with their surroundings in distinct ways. The class and race/nationality position of each group mediated that group's experience with nature at work and at home. . . . For Mexican workers and their families . . . social divisions and labor hierarchies the companies

implemented thus reached the environmental realm. The spheres where this divergence was most pronounced were in lifestyle, health, and safety.[26]

Particularly prior to its nationalization, Mexico's interaction with the oil industry serves as a model for the effects faced by local populations when oil development arrived. Often, when the industry left and the oil played out, local populations alone faced the environmental hazards of spilled oil, ruined water supplies, and flooding and soil runoff. These were the realities of the industry as global corporate entities, based in far-off lands, followed known supplies, harvested them, and brought the oil to market.

Big Oil masked these examples of exploitation as it systematized a flexible workforce to be placed anywhere on the earth. By mid-century, such development often didn't even require a temporary boomtown. The increasingly systematized development of oil also helped to form another crucial aspect of its myth: that oil appeared almost magically, without difficulty or discomfort. While petroleum companies may not have set out to create or to perpetuate a mythology of crude, these dynamics became a powerful part of its public image in the twentieth century.

Figure 3.4. From the earliest days of oil, the enterprise required heavy labor, often from underpaid workers. International developments, such as this one from the oil fields of Romania in 1923, often relied on a local or native workforce for dangerous work, including shoveling out refuse from the hot pools of oil that spouted around a wellhead. (Library of Congress Frank and Frances Carpenter Collection, LC-USZ62-98530)

LABOR CONFLICT IN OIL CAMPS
FOR GLOBAL OIL DEVELOPMENT

Neutralizing labor disputes abroad could be a very complicated undertaking. In order to do so, Big Oil created a unique mechanism to replace boomtowns and to allow for long-term development of supplies in distant lands. The single best example is the camps that were administered in Saudi Arabia after 1944, when the United States formed its "special" relationship with the kingdom that will be discussed below. These American camps functioned as an oasis for U.S. workers but also for laborers from many nations. They followed an organization that had been perfected throughout the globe by companies from a variety of nations.

In the case of developing Saudi's supply of crude, the Arabian American Oil Company (Aramco) was organized in 1933 when the Saudi government granted a concession to Standard Oil of California. After a few unsuccessful years of exploration, Texaco purchased 50 percent of the concession. Aramco was the vehicle for companies, with the support of the U.S. federal government, to search for Saudi's supposed oil wealth. Most of the American employees of Aramco learned their trade elsewhere, particularly in the South American fields of Colombia.[27] Organized similarly to those used in Venezuela, the camps in Saudi Arabia were segregated by the laborers' nationality, with "gross disparities in living quarters, wage scales, and access to services." In such camps, barbed-wire fences often were used to keep everyone but house servants from the Anglos' reservation. In Venezuela, there were at least two major strikes by workers that were specifically focused against these living conditions. In these situations, the army was typically used to break the strikes and to maintain the arrangements established between the government and the outside oil interests.

In Saudi Arabia, the camps' separate reservations included Anglo-Saxons, Bahrainis, Iraqis, and Indians. Americans typically lived in corrugated metal and cement huts while Arabs and Indians typically lived in thatched, palm-frond, and floorless huts known as "barastis." Although many Americans were eventually moved into more permanent, air-conditioned accommodations, other groups remained in their original huts. In addition, only Americans were permitted to have families living with them.

To describe any of the ethnically diverse workers, Americans typically used one general term: "coolie." The development of "coolie" camps preceded World War II but grew significantly after the war. In his study of these camps, historian Robert Vitalis describes the intensified conflict that often occurred between these separated barracks. He writes: "Meeting Americans' often brutal sense of innate superiority with acts of violence or theft would repeat itself regularly over the coming decades, but meanwhile a fence went up around American Camp and company officials secured the right of the firm to police inside its perimeter."[28] When needed, the muscle came from elements of Big Oil—just as through Big Oil the camps had come to exist on foreign soil at all. As American families joined the camps, cultural elements arrived as well, including, very likely, the first films to be shown publicly in Saudi Arabia. Vitalis includes a description of the showing of Ann Harding in *Gallant Lady*: "Arabs were forbidden to attend, but they were about five deep all about the outside of the house peeking in the windows."[29]

As American oil development grew, so too did the apparatus. Workers ran power, phone, fuel, and sewer lines, and a staff hospital, recreation center, and four-hole golf course were added inside the camps. By 1944, the construction of this infrastructure as well as new refineries brought in more roughnecks from the United States as well as skilled Italian masons, many of whom had been working in Eritrea; Indians from throughout the Gulf region; and skilled and unskilled men from al-Hasa, Basra, and Bahrain. Intermittent labor unrest began for Aramco in 1945. Typically, these uprisings were met with disinterest or violence. Vitalis stresses that when local authorities dealt with the strikers, the outcome was often beatings. If negotiations occurred with Aramco, agreements were rarely adhered to and strike organizers were typically shipped out to other locations. Eventually, Aramco formed its own bureau of intelligence gathering to allow it to nip such discontent in the bud.[30]

In the late 1940s, the living conditions of Arab workers were the focus of a meeting at the Monomonock Inn, deep in Pennsylvania's Pocono region, back in the United States. American politicians leveled criticism of Aramco practices, and company officials stressed that there could be no lessening of privileges for Americans in the work camps. And over the course of the meeting, for the first time, company officials considered educating the dependents of Arab workers. For the most part, however, the Pennsylvania Compromise, as the meeting is called, resulted in little improvement for non-American workers. Additional strikes and labor unrest continued through the 1950s.

"To underscore what should be most obvious," Vitalis summarizes, "extractive industries confronted . . . a common set of structural features." What was true in mining fields of Arizona "was true about the oil fields of Dhahran in the mid-twentieth century. . . . The work it took and the costs men and women paid in the course of challenging injustice and inequality in the mines and camps . . . is the even bigger, unresolvable paradox in the tale."[31] Mechanisms of Big Oil functioned to neutralize workers' rights in order to increase production and profit. In examples such as Saudi Arabia, regional authority—government and royal—often worked hand in glove with the international oil interests to keep production running smoothly.

In this emerging industrial form, not only was the frontier myth of the wild-catter neutered, but Big Oil constructed the biggest facade of all: there was no free market for oil. Instead, petroleum became the most managed, controlled, and industrially manipulated commodity of the modern era. None of these details, however, was part of the popular image projected by the industry.

CONCLUSION: BIG OIL PERPETUATES
THE MYTH OF BLACK GOLD

A clear pattern formed for petroleum: as its reality became more managed and corporate, those forming its popular image held more ardently to the mythic dimensions of oil's past. An unintended consequence of the forma-tion of Big Oil was that petroleum remained of ever-increasing interest to the general public. The story line that most attracted the public remained petroleum's capacity to create boom or bust for individual speculators; however, in the 1930s corporate organization also joined the narratives. First and foremost, though, the objective in this ultracompetitive market-place was the corporate version of the rule of capture—to acquire the sup-ply before others did so. Such opportunity, of course, possessed a corrup-tive influence, which was part of oil exploration from its earliest days. The mythic images of oil never entirely allowed these stereotypes to subside; in fact, through its use in popular culture, we see that the corruptive influence of crude became a touchstone of film and television in the United States and helped to define the overall image of Big Oil. The myths, however, go back even farther.

Before J. R. Ewing and the others, the image of oil's potential was estab-lished through popular songs, such as "American Petroleum." The myths initiated in such songs were personified by a few famous characters in the late 1800s, including Coal Oil Johnny. Based on a genuine character, John W. Steele, this legend formed around the ability of oil to generate instant fortune and the corruptive nature of humans who wasted it. Growing up a penniless orphan, Coal Oil Johnny quickly spent his fortune—supposedly as much as $100,000 in a day—and died without wealth. When the *New York Times* published his obituary in 1921, it listed his past opulence: it was said that he bought a hotel for a night, rode around in a bright red carriage adorned with a drawing of an oil derrick instead of a coat of arms, lit cigars with hundred-dollar bills, and had diamonds dripping from his fingers. In recalling the legend, Alexis Madrigal writes, "Coal Oil Johnny was a legend and like all legends, he became a stand-in for a constellation of people, things, ideas, feelings and morals—in this case, about oil wealth and how it works."[32]

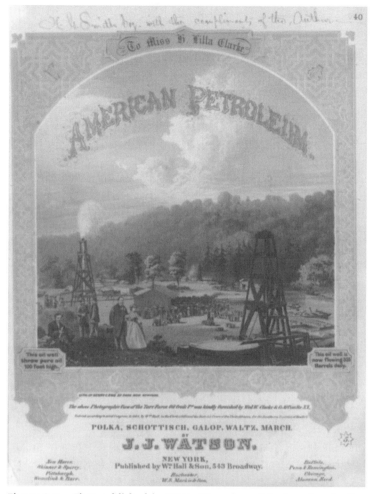

Figure 3.5. First published in 1864, "American Petroleum" and other "oil boom tunes" popularized the mythic elements of oil exploration. Popular culture became an important way to disseminate elements of the ideology that became known as Big Oil. (Library of Congress Prints and Photographs Division, LC-USZ62-86463)

In this legend that would grow through characters such as Jett Rink in *Giant* and the Clampetts in the *Beverly Hillbillies*, oil possessed the capacity to make common people rich beyond their wildest dreams. Boom was the desired portion of the myth of petroleum; however, it almost always wound its way eventually to bust. When Coal Oil Johnny's supply of crude ran out in the early fields of Pennsylvania, he ended up just as poor as he had begun.

The myth continued, however, in music ("Coal Oil Johnny" recorded by Little People Records) and various written accounts so that the main character was treated to a *New York Times* obituary upon his death in 1921. Big Oil sought to remove this ultimate decline from the reality of oil and, eventually, from the myth. Many of the examples of the myth in popular culture that followed wove the entire scenario into a morality play. As the industry developed in the twentieth century, however, the new international model of development included a corporate structure that might insulate individuals from the almost inevitable corruption inherent in crude. This dichotomy within Big Oil also became fodder for popular culture.

The feature film *Boom Town* (1940), which was discussed earlier, tried to capture the differing dimensions of the Big Oil idea. Starring Spencer Tracy, Claudette Colbert, Hedy Lamarr, and Clark Gable, *Boom Town* used Texas wildcatting of the 1930s to pull at every aspect of petroleum's myth—including its capacity for corruption. Similar to Pithole in Pennsylvania, the East Texas in which the film is set has entirely given itself over to oil. Nothing is sacred in East Texas during its boom. To make this fact absolutely obvious to viewers, Tracy's character stands with the church minister in his former sanctuary. Earlier, the congregation had voted to lease out the rights to the land beneath their church. Now, surrounded by the altar and pews, man of God and man of oil watch as the derrick pumps up and down. The scene suggests a community entirely and ultimately committed to oil. Ultimately, Tracy's character leaves the business in order to find happiness, while the unhappy Gable remains a global oil tycoon. Even as a mogul in the industry, Gable's character is worn down and ultimately corrupted. This same parable forms the core of the most famous of all oil films.

James Dean's final film, *Giant* (1956), uses the greed inherent in the expansive oil industry to organize its entire plot. Director George Stevens uses Texas oil as a symbol of newness and change in the older ways of the American West, particularly cattle ranching. Rock Hudson plays Bick Benedict, the patriarch of the Benedict family, a paragon of the stable cattle industry. When one of his employees, Jett Rink, played by Dean, strikes oil, he becomes a symbol of the unethical New West emerging from reckless resource extraction. The young upstart uses his wealth to build a decadent modern metropolis (strikingly reminiscent of portions of Houston), but he can never measure up to the dignity and tradition of Benedict. Rink ends the movie drunk and passed out at the head table of the grand event he has arranged in his own honor. In Rink's closing scene in *Giant*, we see many of the same implications of growth with which twentieth-century America contended. The morality play is complete: greed can't win; oil equals greed. Such images are so familiar that the plot may seem trite; however, these are the primary planks of the myth of Big Oil.

In the hands of a poor hillbilly such as Jed Clampett of the *Beverly Hill-billies*, an oil strike marked one of society's most transformative economic opportunities. Each episode opened with the now-infamous song depicting Jed's serendipitous discovery:

Well, listen to the story of a man named Jed,
a poor mountaineer barely kept his family fed.
Then one day he was shooting at some food,
and up through the ground came bubbling crude—

OIL, that is, black gold, Texas tea.

Well, the first thing you know, ole Jed's a millionaire
and kin folks said, "Jed, move away from there.
California's the place you ought to be."
So they loaded up the truck and moved to Beverly.[33]

In the case of Jed's discovery, part of the appeal was the fact that he did not seek oil; however, the difficulty with locating crude still allowed luck to play an important role for any oil seekers. In the *Beverly Hillbillies* television program of the 1960s, the strength of Jed's character was his ability to withstand most of the trappings and opportunities of petroleum's corruptive potential. Those around him, however, were often less stoic. In the series' ongoing narrative, friends and family members gave in to the wealth brought by petrodollars, while Jed resisted and held to his traditional roots. In the grander image of oil, of course, Jed and his family were a throwback to the early days of oil, and they functioned to counter the reality of Big Oil: an emerging, corporate bureaucracy unlike that seen in any other industry.

The durability of oil in popular culture throughout the twentieth century and into the twenty-first demonstrates the commodity's ongoing importance to human life. Blending elements of the Western with aspects of the action/adventure genre, films about petroleum have only become more popular. In films such as *Syriana* or *The Kingdom*, we find that the public is even intrigued by the latest chapters in humans' relationship with crude: the dominance of Big Oil as its reality is revealed as an inaccessible, largely foreign entity. The action of each film emphasizes human powerlessness over the larger business and political interests that bring oil to market from the far reaches of the globe. Therefore, contemporary viewers are forced to reconcile the crude reality of Big Oil.

Despite its evolution into international models of organizations, Big Oil, as a cultural icon, continued to include the possibility of boom or bust that helped to make it an American original. Its dark potential remained part of its appeal and its legend. The unique culture of oil marks one of the most recognizable and resilient touchstones of American corporate mythology. When the filmmaker Paul Thomas Anderson turned Upton Sinclair's early twentieth-century *Oil!* into a screenplay for the twenty-first-century oil culture, these same characteristics required only a bit of polishing. In the character of Daniel Plainview, viewers of *There Will Be Blood* found a personification of the industrial end of petroleum culture that transcended a century of change. "I drink your milkshake," explained Plainview in an effort to express the ethic of the rule of capture—the ethic of Big Oil. And, in actuality, the ethic that enabled the trickle of petroleum at Drake's well remains at the core of the gusher of Big Oil's commodity found in fields from Baku to Bahrain.

Big Oil, from its start in the late 1800s, merged myth and reality to form a new transborder entity that proved dynamic as it evolved with humans' use of crude in the twentieth century. With a new scale and scope, petroleum's increasing availability changed its potential as well as humans' expectations of it. Big Oil, as a term, encompassed all of this, including mythic dimensions of the resource's past and increasing resentment of the commodity's present. The dynamic term could expand to encompass these different eras, binding one to the other in the ongoing narrative of human use of petroleum. This capability was crucial, of course, because during the interwar years petroleum's essentialness was only in its infancy. In fact, those supporting the critical importance of petroleum supplies were doing so quietly as they sought to ensure sufficient supplies for their own national security. This was just preliminary, though; in one of the most fabulous aspects of petroleum, its essentialness was about to reach into the lives of each human living in developed societies, adding new dimensions to the Big Oil continuum.

INFRASTRUCTURE
Shipping Crude throughout the Globe

Run aground in 1891, the German ship *Gluckauf* did not live up to its name of "lucky." Today, remnants of its hull can still be seen off Fire Island, near New York City. When it launched from Britain in 1886, however, the *Gluckauf* revolutionized the oil industry by connecting the increasingly complex international trade in a profoundly new way. By the time it ran aground loaded with kerosene, approximately seventy similar tank steamships crisscrossed the world's seas.

Tanker ships moving crude oil and kerosene, of course, possessed a distant kinship to the skiffs loaded with crude that had been sent down Pennsylvania's Oil Creek during the 1860s. In fact, the scale had begun to shift when the brig *Elizabeth Watts* sailed for England carrying 224 tons of petroleum in 1861. When the ship arrived safely, it allayed many of the fears of shipping the flammable crude oil across the ocean. Throughout the following decades, however, petroleum and kerosene were shipped as whale oil had been for a generation: loaded in barrels and stowed belowdecks in sailing ships.

The iron-hulled *Gluckauf* was the model for the modern-day tanker because it held loose kerosene or oil. For many years, shipbuilders had resisted the idea of stowing shifting cargo in ships, for fear of the load's instability in rough seas. In *Gluckauf* and similar tankers, the vessel's hull became the oil container, which set the standard for future shipping and greatly enhanced the industry's capability for tying together its complex systems for developing and distributing crude.

The tankers of the 1890s were powered by steam and distinguished from all other sailing vessels by the large funnel placed near their front. Normally, these tankers had two decks and between seven and nine compartments or tanks for oil, each of which could hold approximately four thousand barrels of loose crude. Although such tankers flew Dutch, German, and English flags, most were owned by the Standard Oil Company, connecting its growing global network for extracting, processing, and distributing crude. The tanker fleet was first powered by coal but had shifted to diesel engines by the 1910s.

Tankers were a critical component for allowing the industry to achieve the flexibility needed to collect crude from wherever it was found in the world. By the 1940s, oil tankers had quadrupled in capacity to about 16,000 tons gross, and by the 1960s this amount had itself doubled. By the end of the twentieth century, tanker capacity had eclipsed 100,000 tons, and new classes were named Very Large Crude Carriers (VLCCs) and Ultra Large Crude Carriers (ULCCs).*

Today, the typical tanker is either a crude tanker or a product tanker, with the former hauling raw crude to refineries. Sizes vary for each type, but product tankers are typically much smaller, and all new tankers are constructed with double hulls to improve safety. In addition, the size of tanker used is based on the journey being taken by the ship—particularly whether it is carrying its petroleum from inland or coastal areas or on the open ocean. Together, tankers today carry

---

*Information from: "Tanker History," GlobalSecurity.org, www.globalsecurity.org/military/systems/ship/tanker-history.htm; "Gluckauf (1886–1893)," Auke Visser's German Esso Tanker's site, www.aukevisser.nl/german/id95.htm and www.aukevisser.nl/.

approximately two trillion metric tons of oil each year. Supertankers emerged as a vessel class after World War II, with the largest being the *Seawise Giant*, which was launched in 1979. This fifteen hundred–foot vessel could hold more than half a million tons of crude in its forty-six tanks. Over the course of its use, this ship was renamed the *Happy Giant*, and then in 1991 was renamed again as *Jahre Viking*. In 2009, this vessel was renamed *Mont* and beached in order to await scrapping.

Rapid innovation, however, means that tankers do not stay on the job for long. Operating supertankers is such a massive expense that most operators quickly decommission previous models. Many of these vessels have been anchored and refitted to serve as stationary floating storage facilities near Middle Eastern areas of oil production.

Part II

GOING MOBILE, 1890–1960

INFRASTRUCTURE
Pumping Gas

As an illuminant, petroleum in the form of kerosene had been sold in cans or pumped from tanks and put into cans in general stores and drugstores. Once petroleum became integral to transportation, it needed to be more accessible to the internal combustion–powered vehicles that ventured about. From refining sites that transformed petroleum into gasoline, trucks and train cars were used to disperse the fuel to convenient points for consumers' transportation. Filling stations brought an opportunity for systemizing and regimentating transportation in a way that had never before been necessary. Initially, though, one of the gravest challenges facing use of the internal combustion engine was the storage and dispersal of flammable, explosive gasoline.

In the late 1800s, after refinement gasoline was most commonly stored in bulk stations that housed the liquid in huge cylindrical tanks that rested on wooden frames high above the ground. Gravity-fed into horse-drawn tank wagons, the petroleum could then be dispersed to local liveries, auto repair shops, or even dry goods stores. At these general stores, purchasers often bought gasoline by the bucketful. Other entrepreneurs pushed small tanks full of gasoline on carts through the streets to sell directly to consumers. Many people filled a measuring can with gasoline from any of these outlets and then poured it into their vehicles through a chamois-lined funnel. As more and more drivers chose to bypass these gas brokers and instead went directly to the bulk station, an opportunity for a new business was created as well as an opportunity to organize and systematize traffic, which became snarled by auto drivers waiting for or searching for a fill-up.

By 1905, ingenious American entrepreneurs such as C. H. Laessig in St. Louis, Missouri, had moved gasoline dispersal into its next phase: he stood a hot-water heater on end and attached to it a garden hose and faucet through which he could empty gasoline directly from the storage tank into an automobile. The gravity-fed system made the bucket of gasoline a thing of the past; however, it still did not make acquiring gasoline any more convenient. That innovation arrived in the same year through the insight of Sylvanus F. Bowser, who perfected a pump that would take gas out of a barrel and fill a car's tank. His pump could be utilized by existing outlets, such as grocery stores, but the waterproof cabinets that held the pumps could also be locked and kept secure overnight. Together, these innovations combined to clear the way for "filling stations."

Bowser's pumps finally allowed the distribution of gasoline to divorce itself from bulk stations. The retail outlets, or filling stations, were a critical step in making gas-powered autos more convenient and feasible for everyday use. This influence was not instantaneous, though. Initially, the unplanned streetside refueling stations led to even more serious congestion and traffic. The mixed-use nature of roads in the first three decades of the twentieth century created countless problems, ranging from frightened horses to steam explosions. The first filling station was planned by the Automobile Gasoline Company in the 1910s, though filling stations did not arrive in all communities for quite some time. Historian Daniel Vieyra describes the approach to land use in this fashion:

> On an ordinary city lot, the company constructed a small brick building, paved the yard behind, and erected four gas pumps. These pumps . . . drew not from small, above-ground barrels but from safer, more advanced underground tanks; they combined this convenience with Laessig's hose hook-ups, which funneled gasoline directly into the car.*

Siting such businesses was one of the most significant difficulties of these early decades of automobiling. As hard as it is for contemporary drivers to imagine, roads of the early twentieth century were not yet a fixed entity—they varied daily both in quality and in their very existence. A road could be busy one day and suddenly abandoned the next when a paved alternative had opened elsewhere. Locating the essential filling station became one of the first permanent developments of the new auto landscape that would define human movement in the twentieth century.

---

* Daniel I. Vieyra, *"Fill 'er Up": An Architectural History of America's Gas Stations* (New York: Macmillan, 1979), 7.

Chapter Four

Hitting the Road

Through the mountainous paths and various stages of developed and undeveloped roads, the odd conglomeration of vehicles—filled with drivers sporting a host of languages and nationalities—provides a symbol of humans' emerging automobility at the end of the nineteenth century. The 1895 Paris-Bordeaux-Paris race presented a host of great possibilities growing out of the international quest to provide humans with powered transportation that required no animals. Petroleum actively vied for its future; however, the outcome was anything but certain. Unlike today's NASCAR, in which similar vehicles compete closely with one another, European races of the 1890s were a demonstration of the transitional moment—it was a demonstration of which technology could survive the immediate competition, as well as which might emerge victor in the larger race to power human transportation.

In the 1895 French race, the competitors included steamers, gas-powered, and electric vehicles—and variations within each of these categories. Each of the twenty-two vehicles also included variations on related technologies; for instance one entry rolled on the Michelin brothers' first pneumatic (air-filled) tires. Committed to finding a new mode of human transport, the French bicycle manufacturer Armand Peugeot organized such races through his family's tool business, Les Fils de Peugeot Freres. Through Peugeot and others, Paris emerged as the hotbed for transportation innovation in the 1890s. Engineers from throughout the world, but particularly Europe, compared technologies and then watched them compete in races.

Of the thirteen finishers in the June 11, 1895, race, the key entry had an engineering pedigree that combined German, French, and Belgian know-how. Gottlieb Daimler would only make a dozen vehicles during the 1890s (his company, Daimler Motoren Gesellschaft, which became Mercedes, did not become prominent until after his death in 1900); however, the 1895 race saw his two-cycle, gasoline-powered engine unveiled to the engineering world. Frenchman Emile Levassor drove the vehicle over the 732-mile course at the revolutionary speed of fifteen miles per hour and—even more importantly— with no stop for servicing longer than twenty-two minutes. He completed the course in forty-eight hours and forty-seven minutes, finishing nearly six hours before the runner-up. The product and the effort to perfect it swept up the interest of many European men.

On either side of the Atlantic, the passions of many engineers at the turn of the twentieth century rose to the challenge of improving the speed and efficiency of traveling by automobile. The methodical, microscopic-level improvement of technologies such as spark plugs, gasoline, and starter motors belies the massive revolution that they actually embodied: the conglomeration of such innovations joined to radically alter basic patterns of human movement. From these developments radiated social, economic, and cultural implications that transformed basic aspects of human life in developed nations. Although societies such as that of the United States compelled this shift in human movement with political and economic initiatives that were rooted in a desire to raise its population's standard of living, in doing so they also manufactured a reliance on petroleum sunk so deeply into the fabric of their societies that after only a generation its removal would be unthinkable. In human movement, Big Oil found a rationale for crude's integrality that swept through Europe and the United States. As a consumer product, gasoline's price per gallon or liter became a driver for national economies in just a few decades. From the rather innocent tinkering that took place during races such as that between Paris and Bordeaux, the ecology of oil revised at a basic level how humans moved about in their everyday lives.

In the ancient past, as soon as humans sought to centralize authority, the value of roads was greatly appreciated. In the Roman Empire, for instance, the road was a tool of domination, and, typically, roads were quickly added when a territory was overtaken. This great engineering feat provided easier access for the military, which functioned as a threat to outlying territories, but also served as an avenue by which the same territories could access the capital, Rome. This was particularly important for the payment of taxes. With approximately fifty-three thousand miles of paved roads radiating out from Rome, the Roman Empire's success was at least assisted by this secure infrastructure. The centrality of such corridors within Roman civilization led cultural geographer John Brinckerhoff Jackson to comment on the general landscape function of roads as "the strengthening and maintenance of a social order, the tying together at one central place all the spaces which constitute the territory of a community or state."[1]

Figure 4.1. Even when automobiling was in its infancy, racing was a natural part of humans' new transportation reality. This race from Bennings, Maryland, in 1915 was very likely similar to races being held throughout Europe that helped to test and improve emerging technologies. (Library of Congress Prints and Photographs Division, LC-DIG-npcc-27856)

In theory, the great expansion of roads in human societies during the last few centuries remained true to this original formula. The Romans were the first ancient civilization to build paved roads, which allowed travel during or after inclement weather. Indeed, mud or gravel would hinder, if not completely halt, many vehicles pulled by animals or other people, not to mention discourage travelers on foot. Roman engineers, however, did not stop with just paving Roman roads. Roads were crowned—that is, they were higher in the middle than on the sides to allow water to run off—and they often had gutters for drainage along the shoulders. Probably the most incredible engineering feat concerning the Roman road system, though, is how well the roads were built. Many are still major thoroughfares for cars today. Indeed, Roman road-building methods were unsurpassed until the invention of macadam in the nineteenth century.

The intricacy of this ancient road system grew from the use of primitive modes of transport, almost all of which emanated from and were owned by the central authority. The vision of the modern Western world might have included ancient roads put to new uses; however, great efforts unfolded to create road systems that would take advantage of startling new, widely available modes of transportation. As humans learned to move about in revolutionary new ways, petroleum would be their lifeblood.

Experiments with devices for personal transportation originally took place far from the United States—and from Detroit, Michigan, which eventually became known as "Motown" when it was the center of the global auto industry. Following the 1895 race, the Automobile Club of France was founded, and its ranks counted nearly five hundred members before they swelled to more than twenty-two hundred by 1900. By 1901, 130 Paris businesses listed themselves as automobile manufacturers, clearly distinguishing the city as the world headquarters for the industry. Although there were many options in use, Daimler's gasoline engine used safety and reliability to surge to the head of humans' transportation transition at the start of the twentieth century. With each of these innovations in the automobile, the need for roads expanded the Roman model and refitted the landscape for a new era in human movement. Quickly, this remarkably innovative application of petroleum transformed into a sociological revolution.

A REVOLUTION IN HUMAN MOVEMENT

Within the last five thousand years, humans tied animals into land-based transportation systems. In a sense, the same technology that expanded transportation of this era—the horse and the sailing ship—held court until the mid-1800s. However, they remained the predominant transportation technologies for Americans into the early twentieth century. Even when urban areas such as New York implemented mass transportation by the end of the 1890s, they could not entirely eliminate the use of horse power. Although new methods of transportation were being developed at the close of the nineteenth century, in fact, industrialization increased the number of horses needed in urban areas. The 1870 Census enumerated more than 8 million horses throughout the nation, with 1.5 million employed in cities. Census 1900, however, shows an increase in the number of horses to 21.2 million, with the urban population of the animals at nearly 3 million.[2] Many of these were employed in new approaches to mass transportation, known as omnibuses and horsecars.

Omnibuses operated in most cities throughout the last half of the nineteenth century and could run anywhere without the use of rail lines. In 1850, for instance, Philadelphia operated 322 and New York 683. In New York, the omnibuses claimed to carry more than 100,000 passengers per day.[3] Horsecars, on the other hand, used rail lines, which helped to increase suburbanization by regulating commutes. By 1890, 32.5 million passengers each year rode the horsecars operated by more than seven hundred companies. In addition, horses pulled most delivery wagons and even offered their services as prime movers. In some mills and at various construction sites, horses were used to walk treadmills that were linked to gearage systems that turned other devices. In the 1850 Census, horses provided more than half of the motive power used in American cities. The horse's life cycle became entirely anthropomorphized during this period, with its meaning defined by humans. Historians Clay McShane and Joel Tarr write:

> As one thinks about the horse not as an animal but rather as a living machine in an urbanizing society, its role in the process of commodification becomes clearer. Horses had value assigned to them from their very birth. In the nineteenth century city this value related primarily to their usefulness for work. . . . Even their manure was of value as fertilizer, while at death their hides and hair were transformed into useful products.[4]

Their labor, though, came with a price. In particular, the organic city of the nineteenth century, in which animal and human wastes (among other materials) required management with only primitive technology, had to deal with the waste products generated by work animals, specifically horses.

A working horse drops between fifteen and thirty-five pounds of manure and two gallons of urine each day.[5] In cities such as New York, this amounted to up to 3.25 million pounds of horse manure per day. In addition to the mess and stench, the manure brought flies and the possibility of outbreaks of typhoid, cholera, tuberculosis, or infantile diarrhea. For city reformers, planners, and residents in late nineteenth-century cities, horses were most often considered part of the problem. Yet the urban population was not willing to give up personal transportation. In fact, the sprawling nature of cities demanded more than ever before that transportation be available to residents of a variety of economic classes.

Thanks to the horse and the horse and wagon, humans had a long tradition of personal transportation by the time industrialization brought new experiments with mass transit at the close of the 1800s. Although mass transit made perfect sense in urban areas, particularly those of Europe, the size of the United States and expansive American residential patterns made certain that personal transport would remain crucial. In addition, Americans had already imbued personal mobility with one of the founding principles of the nation: independence. A nearly innate need to prioritize personal autonomy had already made personal transportation part of American cultural tastes and preferences. Therefore, entrepreneurs of American industrialization seeking to create profitable inventions knew that mass transportation would not suffice for most Americans.

Bicycles were a perfect example of this new declaration of transportation independence. In the United States, Bostonians such as Frank Weston started importing bicycles in 1877 and 1878, and Alexander Pope started production of his "Columbia" high-wheelers in 1878. In addition to applying his design ingenuity, Pope flexed legal know-how by gaining control of bicycle patents and taking his competitors to court. This would prove to be a familiar practice for Pope as he sought to dominate nineteenth-century modes of personal transportation.

In addition, Pope made high-wheelers and tricycles more widely available through large-scale advertising and also through mass production and mechanization in the manufacture of bicycles. Primarily of use to urban men, these precarious bicycles failed to revolutionize American transportation patterns. In fact, the most significant influence occurred later, in the 1890s, with the development of the "safety bicycle," which is the basic design still in use today. The safety bicycle made use of the bicycle much simpler and available to young people, both men and women. Using two similarly sized wheels and a rear chain drive, the safety bicycle swept the nation and was manufactured very broadly by both large and small companies (such as that of the Wright brothers starting near Dayton, Ohio). Its development joined with John Dunlop's pneumatic tire to make bicycles a great fit for the new paved streets that were being added to many communities. By the start of the twentieth century, cycling had become an important means of transportation as well as a preferred form of recreational leisure for many Americans. In addition, bicycling began to adjust human expectations. For many bicycle manufacturers, the two-wheeled, human-powered model was just a stepping-stone. They sought other forms of transportation that did not possess the bicycle's limited nature. The switch to petroleum-powered transport, however, was not necessarily an automatic one. Other factors converged to stimulate the viability of the internal combustion engine (ICE).

CONSUMING CRUDE

The massive increase in humans' supply of petroleum spurred the search for new applications for it. While Higgins, Rockefeller, and others worked to increase the supply of crude, the market for potential uses beyond lubrication and illumination began to take shape in fits and starts. Big Oil's increasing influence compelled experiments of every type of petroleum use, including in the transportation sector. Human transportation, however, might have been the most contested frontier of petroleum's future.

There were certainly obvious advantages to using newer technologies to reform and retool human modes of transportation. In American and European cities of the nineteenth century, which were often referred to as "organic cities," filth and inefficiency predominated with the concentrated human population. Transportation was a mighty contributor to the problems inherent in the organic city. Since its domestication, the horse served as the prime mover of choice, whether ridden by an individual or bridled to a wagon or carriage. In the United States, until 1841 there were approximately forty humans for each horse. By 1880, though, the ratio dropped to twenty-five to one as industrial and economic development demanded a new scale and scope of transportation.

Concentrated in cities, the use of horses or animals for transportation created many difficulties, primary among which was managing manure and waste, as discussed above. The numbers are surprising: in 1900 Manhattan had 130,000 horses, Chicago had 74,000, and Philadelphia had 51,000.[6] The number of horses in service declined in the early twentieth century, though, as reformers and planners rethought transportation in a way that led horses to be outmoded.

At the turn of the century, in contrast to most entrepreneurs, most city administrators viewed methods of mass transportation, including trolleys, omnibuses, and subways, as the most sensible improvements to residents' health. European cities such as Paris and London invested in subway systems that remain functional and innovative in the twenty-first century. Underground transportation and many of these transportation innovations relied on electricity, which was rapidly altering urban life.

In mass transportation and illumination, electricity (primarily produced from burning coal) became the major challenger to petroleum as an energy source. Thomas Edison, Nikola Tesla, and other inventors and entrepreneurs were rapidly devising new technologies that allowed electricity to be moved from place to place and applied to a variety of tasks. Although electricity was a technology, its revolutionary capabilities were significant enough to rapidly redefine the basic physics of nature in everyday life, whether in terms of transportation, illumination, or construction. As a source of power, electricity possessed an unparalleled flexibility.

As the capabilities of electricity expanded through American and European cities in the early 1900s, the organic city was replaced by a technological infrastructure that wedded urban life to electric lighting and mass transportation—just as the supply of crude was increasing. By association, petroleum's marketplace dramatically shrank as its supply compounded. Although it represented a more flexible, liquid hydrocarbon form of energy, petroleum lost out in many applications to coal's supply and infrastructure. Powered by electricity made from coal, the United States endured unbelievable growth: In 1860 there were fewer than 1.5 million factory workers in the country; by 1920 there were 8.5 million. In 1860 there were about 31,000 miles of railroad in the United States; by 1915 there were nearly 250,000 miles.

Much to Rockefeller's chagrin, at the turn of the century, petroleum, despite its standardized corporate organization, had little use. Technological infrastructure led American consumers down other paths for lighting, transportation, and construction. In fact, the cultural conception of modern transportation veered dramatically from animal power to organize itself around the most efficient solution: electric-powered mass transit. However, if consumer preferences could be altered, so could the cultural ideas about transportation. The corporate titans of the Gilded Age eventually gave way to entrepreneurs who appreciated the abilities of the new consumer culture to energize and popularize their products. With vast amounts of cheap oil flooding the market by the early 1900s, petroleum seemed to offer great potential for transportation if the emphasis was less on modes of mass transport and, instead, more on individualized methods.

MECHANIZING HUMAN MOVEMENT

In an era of remarkable innovation in nearly all facets of human existence, Americans and Europeans chomped at the bit of limited personal transport. They demanded more. The effort to innovate technical solutions to the limits of the animal- or human-powered modes listed above created one of the most competitive markets of the early twentieth century.

Steam and Biofuels

Attempting to mechanize transport proved to be only one fraction of the challenge of innovation. Throughout the nineteenth century, innovators pursued broad variations in vehicles and, particularly, in their belief about what power source should drive the vehicles of the future. For instance, when Oliver Evans built the first motor vehicle in the United States in 1805, he chose steam for his combination dredge and flatboat that operated on land and water. He built based on the reports of international experiments, including those by Ferdinand Verbeist and Philippe-Marie Grimaldi, French Jesuit missionaries in China, in 1665; the Swiss engineer Nicolas Joseph Cugnot in the late 1760s; and the Cornish engineer Richard Trevithick in 1769. Steam-based inventions followed for a variety of purposes. For instance, Richard Dudgeon's

1867 road engine, which resembled a farm tractor, could carry ten passengers. By the late 1890s, nearly one hundred manufacturers were marketing steam-driven automobiles. The most famous of these steam-car makers were Francis E. and Freelan O. Stanley of the United States—twin brothers who developed an automobile called the "Stanley Steamer" in 1897.

Nations reacted differently to the impending changes to human movement. One of the reasons why steam technology took faster root in the United States than in Britain was the infamous British policy initiative known as the Red Flag Act.[7] Forwarded by interests ranging from railroads to horse-carriage manufacturers, the 1865 act severely limited the speed of "road locomotives" to two miles per hour in town and four miles per hour on open roads. More remarkably, an attendant carrying a red flag was required to walk sixty yards ahead of any such device. Most of the models of steam cars burned kerosene to heat water in a tank that was contained on the car. The pressure of escaping steam activated the car's driving mechanism, which moved the vehicle. In France, Peugeot's great success was a steam-powered tricycle, and many other manufacturers worked in steam. The first lines of the underground Paris Metro opened in 1900 with steam-powered cars. The popularity of the steam car declined at about the time of World War I, and production came to an end in 1929. This was not, however, due to a decline in interest in automobility.

Inventors of early vehicles often experimented with burning a variety of oils, although this was considered somewhat more dangerous. Even though petroleum supplies were overwhelming in the early twentieth century, experiments with the use of biofuels in transportation began in the early days of personal transportation and continued for decades. In fact, the use of such oils for illumination and other work predated the discovery of petroleum in 1859. As early as the mid-1800s, many bio-materials were used for purposes such as making soap. Early feedstocks were corn oil, peanut oil, hemp oil, and tallow. In addition, ethanol was in use prior to the Civil War. Mixed with turpentine, ethyl alcohol (ethanol), which was known as camphene, had become a popular illuminating oil by the second half of the nineteenth century.

In terms of personal transportation, biofuels were an alternative powering option from the first experiments at the close of the century. The first transportation device made by Henry Ford, democratizer of the automobile, was an ethanol-powered quadricycle, built in 1896. Unwilling to give up on biofuels entirely, in 1908 Ford, after his successful design of the Model T, made a model that could run on ethanol, gasoline, or a combination of the two. Ford opened his own plant to make ethanol. Later, he worked with Standard Oil Company to distribute and sell the corn-based fuel at its service stations. Most of the ethanol was blended with gasoline. Ford continued to promote ethanol through the 1930s. But finally, in 1940, he was forced to close the ethanol plant due to stiff competition from lower-priced petroleum-based fuels.

Within the petroleum and automobile businesses, biofuels were seen as a necessary side business—particularly with ongoing uncertainty over the supply of petroleum in the early 1900s. Some developers intended to use such fuels as a substitute for gasoline while others sought to boost octane levels by adding them to gasoline. Most famously, Alexander Graham Bell authored a 1917 *National Geographic* article in which he predicts that alcohol will be the fuel of the future when the oil runs out. It "makes a beautiful, clean and efficient fuel." Bell goes on to say: "Alcohol can be manufactured from corn stalks, and in fact from almost any vegetable matter capable of fermentation. . . . We need never fear the exhaustion of our present fuel supplies so long as we can produce an annual crop of alcohol to any extent desired."

The drive to revolutionize human movement fueled a remarkably exploratory era in auto technology from roughly 1890 to 1920. Innovations occurred with a rare rapidity, and innovators possessed a vicious sense of competition with one another.

Initial Experiments with Electric

During this early era of automated personal transport, some Americans adopted electrically powered automobiles that were being built in Europe by the 1880s. The storage battery, which was the essential element of the vehicle's potential, was perfected in France during the late 1800s. By 1890, electric vehicles were being put to use in Paris; however, there was very little manufacturing of the vehicles in France. Instead, the United States proved to be the hotbed for applying the electric technology.

In the United States, one of the first "electrics" produced was by William Morrison in 1891. About fifty-four U.S. manufacturers turned out almost thirty-five thousand electric cars between 1896 and 1915—the period of their greatest popularity. The Columbia, the Baker, and the Riker were among the more famous makes. Electric cars ran smoothly and were simple to operate. However, they did not run efficiently at speeds of more than twenty miles per hour and could not travel more than fifty miles without having their batteries recharged.

The primary difficulty with electric vehicles then (as now) was the battery's limited ability to retain a lasting charge. In the dawning age of electricity, batteries promised all kinds of opportunity but, in fact, delivered very little. In most designs, a battery received a current of external electricity through its electrodes and passed it on to a series of lead strips that accumulated and stored the charge. Creating the accumulator, as a battery was often called, required as long as two years in order to properly prepare the lead strips. George Brush, an American businessman, brought new French battery designs to the United States in 1882.[8] However, over the following decade his undertaking was mired in litigation with French inventors. Of transportation in the late 1800s, the journalist Edwin Black writes:

> Batteries could make it all sensible, make it all possible. Battery power was, in fact, wireless power. . . . But as much as everyone craved batteries to usher the world into the next century, batteries were synonymous with lying and deception, fraud and speculation, exaggeration and misrepresentation. Who could trust the battery—or any company that offered one?[9]

In 1883 even the world's most famous inventor, Thomas Edison, weighed in, calling the storage battery "a mechanism for swindling the public by stock companies."[10]

However, by the late 1800s, a few large suppliers had steered urban transit toward electric vehicles (EVs). EVs were the first systematic effort at a personal transit system, and, as one might expect, they experienced a host of difficulties. Although any new system would have experienced difficulty, to the public the problems were attributed specifically to electric-powered vehicles. The Columbia and Electric Vehicle Company worked with smaller companies in most northeastern cities to create regional interests that established cab fleets and central charging stations in 1899. In Boston, an inspector's report focused on two primary problems: a total absence of regular daily inspections of the mechanism of the cab and no precautions being taken against normal wear and tear. His report suggests that the undertaking was considered less of a business and more as the introduction of an oddity.[11] Improvements were made, and by the summer of 1900 the New England Electric Vehicle Company operated approximately 175 vehicles in Boston and Newport, Rhode Island. In the Boston area, the company began implementing its plan to construct charging stations within concentric circles from the city hub.

Similar developments were also seen in New Jersey's tourist cities, including Atlantic City and Cape May. In Philadelphia, the era of electric transportation began with Electrobat, a prototype cleared for a test drive on Broad Street in August 1894. The vehicle, which weighed more than 4,000 pounds, carried 1,600 pounds of lead batteries over a series of open benches on which passengers could sit. Similar to the design of a bicycle, a long chain connected the power source to the wheels and moved them forward or backward. Throughout 1894, the Electrobat frequented the boulevards of Philadelphia, particularly its high-culture Fairmount Park. In 1895, Electrobat II entered one of the era's many man-machine races and only required 160 pounds of battery power—after just a year, the vehicle could be propelled with only one-tenth the former battery weight. Innovations moved quickly, and events such as arranged races helped to spur technological improvements.

In each case, a national EV company established local or regional branch companies to develop a specific market. Viewed on an entirely profit-generating basis, these regional undertakings were given a very brief period to succeed. By early 1901, the national EVC declared that it would not purchase additional vehicles for any of the projects outside the New York market. Writes historian David A. Kirsch: "By 1901 the major shareholders of the vehicle operating companies were more concerned about preserving capital than with the ultimate success or failure of the electric cars themselves."[12] In New York, electric cabs, buses, and sightseeing coaches continued to operate in and around the city until 1912. New battery design during this period was put directly to work and allowed the range of a single charge to grow to approximately twenty miles. In this urban environment, Kirsch traces the specific landscape of the electric vehicle: "The large station on the West Side continued to serve as the base of cab operations, although the company eventually acquired substations and standing privileges at a number of remote locations, including the Hotel Astor (44th Street), Café Martin (26th Street), and the 34th Street ferry terminal."[13]

Kirsch's findings make clear that after losing money until 1904, electrics became increasingly profitable in New York. However, just as they reached this point, a mechanics' strike in 1906 was followed by a disastrous fire in 1907 that destroyed two hundred cabs at Central Station. Assessing the situation from a business standpoint, the company imported from France fifty new gasoline-powered cabs for its fleet. Profits increased and the EV's last bastion was gone by the early 1910s. "Far from taking advantage of its pioneering role in introducing electric vehicle service," writes Kirsch, "the cab company ended up paying a steep price for innovating."[14]

The Internal Combustion Engine Unites Supply with Flexibility

As mentioned earlier in the discussion of the 1895 race in France, it was the German auto designers who first emphasized an internal combustion engine powered by gasoline. Gottlieb Daimler and Karl Benz created fuel-injected models that showed how such a design had strengths of range, speed, and weight that placed it ahead of other prime movers. Historian James Flink writes that it is "unequivocal that Continental [primarily French and German] automobile manufacturers were at least a decade ahead of their British and American counterparts in the technological development of the gasoline automobile."[15] German inventor Nicolaus Otto created a four-cycle engine that was on display at the 1878 Paris Exhibition. This was the design that Daimler perfected in the late 1880s. Using this design, Karl Benz brought the automobile to the stage of commercial feasibility. By 1900, Benz had sold a few thousand in Europe and a few sites in the United States. It was largely this single invention, then, that was taken up by other innovators all over the world and adjusted or improved.

By the early 1900s many inventors had entered the auto scene, with the French leading the way. The French company De Dion-Bouton sold 15,000 three-wheeled, gasoline-powered transportation devices between 1895 and 1901. Between 1900 and 1910, the company also began selling its engines to vehicle manufacturers all over the world; these engines combined with initiatives in Great Britain to illustrate the dramatic international effort to create new transportation opportunities. Overall, French auto production jumped from an estimated 320 vehicles in 1896 to nearly 5,000 in 1900 and more than 16,000 in 1904, which was the year when the United States surpassed France to become the world's largest automobile producer. Flink reports that France remained the leading producer of cars in Europe until 1924, after which Great Britain surpassed it.[16] The emergence of the U.S. auto industry allowed gas-powered vehicles to reach their potential to completely remake human life. The growth of the industry in the United States grew both from production capabilities and from the unique American ability to consume numbers of vehicles incomprehensible in other parts of the world.

The American efforts on behalf of internal combustion engines began in 1893 when J. Frank and Charles E. Duryea produced the first successful gasoline-powered automobile in the United States. They began commercial production of the Duryea car in 1896. The obvious drawback of the internal combustion engine was noise and smoke. Early innovators actually tried to turn this critique on its head. Charles Duryea argued: "The history of almost every invention of importance is that in its earlier stages it is met with some of the most unreasonable objections, and the objectors lived long enough to see their objections forced down their throats."[17] Clearly, for Duryea and others, what marked the very drawbacks of burning gasoline to some of its critics were for him positive symbols. He continued by mockingly quoting a critic of gas-powered autos:

> "Imagine a street full of such vehicles! Why, you could not live in the same town!" . . . [But] it is also true that everybody rides behind locomotives which give out not only the products of combustion of coal, but sulphuric gases arising from impurities in the fuel, cinders, and specks of soot and coal blown out by the forced draft. [Passengers] . . . do not revel in these objectionable features . . . but they patronize that method of travel and do not usually complain.[18]

In his final judgment, though, Duryea placed the decision squarely at the feet of American consumers when he wrote, "If Americans were to refuse to ride until better accommodations were afforded, the accommodations would be forthcoming in short order." The passion for the autonomy of personal transportation would only intensify. As Duryea foresaw, consumer demand—and passion—would be the primary instigating force for the preeminence of the internal combustion engine.

A human future with personal transportation devices seemed extremely likely; however, the focus on gasoline-powered engines seemed a dark-horse possibility. The use of the internal combustion engine relied on countless minute innovations that, once pieced together, totaled a relatively reliable device for transportation. It is impossible for this account to single out each one of these breakthroughs; however, one must be discussed. As electric cars surged in popularity in the first decade of the 1900s, one of the most frequently stated rationales of consumers was that despite all of its other difficulties, the electric vehicles could be relied on to start and run for at least a minimum amount of time. Starting gasoline-powered vehicles, on the other hand, most often required that one be or have access to a knowledgeable mechanic. Although today's drivers happily take such innovations entirely for granted, imagine the difficulty and danger of being the first innovator to explore methods for igniting petroleum distillates and other flammable substances in a stationary chamber that could be incorporated into the design of a mobile device for transportation.

This engineering difficulty bedeviled the early automobiles until innovations brought under control what George Baldwin Selden called enough explosive power to "blow your damned head off if necessary" and directed it toward igniting and turning a portable engine small enough to power an automobile.[19] Throughout the late 1800s, Selden had experimented with a variety of substances in his Rochester, New York, laboratory. By the 1870s, he had eliminated kerosene and other petroleum distillates in favor of gasoline. Over the course of the next thirty years, Selden would almost single-handedly clog the efforts of many American innovators to patent engine designs. His own patent for a "road engine" was finally approved in November 1895, and he was granted a seventeen-year control over the technology at its inception. In 1899, Pope—the transportation entrepreneur mentioned earlier for his efforts on behalf of bicycles and then electric vehicles—paid Selden $10,000 for his patent. By this point, the dabbling of countless inventors had concentrated into genuine efforts by a limited number of legitimate manufacturers. Pope intended to stop them all in their tracks while he made America's transportation infrastructure based on electricity. It was a grand strategy, but the legal fights would force Pope's EV company to finance teams of lawyers instead of constructing the power stations in each major city as planned.

Most of the other auto manufacturers combined into a loosely formed group referred to as the Hydrocarbon Association and then fought the Selden patent. In a strange twist of irony, the depleted economic condition of Pope's EVC forced it, by 1902, to begin a policy of allowing the construction of automobiles with internal combustion engines so that the company could collect the patent royalties that it then used to finance the limited electric vehicle projects still under way, primarily in New York. Joining forces in 1903, the manufacturers formed a transportation combine referred to as the Association of Licensed Automobile Manufacturers (ALAM). Operating as a controlled trust, ALAM made certain that most cars cost $1,000 to $2,000, which was unaffordable to most Americans. Challenges to the trust's control soon emerged, particularly from the workshop of one Detroit businessman.

There are inventions, and then there are innovations that alter basic patterns of human life. Within the very small latter group, there are a few innovations that additionally alter basic human relationships with the world around us. In this case, one innovator can be held largely responsible for shifting petroleum from its status as an industrial fuel to its central role as a transportation fuel in the consumer culture of automobiles. Born near Dearborn, Michigan, in 1863, Henry Ford personified a new era in American business. After being trained as a machinist in Detroit, Ford left the area in 1891 to become an engineer with the Edison Illuminating Company. When he was promoted to chief engineer in 1893, Ford concentrated on his own experiments with transportation devices, particularly those powered by the internal combustion engine. His first success came with the Quadricycle in 1896, and he began efforts to open his own company. Finding the transportation market largely locked up by patent disputes, Ford refused to play ball. Demonstrating the independent streak that would fuel his future successes, Ford refused to join ALAM, and in the process he altered the entire game.

FORD DEMOCRATIZES THE
INTERNAL COMBUSTION ENGINE

Defying the existing power structure in American car manufacturing and becoming an international symbol for the industry's future, Ford formed his own company, the Henry Ford Motor Company, in 1901. He continued to focus on perfecting automotive technology, particularly in the form of racing vehicles. Ford's defiance made his a most difficult road forward as both sides of the dispute focused on thwarting his efforts. Ford twice had to restart his undertaking when investors, frustrated with his unwillingness to prioritize profit over quality (and price), abandoned him. Forced out of the company that bore his name, Ford gained a reputation as a maverick. After his departure, his former Henry Ford Motor Company changed its name to the Cadillac Automobile Company. It became one of his greatest rivals during the rest of his business career. Throughout his difficulties, though, Ford's unique vision for American transportation had emerged. "I will build a car for the great multitude," he proposed. To potential investors, he explained his ideas more closely when he said: "The way to make automobiles is to make one automobile like another automobile, to make them all alike, to make them come through the factory just like one pin is like another pin when it comes to a pin factory, or one match is like another match when it comes to a match factory."[20] Spoken at a time when cars were solidifying themselves as a conspicuous trapping of affluence, Ford's proclamation was a radical departure. In hindsight, his vision converged with two very specific trends: first, the emergence of a market of nongenteel, mass consumers at the turn of the century, and, second, the failure of mass transit, steam power, or electric batteries to emerge as an acceptable and predominant mode of transportation.

Ford sought to seize this moment and market, but he did not necessarily wish to confront ALAM.[21] In June 1903, Ford, backed by just $28,000 of private investment, formed his third corporation, the Ford Motor Company. Seen as a direct threat to ALAM's control over the entire transportation marketplace, Ford initially attempted to negotiate with them to pursue his plan. In addition, he sued to break Selden's hold on the industry. With rocketing legal bills and only $223 left in the bank, Ford raced to get his vehicle into production in hopes of generating income. Beginning in the summer of 1903, Ford sold all seventeen hundred vehicles that he had produced, which was more than any other manufacturer had ever sold. The transportation sector took a clear tilt toward the internal combustion engine. As journalist Edwin Black writes:

> Had the EVC invested its capital in a recharging infrastructure, and a distribution network of batteries to hardware stores to be available on shelves right along with the ever-present kerosene and gasoline canisters . . . then the American spirit of freedom, wanderlust, and independence could have been achieved as a safer, quieter one, one that did not foul the air, penetrate the lungs, and dim the sky at noon.[22]

Following this success, the ALAM attacked Ford and his undertaking as a threat to its product and the future it planned to develop.

Although the era of electric cars fizzled due to a lack of coordinated development on the part of vehicle producers, one can't overstate Ford's role in determining what would power the future of American transportation. In a letter published later in 1903, Ford explained that his company's plan was extremely simple. He wrote: "We intend to manufacture and sell all of the gasoline automobiles . . . we can. We regard the claims made under the Selden patent . . . as entirely unwarranted and without foundation in fact. We do not, therefore, propose to respect any such claims, and, if the issue is forced upon us, shall defend not only ourselves, but our agents and customers."[23] While the litigation dragged out, Ford's quasi-Jeffersonian vision took form and redefined the United States. Just as Thomas Jefferson had believed that the autonomy brought by individual ownership of land would best perpetuate the values of American democracy, Ford trusted in a future of automobility—particularly if he personally profited from each vehicle's manufacture and sale. Ford's sales remained consistent until the 1906 to 1907 season when they quintupled to eighty-five hundred. Despite national economic crisis, Ford released the Model T and revolutionized American consumer life. His innovation, because it lowered the price of the automobile below $1,000, allowed personal transportation to become conceivable on a individual basis, particularly for rural and emerging suburban markets.[24]

In addition to its popular low price, the Model T benefited from superior advertising and product identification. This status grew in June 1909

Figure 4.2.   The Model T was not very user-friendly by today's standards. In this 1938 photo from Worthington, Ohio, the driver uses the front crank that predated the self-starter. (Library of Congress Prints and Photographs Division, LC-USF34-054571-E)

when the Model T won the well-publicized transcontinental race between New York and Seattle, which was sponsored by M. Robert Guggenheim to promote the year's Alaska-Yukon-Pacific Exposition in Seattle. In addition to its wide availability due to Ford's revolution in mass production, the Model T could now be appreciated for its capabilities: fairly simple repair thanks to standardization of parts; high clearance, which was a most critical selling feature during the roadless era; and a twenty-horsepower engine and weight of twelve hundred pounds, which allowed drivers to get between twenty and thirty miles per gallon of gasoline.[25] More than fifteen million were to be sold in the next twenty years. The Model T, nicknamed the "flivver" and the "tin lizzie," was probably more responsible for the development of large-scale motoring than was any other car in automotive history.

Riding the new wave of personal transportation that swept the United States (American vehicle registrations rose from 800 in 1898 to 8,000 in 1900 and to 902,000 in 1912), Ford persisted in honing his product and filling his coffers to sustain his legal fight over Selden's patent.[26] After extensive litigation, Ford won. In 1911 a District Court of Appeals held that Selden's patent applied only to a two-stroke cycle engine. The Selden patent had been scheduled to expire in 1912 regardless of the court's finding. During the life of the patent, ALAM (which dissolved in 1912) had collected approximately $5.8 million in fees and artificially forced the personal transportation market first toward the electric and then, after 1910, toward the internal combustion engine in hopes of generating profits from patent fees. Unintentionally, they also had contributed to Henry Ford's legend and the success of his innovations. The 1911 decision led to a cross-licensing agreement among most of the American manufacturers, to be administered by the Automobile Manufacturers Association.[27] Even in the 1910s, though, America's vehicular future was not yet determined. In fact, events of 1914 made it clear that the technical issues behind the automobile were not yet clear even to Ford himself.[28]

A FORK IN THE PATH OF MOBILITY

As technologies competed for the human transportation future at the dawn of the twentieth century, there was a bit of luck involved as well as great technological breakthroughs. Led by innovators and businessmen, the transition to petroleum's use for personal transportation is an example of vigorous efforts to aggressively guide consumption tendencies from the top down. With supplies overwhelming need and additional reserves being found at a rapid clip, petroleum's role in human life was ripe for expansion.

Industrial leaders—not consumers—deserve most of the credit for reconstruing transportation. As urban dwellers, in particular, endured this radical change in their lives, specific industrial leaders, in particular Ford and John D. Rockefeller, almost single-handedly wrestled the energy transition away from electricity and toward a different kind of energy. As if reaching over from the passenger seat of a car already moving into the passing lane, they pushed the wheel further to the left and in an altogether different direction. By 1920, their efforts had wedded the transportation future of humans to petroleum.

Electric-powered transport did not go away completely. Many people continued to believe that commercial vehicles, particularly trucks, could best be powered by electricity. For instance, as a replacement for the horse-drawn wagon, the commercial vehicle had to be reliable for short trips, which played to the limits of electrics. In addition, unlike the pleasure vehicle, the delivery truck had to be run in all weather, which again favored electrics. Also, in an entire society of new drivers, there was great variability in the speed and acuity with which drivers guided gas-powered trucks. Speeding was considered a major problem that derived from the drivers' disrespect for the owners' investment. If owners opted for gasoline-powered trucks, they often installed governors on their vehicles' engines. However, the option of purchasing slower, electric-powered vehicles circumvented these difficulties. Overall, though, the definition of spheres to be served by each technology and the willingness to consider transportation alternatives represented a commercial application of the nascent area of business management inspired by Frederick Winslow Taylor and others.[29] The record shows that, at this early stage, American businessmen were able to think of movement in a complex, flexible, and diverse system of transportation.

For instance, in 1909 Chicago Edison produced a study concluding that an electric truck replacing a horse-drawn wagon increased operating costs per mile by 70 percent; however, by the time the average service mileage reached twenty-seven miles per day, the electric truck cost 5 percent less to operate. Other studies also demonstrated that within a ten-mile radius of a city, the electric truck cost less than the gas-powered one to run.[30] Unfortunately for electrics, as businesses expanded in the 1910s, very few limited themselves to these distances. Their preference, overall, became one of flexible transportation that could travel whatever distance was required. In general, trucking offered a significant opportunity for transitioning modes of transportation. "Motorization offered a wedge into the tradition-bound realms of the stable and shipping room," writes Kirsch. Most businesses, he continues, motorized at the same time as implementing organization changes. They did not intend that the truck would immediately do away with the horse, only that it would increase overall efficiency of transporting and delivery.[31]

Even as late as 1914, the future of personal transportation was not clear. Thomas Alva Edison, the United States' greatest inventor, had dedicated a 200,000-square-foot, four-story factory in his West Orange, New Jersey, complex to perfect a battery that could last more than forty thousand miles in cars and serve for various other duties as well.[32] The existing manufacturers of batteries, though, did not wish to see Edison's Type A battery succeed. In addition, although the battery had been successful in trucks and other uses, Edison did not wish to commit to becoming a manufacturer of vehicles. Simultaneously, writes Edwin Black, Henry Ford came to a quiet realization about his own innovation: his vehicles possessed "a faulty electrical ignition system to drive the pistons."[33] With the settlement of the Selden patent suit, Ford no longer needed to steer entirely clear of the concept of electrically powered transportation. Therefore, in the fall of 1912 Ford joined forces with Edison to further revolutionize transportation.

In September 1912, the *New York Times* announced that Edison had perfected "a combination of gasoline engine, generator, and storage batteries by which, for a modest expense, every man can make his own electricity in his own cellar."[34] The first fully operational home of this sort was Edison's mansion in Llewellyn Park, New Jersey. Among the many items that could be charged from the central generator was the Type A–powered electric vehicle that Ford planned to mass produce—in fact, he had committed to build 12,500 per month in just the first year of production. Black writes:

> Finally. It was happening. The automobile revolution which began as an electrical phenomenon, would return to the concept advanced nearly a generation earlier. The automobile revolution could become a cleaner, quieter, more efficient place, drawing its strength from nature, from electricity. The American spirit of independence would be achieved not only by permitting mobility but by enabling stunning individual self-sufficiency.[35]

Ford announced his plan on January 9, 1914, with the promise that each vehicle would cost between $500 and $700. He also directed that his son, Edsel, would head up the new electric vehicle company.[36]

In the midst of such positive spin for the new vehicles, internal experiments with the batteries began to show problems. Keeping a strong public face, however, Edison said in an interview with the *Wall Street Journal*, "I believe that ultimately the electric motor will be used for trucking in all large cities, and that the electric automobile will be the family carriage of the future. . . . All trucking must come to electricity."[37] In the fall, however, while Edison's batteries, which had worked successfully at the lab, continued to fail in Detroit, word arrived that Dodge was also going to release an inexpensive electric car. Finally, October 1914 brought ominous news of potential war on a massive scale in Europe. While each of these developments factored into the death of the American initiative for electric transport, they converge on an actual event: on December 9, 1914, with a flash in the crisp evening, Edison's complex went up in flames.

Fires escalated quickly, and Edison immediately ordered his fire brigades to give first priority to protecting the storage battery building. Although the complex was outfitted with "fireproof" buildings, fires burned until the following day. Ultimately, only his private laboratory and the storage battery factory were saved. Edison would never fully regain his career, and he ultimately suffered a nervous breakdown. With his personal tragedy and difficulty, the future of electric vehicles was easily extinguished by the panic of war and of survival.

THE INTERNAL COMBUSTION ENGINE
ALTERS THE HUMAN LIVING ENVIRONMENT

While Ford and Edison experimented with mass production of electric vehicles, general automobile manufacturing remained a global undertaking. By 1907, however, the U.S. production capabilities were distancing it from other nations. When the U.S. production rose to 44,000 vehicles, France was next with 25,000 vehicles; other nations' production was much lower, with Great Britain at 12,000 and Germany just over 5,000.[38] In 1910 the American vehicles were made by approximately 250 companies, and, thanks to Ford's innovations, mass production allowed their capabilities to far surpass those of any other nation. Additionally, the United States organized its emerging society around individual consumption, which created an incomparable economy of scale for the industry. European manufacturers, for instance, did not adopt the assembly line until the 1920s.[39] By 1913, U.S. vehicle registrations stood at 1.25 million, which was approximately 1 car for every 77 people. Historian Rudi Volti offers the following ratios in European nations for contrast: Britain, 1 car for every 165 people; France, 1 car for every 318 people; Germany, 1 car for every 950 people.[40] The implications of the new mode of transportation were significant, and, therefore, it makes sense that they were felt first in the United States, where one found approximately 80 percent of the world's autos in 1913!

Like a great actor emerging on stage, the transportation revolution immediately brought changes to all that surrounded it. Regardless of what power source was in use, the changes in human movement created new needs and relationships between humans and their environment. Adaptation of the living environment occurred most easily in the United States, but similar patterns could

Figure 4.3.   The centrality of petroleum was embodied by the service station attendant who tended to every detail of each vehicle that visited. (Library of Congress Horydczak Collection, LC-H814-T01-1504-001)

be seen wherever humans relied more heavily on the automobile. Ultimately, in the United States, the primary outcome was decentralization; however, this was a gradual human shift. The first few decades of the twentieth century were instead defined by grassroots efforts to accommodate the needs of the automobile and a society of drivers.

The truly vernacular effort to create an automobile landscape began in the 1910s and lasted until World War II. During this fascinating era, only a small portion of the landscape design was carried out by the large-scale industries that would define post–World War II sprawl. Instead, most of these early businesses sprang from the bona fide realization by a few entrepreneurs that the future for Americans would be behind the wheel of autos. Individually, these entrepreneurs identified opportunity in providing the necessary services to auto travelers and, ultimately, a landscape form emerged as these businesses coalesced along thoroughfares.

Human drivers required maintenance. Tearooms and coffeehouses, providing sustenance in a form becoming popular in urban areas, were some of the first businesses to initiate our roadside culture. Tied to high society and gender independence, tearooms had grown out of the tradition of tea parties and high teas from the Victorian era. By the early twentieth century, tearooms had become places to relax for a light lunch or afternoon tea. By 1910, many city hotel owners came to notice that their tearooms did a better business than their barrooms.[41] Stand-alone tearoom businesses began to develop, and it followed that tearooms would become a popular roadside business as driving became more popular. Particularly during the early decades of driving, car rides were often a leisure activity, and this synched nicely with the clientele and culture of the tearooms. By 1912, roadside tearooms sprang up in rural areas. Women's magazines, then, passed the information along to create destinations for women travelers and their friends that could be reached from urban areas in a day's excursion.

Vehicle sustenance was also required in the form of gas pumps and stations. In the late 1800s, kerosene was sold in cans at general stores or groceries, or it was refilled by clerks in storerooms. Once vehicles with internal combustion engines began venturing about, though, a supply of fuel was essential. The refining process helped to compound the supply of gasoline through "thermal cracking," a practice begun in 1912 that doubled the amount of gasoline yield from crude.[42] Trucks and train cars were then used to disperse the fuel to convenient points for consumers' transportation. Filling stations, described above, systematized and regimented transportation in a way that had never before been necessary. Unlike the tearoom and other consumer forms that had been devised without the automobile, the filling station was first and foremost a technological innovation—eventually, it became integrated as a cultural form of the vernacular landscape. Initially, though, one of the gravest challenges facing use of the internal combustion engine was the storage and dispersal of the flammable, explosive gasoline. These concerns became anchors for a new auto-oriented landscape.

CONCLUSION: SOCIAL AND POLITICAL
DIMENSIONS OF AUTOMOBILITY

The races, such as 1895 Paris-Bordeaux-Paris, did much more than fulfill a human need for speed. They initiated a process in which humans all over the world learned what was required if societies began to rely on mechanized transportation. The effort to apply these lessons to the landscape in which humans were already living their everyday lives defined the first decades of the twentieth century. These years also marked a dramatic energy transition as humans struggled to decide how these vehicles would be powered. In the case of electricity, clearly, the technology was flawed and the patterns of innovation were fractured and spread throughout various tinkerers. For a technology that required centralized innovation and capital, electric-powered transportation could not become cost-effective quickly enough to remain

Figure 4.4. Even in 1938, with gas prices at only twenty cents per gallon, the public wondered how the companies arrived at the figure. This gas station owner in Santa Fe, New Mexico, sought to break it down for his customers. (Library of Congress Prints and Photographs Division, LC-USZ62-96465)

competitive. It did not fail necessarily; more precisely, it did not succeed rapidly enough to snuff out the rise of what many observers agreed was a less desirable solution fraught with significant drawbacks: powering transportation by burning gasoline.

The marketplace for personal transportation marked a source of economic growth during the first decade of the twentieth century for all developed nations. While entrepreneurs of electric and steam transportation struggled to overcome each technology's difficulties in order to seize the historic moment, innovators of the internal combustion engine did the same. With no thought to long-term implications, developers quickly realized that burning gasoline offered the most rapidly available solution to the desire for personal transportation. In addition, historical events contributed additional incentives to drive gasoline ahead of any competitors for personal transportation. Taken together, these events demonstrate the unique historical convergence that made personal transportation veer toward gasoline and, by association, made the twentieth century a petroleum-powered era for developed nations.

In other nations, these new opportunities were not necessarily seized by free-market entrepreneurs; instead, the centralization of road building in this new era came to resemble the rationale of the Romans, centuries before. As European nations struggled with political shifts in the first decades of the twentieth century, roads represented an important tool of modern economic development undergirding centralized authority. In Fascism, in particular, road development cohered with a push for militarization and an emphasis on internal development and trade. This was seen in Italy during the 1920s but became most pronounced during the "Reinhardt Program" in Germany during

Figure 4.5. This remarkable photo of a Graf zeppelin over 13th Street in Manhattan, New York, captures an energy crossroads in the early twentieth century. Particularly during the first decades of the 1900s, transportation utilized various sources of power simultaneously—the future, however, was quickly seized by petroleum. (Library of Congress Horydczak Collection, LC-H832-2070)

the 1930s. In hindsight, these road projects were clearly part of Adolf Hitler's war preparations: Germany needed a state-of-the-art highway system in order to be able to move troops and matériel quickly.

Standardizing transportation networks functioned as a tool for enforcing ideology, just as the Romans had learned. In the United States, the new American auto landscape seemed functional and utilitarian; however, the tearooms, diners, and gas stations contained the economic ideology of capitalism at the nation's root—and that ideology dug consumers more and more deeply into consumption based on the use of petroleum. Figuratively and literally, road building in the United States helped to tie all Americans into the same ideology and economic system. In most aspects, the central authority and federal influence reinforcing this transformation took the form of boosterlike economic development. By 1910, though, efforts to construct similar infrastructure for the auto age often served as a tool and expression of radical shifts in ideology. Roads, it appears, were viewed by leaders as a method for demonstrating their government's centrality and connectivity—its dominion.

Chapter Five

Marching for Petroleum: Supply and Weapons

World War II has left on the human psyche a number of indelible images, including the concentration camps of the Holocaust as well as the mushroom clouds generated by atomic technology. Another image, more prevalent among Europeans, was what the Nazi war machine did to modern warfare. Or, more precisely, what the Nazis' integration of petroleum did to modern warfare.

Nazi technical innovations combined with a strategy to match the name by which they were known: blitzkrieg, or "lightning war," meaning short, concentrated battles carried out over a broad area by mechanical forces. Gefreiter Mollmann, a German soldier, recalls the scene:

> The tanks roar ahead of us. It is a massive show of military might. They have smashed through all resistance, so that until now we have driven unopposed through enemy towns and villages. . . .
>
> The drivers are the silent heroes of this march. They clench their teeth. Stay awake at all costs! Roads, roads, roads—always the same. . . . We roll onwards, devouring the kilometres. . . . We advance—on and on. Past endless ditches by the roadside. For us there is a kind of "mystery" in roadside ditches. They characterize the nature of the advance! Abandoned vehicles, broken weapons, discarded ammunition of all kinds, helmets, uniform items. And everywhere the bodies of fallen enemies. We can see from the ditches exactly what happened here.[1]

Another soldier, Oberleutnant Dietz, adds: "There is no pause for rest: forwards—surprise attack—breakthrough—pursue, destroy and throw everything into it without keeping back even the very last reserves! Those are the mottoes in this war of fast-moving troops. The men's achievements are superhuman."[2] In fact, these accomplishments were only possible for humans who had mastered the use of petroleum and integrated it into their approach to battle.

The aggressive application on the battlefield of new devices, many of which were powered by burning gasoline, was an uneven revolution that had arrived rapidly in World War I, and by World War II it had crystallized into a new strategic approach to battle. The military journalist *Leutnant* Werner Shafer, who moved across Europe with the invading Nazi forces, drew the distinction dramatically:

> The great hope of both officers and men is—the tanks! . . .
> Marching? We'll be racing. We're going to be asking a lot of our vehicles. . . . This Panzer army is fantastic! Like a creeping barrage it pushes forward at incredible speed toward the Marne. . . .
> We really only do measure distance in kilometres now. Our dynamic Panzer arm has spoilt us for any other kind of calculations. Would front-line soldiers in the Great War have believed that the [Nazi forces] could keep up this pace not only in the Polish blitzkrieg, but in France?[3]

Panzer tanks joined with motorcycle corps, autos, and trucks, as well as airplanes and rockets, to use petroleum-based fuels that altered human warfare forever. As Nazi forces brought each of these innovations to the battlefield, the Allies sought to measure up and, ultimately, better them. And in the Pacific theater, Japanese warriors directed their imperialistic wishes through airplanes known as "zeroes" that could be delivered by massive aircraft carriers.

A revolution in human transportation was a vital component of the growing ecology of oil; however, applying these innovations to the needs of national security was another thing altogether. Big Oil was built on a foundation of petroleum's increased supply and its growing essentialness. The corporate expansion into petroleum required the involvement of national governments because of the industry's scale and scope. And the need for petroleum in warfare meant that national governments were already cuddling with industry. Simply, there was no other industry that so easily and consistently accessed the ear of national leaders by the 1920s.

Building on the commitment to petroleum by navies in Britain, the United States, and other nations, warfare in the first half of twentieth century grew increasingly reliant on petroleum. In the case of the United States, the new pressure on supplies was seen on the domestic front—most supplies were drawn from within the country. Once the United States fell in line with other nations that drew significant portions of their oil from abroad, that tenuous supply also needed to be secured through transnational corporate interests, diplomacy, and even military intervention. Although American domestic supplies buoyed consumer consumption, national leaders on the battlefield recognized the reality that they relied on crude obtained elsewhere. World War I proved to be the primary hinge point for defining the twentieth as a century of petroleum. Beginning with the use of petroleum on the battlefield from 1914 to 1918, petroleum became so integral to industry and military alike that by the end of the century wars would be fought to ensure its supply.

CONFLICT AND INNOVATION IN THE GREAT WAR

World War I relied on the use of new vehicles, and, simply put, electrics did not offer a secure option. During World War I the manufacture of automobiles for civilian uses was virtually halted as the industry mobilized to produce vehicles, motors, and other war matériel for the armed forces. The role of cars emerged immediately when a fleet of Parisian taxicabs were used to bring troop reinforcements forward during the Battle of the Marne in 1914.[4]

The Allies used 125,000 Model Ts on the battlefields of World War I. In addition, truck production doubled. Even though the American auto and truck industry diversified during the war to make other products such as shells and guns, the need for more vehicles grew at a rate faster than ever before. Historian David Kirsch notes that in France, Britain, Germany, and later Russia,

Figure 5.1. This photo of a German convoy in World War I captures the energy transition of the 1910s as it appeared on the battlefield. The emergence of the internal combustion engine played out on the battlefield first and then the engine found its way toward dominance in each developed nation. (Library of Congress Prints and Photographs Division, LC-USZ62-136090)

truck purchasers received up to $1,200 from the government for the purchase of an approved vehicle—which stipulated ICE-powered vehicles over the electric alternatives. In 1916 and 1917 U.S. manufacturers established designs for a standard war truck, and they subsequently began exporting vehicles to the front. Kirsch writes: "The dramatic role of motor trucks in the conduct of the Great War reinforced and accelerated the standardization of the commercial peacetime truck. . . . By 1919 electric trucks accounted for less than 1 percent of the total number of commercial vehicles produced in the United States, down from 11 percent in 1909."[5]

Mobility on the U.S. home front was influenced in basic ways by the needs of the war. For instance, in the United States the strain on the nation's railroads led the military to emphasize long-distance trucking and to call for the roads that these routes made necessary. In addition, most trucks for the war effort were manufactured in the Midwest and needed to be brought to the eastern seaboard for shipment abroad. From 1917 to 1918, an estimated eighteen thousand ICE-powered trucks made this trip. In the United States, these trips, which were driven by necessity, demonstrated that such vehicles could be used reliably for interstate shipping, in lieu of railroads. Federal funds had begun in 1912 to develop such roads, which primarily focused on rural access for the U.S. Post Office. In 1916, the Federal Aid Road Act focused federal funds on roads that would help farmers get their products out of rural areas with more ease and flexibility.[6]

Following the war, commercial trucking in the United States became a dramatic example of technological selection: consumers chose the ICE-powered vehicle over the electric alternative. The dominant form of commercial transport within urban areas remained horse-drawn carts; however, electric-powered trucks seemed a superior alternative for short-haul delivery systems. After World War I, though, explains Kirsch, standard practices within the industry—including the use of rail for long-haul transport—forced the "appropriate sphere of the electric truck [to grow] smaller and smaller."[7] Although proponents of electrics pushed for separate spheres of transportation with separate technologies, business owners could not support hybrid fleets. In making their decision for ICE-powered trucks, businesses accepted a cost-benefit scenario that allowed them to succeed across the board, even if another technology (electric power) made more sense for short hauls. These decisions, fed by cheap fuel prices and government-sponsored infrastructure, helped to determine future patterns in human mobility.

During World War I, having a domestic abundance of crude put the United States in a powerful position, no matter what regulatory choices it made. For other developed nations who did not possess petroleum, their growing reliance on oil dictated new patterns of trade and diplomacy. Even before naval forces reserved their oil supplies, though, the battlefield proved petroleum indispensable in modern warfare. The energy transition that stemmed from Britain's commitment to petroleum had an obvious influence on battlefield strategy, first in World War I and then in World War II. Less noted by historians, petroleum's importance in matters of national security and diplomacy frames the grander patterns of this era, tying together both wars and the period that separates them, particularly as it shapes the civilian economy.

Although neither conflict grew entirely from disagreements associated with petroleum supply, new systems of negotiation and need had emerged that would eventually be referred to as "geopolitics." This concept included spheres of influence and trade, each of which was dictated by location as well as by specific resources that were needed. By considering some of these larger patterns from 1915 to 1945, we see petroleum moving to the forefront of the many security concerns of industrial nations. Conflict was increasingly less focused on border disputes and more often emphasized important resources such as energy and particularly the fickle supplies of petroleum that occurred in very limited locations.

The European conflict mentioned above, of course, became known as the Great War, or, in historical retrospect, World War I. It was a disastrous blend of old-world strategies and new, modern-era technologies. Thirteen million people died and millions more were injured or lost their homes and livelihoods. "It was a war," writes Yergin, "that was fought between men and machines. And these machines were powered by oil."[8]

When Britain set out to create its petroleum-powered navy during the spring of 1914, European war seemed a remote possibility. Just eleven days after Parliament approved Churchill's bill about petroleum, though, Archduke Franz Ferdinand of Austria was assassinated in Sarajevo. Russia's army mobilized on July 30 and Germany declared war on it on August 1. British hostilities against Germany began three days later on August 4, 1914.

When the war broke out, horses and other animal participants organized military strategy. With one horse on the field for every three men, such primitive modes dominated the fighting in this "transitional conflict." Over the course of the war, an energy transition took place from horses to gas-powered trucks and tanks and, of course, to oil-burning ships and airplanes. Innovations put new technologies into immediate action on the horrific battlefield of World War I. It was the British, for instance, who set out to overcome the stalemate of trench warfare by devising an armored vehicle powered by the internal combustion engine. Once again, Churchill is given credit for bringing the project—under its code name "tank"—to reality when other British politicians wished to continue with existing practices. Although the tank was first used in 1916 at the Battle of the Somme, its decisive use arrived in August

Figure 5.2. Devised by the British in World War I, tanks were primarily designed to literally plow through the German lines and the trenches in which soldiers hid. Gasoline-powered machines such as this one near Saint Michel, France, in the late 1910s were not outfitted with guns at this time. (Library of Congress Prints and Photographs Division, LC-USZ62-115011)

1917 when at the Battle of Amiens a squadron of nearly five hundred British tanks broke through the German line. In addition, the British Expeditionary Force that went to France in 1914 was supported by a fleet of 827 motorcars and 15 motorcycles; by war's end, the British army included 56,000 trucks, 23,000 motorcars, and 34,000 motorcycles.[9] These gas-powered vehicles certainly offered superior flexibility on the battlefield; however, their impact on land-based strategy would not be fully realized until future conflicts. Therefore, World War I presents a blend of new technologies alongside traditional methods of warfare.

In the air and sea, the strategic change was most obvious. By 1915, Britain had built 250 planes. In this era of the Red Baron, primitive airplanes often required that the pilot pack his own sidearms and use them for firing at his opponent. More often, though, the flying devices could be used for delivering explosives in episodes of tactical bombing. German pilots applied this new strategy to severe bombing of England with zeppelins and later with aircraft. Over the course of the war, the use of aircraft expanded remarkably: Britain used 55,000 planes; France, 68,000 planes; Italy, 20,000; the United States, 15,000; and Germany, 48,000.[10] The disagreement over using petroleum at sea helped to exacerbate existing conflict leading up to the war. Ironically, the use of petroleum in ships led to what Yergin calls a "stalemate" in the use of ships during the war, with only one battle at sea (the Battle of Jutland in 1916). However, part of the explanation for this is the great chasm that separated Britain's emerging petroleum-powered shipping fleet from the entirely coal-burning one of Germany. It made little strategic sense for Germany to confront the British Navy; therefore, it used submarine warfare. These early submarines ran primarily as diesel-powered ships on the surface, but they were also capable of briefly diving for attacks while they ran on battery power.

With these new uses, wartime petroleum supplies became a critical strategic military issue. Royal Dutch/Shell provided the war effort with much of its supply of crude. In addition, Britain expanded even more deeply in the Middle East. In particular, Britain had quickly come to depend on the Abadan refinery site in Persia, and when Turkey came into the war in 1915 as a partner with Germany, British soldiers defended it from Turkish invasion. In addition, British soldiers pushed in to take control of Basra and eventually Baghdad. These defensive efforts allowed British fuel to continue to come from the Abadan refinery. Oil production in Persia grew during the war from 1,600 barrels per day (bpd) to 18,000 bpd. Of course, the growth and stability of the supply grew from Britain's Anglo-Persian corporation, which by the end of the war had purchased the British Petroleum distribution company from the Crown. In order to move the supply where it was needed, the company quickly became a pioneer in the tanker business. By 1917, for the reasons listed above, oil tankers had become one of the German submarine fleets favorite targets. Late in this year, the loss of tankers had become so extreme that British leaders worried that the war effort would be stymied.

When the Allies took renewed measures to prosecute the war in 1918, petroleum was a weapon on everyone's mind. The Inter-Allied Petroleum Conference was created to pool, coordinate, and control all oil supplies and tanker travel.[11] The entry of the United States into the war made this organization necessary because it had been supplying such a large portion of the Allied effort thus far. As the producer of nearly 70 percent of the world's oil supply, the United States' greatest weapon in the fighting of World War I may have been crude. President Woodrow Wilson appointed the nation's first energy czar, whose responsibility was to work in close quarters with leaders of the American companies. These policies began more than a century of close relations between the U.S. government and the oil executives of Big Oil. As a result of this cooperative relationship, when domestic prices for crude rose during the war, the czar made an appeal for "gasolineless Sundays" and other voluntary conservation measures.

On the battlefield, the Allies also designed their strategy to disrupt even the limited supply of petroleum. Although Germany was heavily dependent on the Romanian oil fields, the small nation refused to join it in the war effort. Finally, in 1916, Romania declared war against Germany. As a result, German troops advanced on the oil fields and stored reserves. With Romania's limited ability to rebuff Germany's advances, Britain moved forward with its own solution to the problem: to destroy the Romanian industry so that it could be of no assistance to their opponent. By the end of 1916, British explosives had been used to relegate the entire Romanian industry—fields, reserves, and other apparatus—to waste. The destruction was total; however, Germany took back the Romanian fields and by 1918 had restored approximately 80 percent of the oil supply. In addition, Germany had made significant movement toward acquiring the Baku supply after the Russian Revolution of 1917. More rapidly, though, their own ally Turkey advanced on the valuable resource, suddenly unguarded. By mid-1918, British forces responded to Baku's cries for help and arrived to defend the fields from the Germans—with instructions to destroy the oil fields if their defense became untenable.

Before World War I, writes historian of minerals Alfred Eckes Jr., "national power depended less on the availabilities of resources for mechanized industry and urban populations than on the qualities of soldiers engaged in hand-to-hand fighting." The new imperatives introduced in World War I elevated the importance of minerals, including coal, iron, and petroleum.[12] In each developed nation, securing supplies of these resources had clearly become a matter of national security.

THE MILITARY-PETROLEUM COMPLEX
TAKES SHAPE IN THE UNITED STATES

On July 7, 1919, a group of U.S. military members dedicated Zero Milestone just south of the White House lawn in Washington, D.C. The next morning, they helped to define the domestic future of the nation that they served. Instead of an exploratory rocket or deep-sea submarine, these explorers set out in forty-two trucks, five passenger cars, and an assortment of motorcycles, ambulances, tank trucks, mobile field kitchens, mobile repair shops, and Signal Corps searchlight trucks. During the first three days of driving, they managed just more than five miles per hour. This was most troubling because of their goal: to explore the condition of American roads by driving across the United States.

Leading this exploratory party was U.S. Army Captain Dwight D. "Ike" Eisenhower. Although he played a critical role in many portions of twentieth-century U.S. history, his passion for roads might have carried the most significant impact on the domestic front. This trek literally and figuratively caught the nation and the young soldier at a crossroads. Returning from World War I, Ike was entertaining the idea of leaving the military and accepting a civilian job. His decision to remain proved pivotal for the nation. By the end of the first half of the century, the new roadscape would remake the nation and the lives of its occupants. For Ike, though, roadways represented not only domestic development but also national security.

This realization is embodied in the person of Eisenhower, who termed the travelers' progress over the first two days "not too good" and as slow "as even the slowest troop train." Ike described the roads they traveled as "average to nonexistent." He continued: "In some places, the heavy trucks broke through the surface of the road and we had to tow them out one by one, with the caterpillar tractor. Some days when we had counted on sixty or seventy or a hundred miles, we could do three or four."[13] Eisenhower's party completed its frontier trek and arrived in San Francisco, California, on September 6, 1919. Similar to Lewis and Clark and the builders of the transcontinental railroad, their effort proved to be a pivotal national moment. The significance of their one step for mankind, though, culminated with neither a golden spike nor an American flag; instead, they sparked an awareness of the importance of roads that initiated a century's worth of reaction from Americans. Unstated, however, was the symbolic suggestion that matters of transportation and of petroleum now demanded the involvement of the U.S. military.

In typically understated language, Ike's recollection misdirects listeners from the dramatic shift that lay below the surface. "The old convoy," he explained, "had started me thinking about good, two lane highways." The emphasis on roads and particularly on Ike's Interstate system was transformative for the United States; however, Eisenhower was overlooking the fundamental shift in which he participated. The imperative was clear: whether through road-building initiatives or through international diplomacy, the reliance on petroleum by his nation and others carried with it implications for national stability and security.

Seen through this lens of human history, petroleum's road to essentialness in human life begins neither in its ability to propel the Model T nor its ability to give form to the burping plastic bowl. The imperative to maintain petroleum supplies begins with its necessity for each nation's defense. Although petroleum use eventually made consumers' lives simpler in numerous ways, its use by the military fell into a different category entirely. If the supply was insufficient, the nation's most basic protections would be compromised. In

1919, Eisenhower and his team thought they were only determining the need for roadways. In fact, they were declaring a political commitment by the United States that would guide diplomacy for decades. And, in fact, thanks to its immense domestic reserves, the United States was late coming to this realization; it was a commitment already being acted upon by nations that lacked essential supplies of crude.

The reliance of the military on petroleum set the tone for humans' twentieth-century commitment to crude. Unlike any other resource, petroleum received administrative attention at the highest levels of government once it served as the lifeblood of the military infrastructure. Historian David S. Painter writes: "The result was a public-private partnership in oil that achieved US political, strategic, and economic goals, accommodated the desires of the various private interests, conformed to United States ideological precepts, and palliated congressional critics."[14] From the marriage of security and petroleum, twentieth-century America received a less noticeable but even more critical rationale for ensuring a stable—or even increased—supply of crude. In a manner similar to a species' awareness of its most basic and essential relationship with a food source, political leaders by 1920 included petroleum supplies on the shortest list of critical priorities, essential to the security and future of the United States and other developed nations. Negotiations between nations now had to factor in this key logic and rationale, giving rise to one of the basic components of the concept of geopolitics.

GLOBAL EMERGENCE OF GEOPOLITICS
DURING THE INTERWAR YEARS

Yergin writes that the denial of Baku's supply at the close of World War I proved "a decisive blow for Germany."[15] In the meeting of the Inter-Allied Petroleum Conference immediately after the armistice had been signed, the lead speaker declared: "The Allied cause had floated to victory upon a wave of oil." A later speaker from France offered that just as oil had been the blood of war, now it must "be the blood of the peace."[16] This realization defined most human lives during the coming decades as petroleum became a critical domestic commodity.

More important, though, as a strategic commodity, petroleum would never leave center stage. As Woodrow Wilson led world leaders to think cooperatively of a League of Nations, British forces secured their control over Mesopotamian oil by taking Mosul. In addition, ensuing agreements secured British dominance over the area now known as the Middle East. Their interest fueled further exploration by oil companies and by petroleum geologists. By the 1920s, the findings established a red line spanning the nations reaching from Turkey to Oman that held the largest supply of petroleum on earth. By 1928, this arrangement took more official form as the "Red Line Agreement," in which Royal Dutch/Shell, Anglo-Persian, an "American Group" (five private companies), and French interests agreed to work within this region only in cooperation with the Turkish Petroleum Company, which was led by Calouste Sarkis Gulbenkian, an Armenian entrepreneur who was also responsible for the agreement. Members of the group were given a 23.75 percent share in the consortium and asked to subscribe to a self-denying ordinance that prohibited the members from engaging in independent oil development within the designated region.[17]

Further agreements to manage oil markets were less inclusive, particularly excluding the United States, which feared the agreements would violate the nation's antitrust laws. While the United States spent the early 1930s settling the public-private partnership that would administer its domestic supplies, the other Red Line nations secured their global spheres of petroleum influence. In 1934, Gulf and Anglo-Persian joined forces to develop Kuwait's oil. Not wanting to miss out on the Middle Eastern prize, throughout the mid-1930s representatives of U.S. companies conducted testing in Saudi Arabia. In 1930, Standard Oil of California (SOCAL) had obtained a concession on the island of Bahrain, which lay off the coast of Saudi Arabia, and followed it with a concession in Saudi Arabia in 1933. Joining forces with a Texas company to form Caltex in 1936, SOCAL's claims in the area became the rationale for U.S. development of Saudi Arabia's oil. By the end of the decade, massive strikes had come in for American companies in both places.

Efforts by the United States and Britain to gain access and control to petroleum and other mineral resources were noted by other nations. Germany, Italy, and Japan, writes historian Alfred E. Eckes, "complained vigorously and repeatedly that the uneven distribution of these key materials was both inequitable and intolerable." In 1939, he continues, Britain and the United States controlled more than three-fourths of all mineral resources and Germany, Italy, and Japan only 11 percent.[18] Although there are additional complications, Eckes argues that these deficiencies helped drive these nations to consider warfare as a viable option to close the mineral gap. And petroleum may have been the most significant of these minerals.

In the long-known oil regions of Baku, which were discussed above, Soviet occupation restored production in the 1920s and 1930s so that oil extraction in Azerbaijan in 1940 reached 22.2 million tons, which comprised 71.5 percent of the entire oil extraction in the USSR. During this period, the industry opened new fields, drained the Bibi Heibat Bay (1927), constructed the Baku-Batumi oil pipeline (1925), and drilled the first oil well in the open sea. These were monumental—even heroic—accomplishments for the pursuit of crude and demonstrated the growing geopolitical significance of crude between the world wars.

WORLD WAR II AS A WAR FOR OIL

By the late 1930s, crude had become a matter of urgency for every industrialized nation. While oil was not yet scarce, existing reserves brought immediate interest from other nations. In the waning days of colonialism, oil reserves in the Middle East attracted the competing interest of many nations. None more than the immense—and largely unclaimed—reserves of Saudi Arabia. As this struggle for influence unfolded, the world slid into World War II, what some scholars call a "war for oil." In particular, although the former Allied powers had locked up the known supply, geologists promised that Saudi Arabia's supply was beyond any comprehension. Painter writes that American interest in Saudi Arabia was threefold: "growing concern over the adequacy of U.S. oil reserves, growing awareness of the extent of Saudi Arabia's oil potential, and growing fear that the British might use their influence in Saudi Arabia to the detriment of U.S. oil interests."[19]

In general, the need to secure crude became one of the great rationales for war among nations who were not engaged in power-brokering efforts in the Middle East. Although the U.S. production of oil in 1941 stood at 64 percent of the world's supply, its consumption of energy had climbed at a similar rate. From 1920 to 1941, even though the American population grew from only 106 million to 133 million, annual consumption of oil and oil products increased from 4.3 barrels to 11.2 barrels per capita. And, on the eve of the war, writes Painter, "the first 'Anglo-American petroleum order' had broken down under the impact of depression, world war, and the growing ability and desire of producing countries to control their economic destiny."[20]As each of the soon-to-be Axis powers confronted their own energy needs, they sought drilling agreements with Saudi Arabia by lavishing the king with gifts and offers of huge payments while also carrying out military expansion directed at controlling oil-producing nations.

Fuel for Japanese Imperialism

Particularly in the case of Japanese imperialism, the quest for oil fueled the drive toward World War II. The United States, which supplied approximately 80 percent of Japan's oil, joined other Western nations in condemning Japan's expansionist attacks on China and other neighbors. In 1937, President

Figure 5.3. The use of airplanes revolutionized wartime strategy during World War I. These British planes were part of the force that opposed the infamous Red Baron and others. (Library of Congress Prints and Photographs Division, LC-USE6-D-008870)

Franklin Roosevelt began publicly discussing an economic war, known as a "quarantine." With this threat being discussed openly, Japan tried to find ways of internally rationing petroleum so that it would still be available if the United States refused to supply more. On July 2, 1940, Roosevelt signed the National Defense Act after the Nazis invaded Western Europe. This policy provided him with the executive privilege to freeze economic activity to hostile nations. In retaliation, Japanese forces pushed deeper into Southeast Asia in order to access additional supplies of crude in the Dutch East Indies. As American leaders argued over whether or not to completely cut off Japan's supply in 1940 and 1941, Japanese leaders assumed it would be cut off and, therefore, feeling encircled by the Allied powers, devised a plan for a decisive attack that would bring the United States into the war. This attack was the naval and air assault on Pearl Harbor, headquarters of the navy's Pacific Fleet.

Launched from aircraft carriers toward a distant, unsuspecting site, the Japanese attack on Pearl Harbor was made possible by the use of petroleum in warfare. Ironically, though, the devastation was not as significant to the U.S. Navy as it might have been with more careful and thoughtful planning. The Japanese attack destroyed a number of naval ships and nearly two hundred aircraft while killing more than twenty-four hundred U.S. service personnel; however, the U.S. fleet's stored supply of petroleum on Oahu remained largely unscathed. Some scholars have credited this to oversight, while others suggest the opposite—that the Japanese hoped to put the supply to use in its own fleet following a full-scale invasion and occupation.[21] With a military strategy that depended on a ready supply of airplane fuel, such logic seems very likely.

Hitler's Blitzkrieg Guzzles Fuel

In Europe, few thinkers had identified the critical importance of fueling war machines more quickly than had Adolf Hitler, Germany's head of state. One historian refers to World War I as a static war and World War II as a war of motion.[22] Forming his government in 1933, the same year that Roosevelt came to power in the United States, Hitler had plans and ideas that knew no limits. A portion of his vision of an all-powerful Germany derived from what today we might call "energy independence." Synthetic fuels offered German scientists the ability to deliver new forms of energy. These experiments, though, had begun earlier; in fact, some of them were carried out in the United States. I. G. Farben, the German chemical manufacturer, worked with Standard Oil to experiment with hydrogenation processes that synthetically derived additional fuel from petroleum. In 1931, the leader of Farben, Carl Bosch, shared the Nobel Prize in chemistry for the development of this important process.

With Hitler in power, such technical innovations became part of the German machine. Whereas the security importance of energy resources had led to close relationships between private oil companies and the governments in the United States and Great Britain, Hitler's Germany simply made I. G. Farben part of the Nazi state. In each situation, though, energy from petroleum was clearly identified as a matter of national security. Hitler expanded the application of synthetic fuels while also making the seizure of petroleum supplies a primary component of the imperialist expansion occurring after 1939.

His basic strategy, which was called blitzkrieg, or "lightning war," was organized around short, concentrated battles carried out over a broad area by mechanical forces. A portion of his desire for rapidity derived from a need to complete fighting before petroleum supplies ran out. Although petroleum supplies affected all of the Nazi commanders, it was the push of General Erwin Rommel across the wide expanse of North Africa that most acutely demonstrated the importance of supply. His advance was forced to stop when his supplies ran out far from any German base. In hindsight, Rommel recalled: "The bravest men can do nothing without guns, the guns nothing without plenty of ammunition, and neither guns nor ammunition are of much use in mobile warfare unless there are vehicles with sufficient petrol to haul them around."[23] In addition, Hitler's revolutionary use of rocket technology for attacks on Europe used devices powered by synthetic fuels (primarily manufactured by slave labor). The realization of energy's importance had led him to create the most formidable military the world had ever seen—at least for the moment.

Fueling the Allied War Machine

In order to fight this war machine effectively, the Allies emphasized their greatest resources, including the courage of soldiers, the strategy of leaders, and, finally, a nearly endless supply of petroleum. This tremendous advantage was immediately transferred into strategy on the battlefield. At the peak levels of activity, American forces used one hundred times more gasoline in World War II than they had in World War I. Yergin estimates that the typical American division in World War I used 4,000 horsepower while in World War II this rose to 187,000 horsepower. In planning the military efforts of 1942, the U.S. Army estimated that each soldier in the field required approximately sixty-seven pounds of supplies and equipment to support him, of which half were petroleum products.[24] Between 1939 and 1943, U.S. oil consumption shot up by 28 percent.[25]

Although most of the Allies used American crude, the Soviets drew from the supplies in Baku that they had developed between the wars. Taking into consideration the growing requirements of petroleum in any war effort, the oil workers of Baku reached a record level of oil extraction in 1941: 23,482 million tons. When thousands of oil workers had to leave the fields to fight in World War II, many of their industrial tasks were carried out by women. By the summer of 1942, an estimated twenty-five thousand women worked in the oil industry in Baku, accounting for approximately 33 percent of all Soviet workers. As the hub of the Soviet oil industry, Baku became a crucial target for Hitler.[26] On September 25, 1942, Nazi forces sought to gain control of this great supply of crude.

Prepared for evacuation, workers in Baku stopped production of 764 wells in 1942 and prepared to destroy them. Additionally, the industry sought to circumvent German blockades on the traditional modes of transportation by shipping the oil through Central Asia. For this purpose, the industry employed the first railway cisterns that were tugged afloat in the sea from Baku to Krasnovodsk. The Soviet State Defense Committee ordered the evacuation of approximately eleven thousand oil specialists and a great amount of equipment from Baku to Tataristan and other regions of Russia in October 1942. Most of these workers were transported to the vicinities of the city of Kuybishev (Tataristan), where workers established "a second Baku." Restoration of the industry began at the end of 1943 and after the Battle of Stalingrad, when the danger around Baku had passed. However, the war's impact was significantly reflected in Azerbaijan's level of oil extraction, which fell to 11.5 million tons in 1945.[27]

On the battlefields of World War II, petroleum made a dramatic difference. Actually, a significant change came *above* the battlefield. Using 100-octane gasoline, British Spitfires demonstrated a definite advantage over German Messerschmitt 109s (burning 87-octane) in air combat as early as 1940. Created in the United States and treated much like valuable gold, 100-octane gasoline was shipped through U-boat-infested waters under the strictest secrecy. Thus, one of the greatest Allied resources for war was the advanced U.S. refining industry that utilized thermal cracking techniques to create fuels, such as 100-octane gasoline, that increased engine performance on the battlefield. No moment demonstrates this new strategic importance, though, as clearly as does the Allies' invasion of Normandy. The delivery of fuel supplies presented a major component of the invasion. In fact, once the Allies moved through France, the difficulty facing General George Patton and others was that the fuel supply remained at the point of invasion, back in Normandy. The fast-moving Allied armies simply outran their supply line of petroleum. Yergin reports:

> Down to a half-day supply of gasoline, Patton was furious. He appeared "bellowing like an angry bull" at the headquarters of General Omar Bradley, commander of the American forces. "We'll win your goddam war if you'll keep Third Army going," he roared at Bradley. "Dammit, Brad, just give me 400,000 gallons of gasoline, and I'll put you inside Germany in two days."[28]

In the United States, which remained the world's largest oil supplier, Roosevelt forced the industry into new methods of organization, including systematizing distribution, standardizing products, and even such mundane tactics as using uniformly sized five-gallon gasoline cans—complete with revolutionary, built-in nozzles. To oversee these new standards and systems, President Roosevelt created the post of Petroleum Coordinator for Defense and moved Secretary of the Interior Harold Ickes to the task. One of Ickes's primary tasks was to alter the culture of those leading the petroleum industry, which was entirely organized under the concept of production surpluses. Appointed by letter, Ickes was assigned to "obtain . . . information as to (a) the military and civilian needs for petroleum and petroleum products and (b) any action proposed which will affect such availability of petroleum and petroleum products."[29] Although his post focused on gathering information, the needs of the war effort forced him to openly discuss a new concept: conservation. Spring 1942, for instance, brought the first episodes of consumer rationing in the United States.

The rationing during World War II represents a direct link to the importance of petroleum for security purposes. Throughout the war, in which the United States was involved from late in 1941 to August 1945, the scale and procedure for domestic gasoline rationing evolved. Initially, the use of gasoline for auto racing was banned throughout the United States. The next step came in May 1942 when rationing cards, which would be punched when a driver filled up at a gas station, were put into service in the eastern United States. Eventually, the cards gave way to the widespread use of coupons for gasoline purchases; in general, though, rationing of gasoline focused on the more densely populated Northeast and allowed westerners and others to pump gasoline largely at will. Other measures implemented a thirty-five mile-per-hour speed limit and also sought to restrict "nonessential driving." This latter effort resulted in a rationing system of five separate grades of driving (from essential, including driving by doctors and clergy, to nonessential) to be demarcated by stickers that drivers displayed in their automobile windows. Typically, citizens at the basic level of nonessential driving received one to four gallons per week; essential drivers had no limit whatsoever. In addition, driving was influenced by other forms of rationing, including the conservation of rubber.

It is only a slight exaggeration to say that petroleum—and, by an overwhelming margin, petroleum from the United States—enabled the Allied war machine to defeat the Axis powers. Although American consumers might have been largely shielded from this reality, U.S. leaders were not. In the halls of Washington, D.C., there was little doubt that a diplomatic strategy was required to at least consider the flow of and access to petroleum supplies.

EXTENDING THE GEOPOLITICS OF WORLD WAR II INTO THE COLD WAR AND COLONIZATION

As World War II revealed petroleum's new importance, some of the most significant geopolitical shifts concerned regions with the largest reserves. In particular, the mid-twentieth century witnessed a wholesale recalculation of the geopolitical importance of the Middle East. In the United States, for instance, a version of the wartime management of petroleum extended through the 1950s as Eisenhower's strategic materials commission. Thus, while the American public spent the postwar years basking in supplies of cheap petroleum—decadently finding ways of using it for even the most frivolous everyday tasks—military and political leaders began the process of fully integrating the resource into the strategic planning of the nation's future. Specifically, they followed the model of Britain and France to increase their strategic connectivity in the oil-rich northern areas of the African continent. As early as 1943, Ickes had written: "We're Running Out of Oil!" He went on to stress that World War III would have to be fought with someone else's petroleum, because U.S. supplies were dwindling.[30]

The effort to reach out to King Ibn Saud and other regional leaders was carried out by government officials and American oil companies. Even during World War II, this effort was viewed by some American officials as a competition for favor with allies, particularly Britain. During the war, Ickes's efforts resulted in Roosevelt's creation of the Petroleum Reserves Corporation (PRC). In this experience, Ickes quickly learned the limits to involving the U.S. government directly in matters of the oil industry. He retreated, and the emphasis of any future federal initiative became forging diplomatic ties largely out of the view of the general public. These efforts, though, formed the relationships that would define U.S. relations and energy prominence into the twenty-first century—and they were not only with the governments of the Middle East.

Before the end of World War II and prior to Roosevelt's death in 1945, Churchill (now prime minister) chose to stare directly into the ongoing efforts by Ickes and others to compete with the British inroads to secure Middle East oil. On February 20, 1944, Churchill wired Roosevelt to say that he had been watching the telegrams from the United States about oil with "increasing misgivings." "A wrangle about oil," he continued, "would be a poor prelude for the tremendous joint enterprise and sacrifice to which we have bound ourselves. . . . There is apprehension in some quarters here that the United States has a desire to deprive us of our oil assets in the Middle East on which, among other things, the whole supply of our Navy depends."[31] He concluded that some British officials felt they were being "hustled" by the United States. Roosevelt did not back down, and their exchange went back and forth before finally concluding with mutual assurances that each nation would give way to the efforts of the other: British entered into Iran and Iraq and the United States into Saudi Arabia. The result was the Anglo-American Petroleum Agreement, which was signed on August 8, 1944, and assured the equity of all parties and the cooperative application of technology and developmental systems to extract petroleum from the Middle East and to bring it to the Allied powers. Unlikely to be approved in the Senate, the bill was pulled by Roosevelt and made part of the negotiations in Yalta in January 1945.

Is it an oversimplification to say that the U.S. energy future relied on the immense personal charm of its then-dying president? Indeed, these deals were not just about FDR; however, despite the absence of a record of what transpired on board the USS *Quincy* in February 1945, just after the Yalta Conference, there is no doubt that FDR set the course for a new relationship between these nations. As the ship sat in the Suez Canal Zone off Egypt, one ship brought Roosevelt and another brought Saudi king Ibn Saud. The existing record shows that the men bonded: the chain-smoking Roosevelt abstained in the king's presence; the king, injured at war and left with largely immobile legs, coveted Roosevelt's wheelchair and called the two men "twins." The two leaders talked for five hours about a Jewish homeland, the postwar configuration of the Middle East, and Saudi oil supplies. When Ibn Saud left the ship, Roosevelt sent with him his backup wheelchair. Over the next half century, as American petroleum supplies diminished, Saudi Arabia became the nation's most trusted supplier.

Within twenty-four hours of Japanese surrender in August 1945, domestic gas rationing was ended in the United States. Consumers rebounded by designing their postwar lives around energy decadence, which will be discussed in the next chapter. During 1946, behind-the-scenes talks with Standard Oil of New Jersey and other companies divvied up the opportunity to develop Arabian oil. By applying the concept of "supervening illegality" that Britain had used to seize shares and properties of any owner associated with the Axis powers, the oil executives voided the Inter-Allied Petroleum Conference agreement that had created the "red line" and divided up Middle Eastern oil prior to the war. Forcing their way to the table, American oil executives demanded to have an official cut of the Middle Eastern reserves. Although Aramco and British leaders eventually agreed to proceed with a new arrangement, France refused. When the parties approached Ibn Saud, possibly recalling his meeting with FDR at the close of World War II, he demanded only that the Americans be included. Ultimately, the Group Agreement of November 1948 laid out a new structure for the world—a geopolitical organization.

This new petroleum-centric worldview had taken shape during World War II. By 1941, Max Weston Thornburg, one of the vice presidents of the Bahrain Petroleum Company, had been brought into the U.S. State Department as an adviser. The seriousness of petroleum access is demonstrated by its growing importance to the State Department, and Thornburg worked to exactly this end through the war years. Petroleum diplomats, in addition to interacting with foreign competitors for supplies, were also needed to manage a growing desire for resource nationalization in Mexico and Venezuela. Across the board, Thornburg argued that if the United States were to maintain its dominant position in world oil, "it would need a 'positive' foreign oil policy that protected its interests and anticipated problems between U.S. companies and foreign governments before they developed into crises."[32] In cases such as Venezuela, policies might require the United States to support political leaders who were more likely to work closely with American oil interests. Through the mid-twentieth century, such efforts, on the whole, proved more successful in Venezuela than in Mexico. Regardless, though, the place of the United States in a post–World War II world was obviously predicated on accessing critical energy resources.

The primary focus of this new world order remained the Middle East. U.S. State Department economic adviser Herbert Feis, who worked with Thornburg, noted of this moment in history: "In all surveys of the situation, the pencil came to an awed pause at one point and place—the Middle East."[33] In a manner similar to a child's game of musical chairs, as the music stopped and each Western power paired up with oil-possessing regions or nations, the late-starting United States sat where no other nation was interested: Saudi Arabia.[34] Throughout 1943, amid fear of British encroachment, the U.S. State Department used finances and diplomatic favor to lay the groundwork for its relationship with the Saudis. With the creation of the PRC in 1943, the United States made its task "to buy or otherwise acquire reserves of proved petroleum from sources outside the U.S." This agency became the major mechanism for joining public and private efforts needed to secure American energy interests in Saudi Arabia.[35]

In a lopsided and largely exploitative arrangement, petroleum companies associated with Allied powers used this moment in history to secure the world's precious supply of petroleum, and this agenda became a primary component of what became known as the "Cold War." In 1950 U.S. President Truman wrote to Ibn Saud: "I wish to renew to Your Majesty the assurances which have been made to you several times in the past, that the United States is interested in the preservation of the independence and territorial integrity of Saudi Arabia. No threat to your Kingdom could occur which would not be a matter of immediate concern to the United States."[36] Similar arrangements would eventually bring Kuwait into the American sphere of influence and also help to involve the United States in the internal politics of nations such as Iran.

While the United States focused on opportunities in the Middle East, Soviet officials expanded Baku's production. One of the greatest efforts focused on creating the world's first deep offshore wells near Oil Rocks (Neft Dashlari), which lay approximately 110 kilometers from Baku on the Caspian Sea. On November 14, 1948, the first troop of oil workers headed by Nikolay Baybakov landed in the open sea on a group of rocks called "Gara Dashlar" ("Black Rocks"). In his troop was the geologist Agagurban Aliyev, who authored the idea that there is oil in the sea.[37] After constructing a small electric power station on the rocks, they started drilling the first well on June 24, 1949, and it came in on November 7 at a depth of eleven hundred meters. Within a few months, tankers had begun taking the oil to shore. Soon, one island and then another was constructed on the site of Oil Rocks. In 1952, piers were added to connect each of the artificial islands. Soon, Oil Rocks had five-story and even nine-story buildings, including hostels, hospitals, palaces of culture, bakeries, and factories; a park with trees was also constructed. Since 1949 nearly two thousand wells have been drilled on Oil Rocks, and it has produced a total of more than 160 million tons of oil and 12 billion cubic meters of gas.

Additionally, the Soviets built the world's longest pipeline during the 1960s. The Druzhba, which is also referred as the Friendship Pipeline and the Comecon Pipeline, extends four thousand kilometers (2,500 miles) from southeast Russia to points in Ukraine, Belarus, Poland, Hungary, Slovakia, Czech Republic, and Germany. Binding together the Soviet empire since 1964, the pipeline carried Russian crude to the energy-hungry western regions of the Soviet Union, as well as to "fraternal socialist allies" of the former Soviet bloc and to Western Europe. Today, it is the largest principal artery for the transportation of Russian (and Kazakh) oil across Europe.

Despite this increasing infrastructure, some scholars believe that fluctuation in global oil prices and in Soviet oil production during the 1980s contributed to the collapse of the Soviet Union by the end of the decade. During the 1970s, the Soviet Union weathered the first oil shocks relatively unscathed by maintaining its own stable supply of crude. However, the Soviet price of oil had been artificially set much lower than the world price and much lower than its scarcity value within the Communist system. This low price, coupled with virtually unlimited supplies up to the 1980s, subsidized the Soviet and Eastern European economies. However, Soviet oil production dropped by approximately 30 percent between 1988 and 1992, and the internal price needed to increase. This pressure created an oil crisis within the Soviet Union, and much of the export of oil to Eastern Europe ceased. Therefore, production decreased first and then consumption declined, which forced conservation and high prices—neither of which could be supported by Soviet and Eastern European economies. This internal economic decline, argue some scholars, played an important role in the Soviet Union's inability to compete globally, which destabilized the bipolarity that had defined the Cold War.[38]

Whatever the cause of Soviet decline, the end of the Cold War brought new opportunities for Baku oil, primarily in the form of new pipelines. The best known is the Baku-Tbilisi-Ceyhan pipeline that extends 1,768 kilometers (1,099 miles) from the Azeri-Chirag-Guneshli oil field near the Caspian Sea to the Mediterranean Sea. The pipeline provided Azerbaijan with great support of its new autonomy by tying Baku, the capital of Azerbaijan, with Tbilisi, the capital of Georgia, and with Ceyhan, a port on the southeastern Mediterranean coast of Turkey. Today, it is the second-longest oil pipeline in the former

Soviet Union after the Druzhba. Although the pipeline is only partly in the former Soviet Union, it has delivered crude to Ceyhan since 2006.

This pipeline and its immense capacity influenced global politics immediately. The United States and other Western nations have become much more involved in the affairs of the three nations through which oil flows. The countries have been trying to use the involvement as a counterbalance to Russian and Iranian economic and military dominance in the region. In recent years, Chinese influence has also grown. In short, after the Cold War, the Baku oil supplies have made these remote nations important power brokers on the world stage.

CONCLUSION: FROM COLD WAR TO RESOURCE WARS

Cold War stratification held parts of the world in check for decades. Some of the earliest fractures in this bipolar world appeared in the growing importance of resources, particularly crude oil, as they transcended the imposed ideological boundaries of nations. For nations possessing crude as well as those needing it, such developments marked a foretaste of a new world order.

In 1950, a Jersey Oil Company executive said simply: "It appears that in the future, Mideast crudes . . . may exceed requirements substantially."[39] By 1960, independence movements and decolonization influenced many of the nations of the Middle East. With this increasing autonomy, oil-producing nations sought to rectify the exploitative arrangements by banding together. In 1960, the oil-exporting nations joined forces to combat the unfettered influence of international oil companies by establishing the Organization of the Petroleum Exporting Countries (OPEC), which will be discussed further in chapter 6. During the subsequent years, OPEC would gain political clout through some activities of its own but also through the fuel dependence of developed nations such as the United States. Between 1948 and 1972, consumption in the United States grew from 5.8 million to 16.4 million barrels per day. This threefold increase was surpassed by other parts of the world: Western Europe's use of petroleum increased by 16 times and Japan by 137 times. Throughout the world, this growth was tied to the automobile: worldwide, automobile ownership rose from 18.9 million in 1949 to 161 million in 1972; the U.S. portion of this growth was significant, from 45 million to 119 million during the same years. New technologies enabled some refiners to increase the yields of gasoline, diesel and jet fuel, and heating oil from a barrel of petroleum, but the needs remained greater than anything the world had ever seen.

Such reliance on fuel forced the U.S. government to consistently question relevant policies. In 1969, the administration of President Richard Nixon began debating the quota program again. In April 1973, Nixon delivered the first-ever presidential address on energy, in which he announced that he would abolish the quota system capping the import of crude oil into America. The new reality, however, was that domestic production—even with quotas—could not keep up with the American needs. Clearly, quotas were meant to manage and limit supplies of crude oil in a surplus market, not in the world of shortages that was taking shape. Without the import barriers, the United States was a full-fledged and very dependent member of the world oil market. At the end of the Cold War in 1990, the global landscape of petroleum had changed in at least one very dramatic way: the United States would need to queue up with all other nations in need of a consistent supply of crude.

INFRASTRUCTURE
"Want Fries with That?"

The year was 1954 in sunny California; the Cold War was reaching across the globe, and for many reasons it was very likely unacceptable for a middle-aged man to sit in his car in the restaurant parking lot for long hours. In this case, the man didn't eat, order, or stir. He watched. Similarly to Frederick Winslow Taylor or Henry Ford, Ray Kroc was observing a system. Or at least, he observed something that had the capacity to be such. As he watched the activities at the burger joint in 1954, the actual system of consumption was in only its germ stage. Kroc and others created ways to extend the consumptive culture that grew from the United States' increasing petroleum use. During the Cold War, American patterns of consumption helped to make each citizen a soldier in a war of ideology.

Maurice and Richard McDonald had intentionally located their McDonald's Famous Hamburgers Drive-In just off Route 66 in San Bernadino, California. Kroc, a salesman for Multimixer, a machine for making milkshake drinks, had received an order from the hamburger joint for eight shake machines and, therefore, had come to see what kind of establishment required such a significant investment in milkshakes.

Kroc found a large parking lot with a small octagonal building in its center. As he watched, lines developed almost immediately by 11:00 a.m. but never grew overwhelming. Customers ordered food at one window and then moved to other windows where they received their order. To really move the customers along, each different food was handed out from its own window; however, the possible variations were kept to a minimum: hamburger, fifteen cents; fries, ten cents; and shakes, twenty cents. There was no seating for customers; the assumption was that the food would be eaten in the parking lot or personal vehicle. When Kroc returned to the Midwest to open his own hamburger stand in Des Plaines, Illinois, he convinced the McDonald brothers to lend him their name and know-how in exchange for royalty payments, but Kroc retained the right to make adjustments to his new establishment. In particular, he changed the McDonald's model by setting out to create meals in just fifty seconds. He began to sell franchises in 1955, and by 1957 thirty-seven restaurants were in operation.

Kroc and other entrepreneurs observed that conspicuous consumption fueled the creation of a new cultural and social landscape; however, the inverse was true as well. Specific elements of the landscape dictated new behaviors and habits. Once movement was primarily organized by automobile travel, revolutionary and systematized new designs for human activity could be created. During the twentieth century planners and designers gave Americans what they wanted: a life and landscape married to the automobile. Most details of the new, planned landscape reflected this social dynamic but additionally sought to formalize practices and developments that had been largely informal during the era of automobility prior to World War II. Great possibilities unfolded from these roots that were unthinkable for humans in previous eras.

What excited Kroc was the dawning of the age of formalized human acquisition of food by automobile—foraging on four wheels. "Fast food," for instance, became a primary source of food for many Americans by the end of the twentieth century.

The tradition started with fast-food stands that began cropping up at the edges of towns in the 1920s and 1930s and became so ubiquitous by the 1970s that Americans exported the model to other nations, even to societies less committed to the driving lifestyle that petroleum made possible.

Kroc's McDonald's format took the evolving form of "fast food" and perfected it. He stressed standardization, cleanliness, and appeal for the entire family. By 1959, Kroc had sold one hundred franchises. He helped franchise owners to select the most effective property for their restaurant: by prioritizing center-block locations along busy thoroughfares in the 1950s and 1960s, Kroc's McDonald's became anchors in the new automobile landscape. In fact, when McDonald's later moved to more urban locations, these valuable previous locations became an important real estate empire for the restaurant. Ultimately, McDonald's became the symbol of the consumer society as, unlike any other chain business, it wore its priority of efficiency as a badge of honor: the customer count on an every-changing sign assured guests of "10 billion served." Could food be *good* on such a scale? This question was unimportant.

Kroc had founded his fast-food chain by prioritizing increased scale, and serving billions the same food was the natural result. His aspirations formed a new American ideal that would ultimately influence consumers all over the world.

Part III

THE GLOBALIZATION OF PETROLEUM DOMINANCE, 1960–PRESENT

Increasing supplies compelled a great rise in global uses of petroleum at the start of the twentieth century. New technologies aided petroleum development at each stage, but none more than the effort to access new supplies. While these new technologies have allowed oil companies to drain difficult-to-access reserves, they have also added a greater degree of certainty to geological estimates of the extent of supplies.

The modern search for oil is organized around reflection seismology, in which seismic energy waves are sent out from an air gun or seismic vibrator that can be housed on a boat or a truck. By noting the time that it takes for this energy wave to be reflected and arrive back at the receiver, geophysicists estimate the earth's underground structures, including the depth and extent of mineral reserves. These reflected energy waves are recorded over a predetermined time period (called the record length) by using hydrophones in water and geophones on land. The reflected signals are recorded by a receiver, usually on magnetic tape. These recordings can be read by computer software that creates a seismic profile—a map—of the earth, including possible hydrocarbon reserves. It is very similar to an X-ray of the earth and can also be used on the ocean bottom.

Such remarkable technical abilities emerged at the start of the twentieth century but only found widespread use in the last twenty years. The technology was first used by a Canadian inventor, Reginald Fessenden, to detect submarines during World War I. In 1924, Ludger Mintrop, a German mine surveyor, first used the technology to locate commercial oil wells in Texas and Mexico. Recognizing tremendous applications in the commercial sector, geological specialists at the University of Oklahoma and elsewhere created corporations—including Geophysical Service Incorporated (GSI), Texas Instruments, and Western Geophysical—to make seismic exploration the norm for the entire petroleum industry. Although these service companies work all over the world, large oil companies also have their own divisions for the use and development of seismic technologies. The only problem with the technology is not really a problem at all: seismic data is conclusive and leaves very little opportunity for surprises. Therefore, seismic mapping has led to the most conclusive knowledge of petroleum supplies in human history.

Once a reserve is located and harvesting is determined to be cost-effective, much of the drilling effort closely resembles that seen from the early years of petroleum extraction. One primary difference, of course, is the remarkable technology used to develop offshore supplies. The first offshore wells were marvels in their own right: they were drilled in the middle of Oil Creek in Pennsylvania during the 1860s, and then later in the 1800s wharfs were used to permit drilling off the California coast. These were oil wells built in shallow water. Today, one of the world's tallest freestanding structures is Petronius, the $500 million deep-water oil platform operated by Chevron and Marathon off of New Orleans in the Gulf of Mexico. While the structure reaches more than 2,000 feet (609.9 meters) above water, it runs up to twenty-one well slots that reach the seabed more than 1,700 feet (535 meters) below. The structure is built to sway with the sea, and it is supported by twelve piles (three at each corner) that extend from the tower's legs through the Gulf and 450 feet into the seabed. The field below Petronius warranted this remarkable investment because it is estimated to contain approximately eighty to one hundred million barrels of oil.

Petrobras 36 is the other part of the offshore story. Built and operated by the Brazilian oil company whose name it bore, this floating platform was the world's largest when it sank on March 20, 2001. Costing $350 million, Petrobras 36 operated off the Brazilian coast and produced approximately 84,000 barrels per day. Explosions on board killed eleven crew members and compromised the structure so that it slowly sank—along with the 395,000 gallons of diesel fuel and crude oil that it stored on board—and compromised all twenty-one of the pipelines connecting it to the wells below. In a manner similar to that used in the BP Gulf oil spill of 2010, Petrobras was able to cap the deep-ocean wellheads. Petrobras was able to avert a spill that would have approached the magnitude of the *Exxon Valdez*; of course, the 2010 spill (which will be discussed later) did not have such a fortunate result. In the case of Petrobras, the platform was a total loss and sank to the ocean floor.

Innovations have been a necessary part of satiating humans' growing need for crude. Although we have improved collection techniques, the possibility of failure, which normally takes the form of spills, always remains. Clearly, however, technology has made supplies of crude measurable and allowed humans to better estimate how long supplies will last.

Chapter Six

Consuming Cultures

Calamity came around 1:00 a.m. on Monday, December 3, 1984, in a densely populated region in the city of Bhopal, located in central India. The British company Union Carbide had located its pesticide plant in this populous location to facilitate hiring cheap laborers. India was a particularly hospitable location for chemical manufacturers as environmental regulations tightened elsewhere in the world after 1970. On this day, though, a poisonous vapor burst from the tall stacks at the plant and leaked a toxic cloud of methyl isocyanate (MIC). Of the eight hundred thousand people living in Bhopal at the time, two thousand died immediately, and as many as three hundred thousand were injured. In addition, about seven thousand animals were injured and about one thousand were killed.

Industrial accidents might occur anywhere; however, the Bhopal incident represented a dangerous new era of quasi-industrial colonialism. In such a culture of economic development, was it right to refer to this incident as an accident, disaster, catastrophe, or crisis. Or was it more appropriate to call it cultural sabotage, conspiracy, or massacre? In *The Bhopal Tragedy* William Bogard writes, "Each of these descriptions, in its own way, minimizes the problem of human agency and intention, and thus refuses to address directly the issue of responsibility."[1] For Bogard and others, Bhopal is a "tragedy" created by many dimensions of twentieth-century geopolitics (the relationship between geographical location, resources, and international diplomacy). Its connection to petroleum comes not from oil extraction, but from the petrochemical industry, which by the late twentieth century made up a critical portion of humans' relationship with crude.

Petrochemicals, including consumer goods such as herbicides and plastics, dramatically altered the use of petroleum by offering a seemingly endless stream of applications. A selection of these chemical applications dramatically improved living conditions for many people in both the developed and less-developed world. Producing these chemicals, however, often created health hazards for surrounding communities. Fully aware of these outcomes, some manufacturers placed their factories in communities and nations that either would not complain or would not be noticed if they did so. Such planning serves as an example of environmental injustice or racism. Often, the products made with these high human costs were part of a system of "planned obsolescence," designed for a limited life span that would thus require replacement. In the United States and many Western societies, this fed a sociological cycle known as "mass consumption" in which citizens' civic participation went beyond voting to include purchasing goods—feeding the economy.

The sociological shifts of this new era in the ecology of oil possessed deep layers of irony for humans, particularly when petroleum reserves became increasingly difficult to locate. International corporations, the behemoths that had evolved from the oil companies described above as initiating an age of "petrocolonialism," exercised the ethic of extraction with a ruthless precision that dwarfed efforts of Standard and others to break into the jungles of Mexico and South America in the first decades of the twentieth century. In cases such as the Niger Delta, corporations such as Shell Oil worked out arrangements with political or military leaders that left residents with no financial benefit from oil exploration and all of its impacts on human health

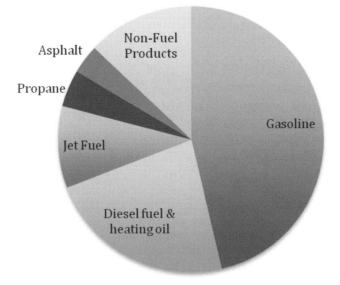

Figure 6.1.   Products from a Forty-Two-Gallon Barrel of Oil
(Data from U.S. Energy Information Administration)

and regional ecology. Whether to harvest oil or to process it for consumption, entire societies were threatened to support the new formula that developed societies called "modern life." In addition to cities such as Bhopal, the ecology of oil crept into societies such as Nigeria that had little use for crude itself.

In short, the ecology of oil had woven petroleum deeply into the fabric of Western life after World War II. The formation of the economic gap between nations discussed by Robert Marks, cited in the introduction, was both complicated and exacerbated by an increasing reliance on petroleum. For a century, many nations of petroleum consumers excelled and prospered. As a long-term development strategy, conspicuously consuming crude was destined to fail eventually because of finite supplies. Even in the short term, however, surprising outcomes of the addiction of the developed world revealed themselves in distant locales and among people with little use for the petroleum or the products it created. Resembling what ecologists call feedback loops in the natural world, the outcomes of this phase in the culture of oil demonstrated that the crude needed by others could be deadly on both physical and social levels.

CONSPICUOUS CONSUMPTION FOR A GLOBAL SCALE

Petroleum remained useful but not essential until humans, and particularly Americans, pursued and modeled a human condition wholly different from that of the nineteenth and even the early twentieth centuries. Tied to ideas of prosperity and patriotism, Americans did not hide their passion for making human life more automated and mechanical. These ideals were presented to the world in venues such as the 1939 World's Fair in New York City. With the United States not yet involved in World War II, Americans used the opportunity to escape the present and wax utopian. Although these dreams took many forms, they were synced together by an invisible hand—more specifically, by a basic assumption that was hidden from each of the scenes: bountiful supplies of cheap energy. Novelist E. L. Doctorow recalled the General Motors Building's "Futurama" exhibit:

> In front of us a whole world lit up . . . [and] demonstrated how everything was planned, people lived in these modern streamlined curvilinear buildings, each of them accommodating the population of a small town and holding all the things, schools, food stores, laundries, movies, and so on, that they might need, and they wouldn't even have to go outside.[2]

The exhibition helped to construct a three-dimensional snapshot of a lifestyle entirely different from that of the past. Although unattainable for many human societies, the aspirations formed by developed nations were based on the merging of science fiction–like visions with the modernist ideas of intellects such as Lewis Mumford. Modernism was no longer an artistic genre restricted to the few artists and designers in European salons; now, modernist design and "the new" were the stuff of the emerging middle class, particularly in the United States. Consumer expectations—such as those shaped by the scene of "Futurama"—became a primary engine behind these radical shifts in patterns of human living. In the United States, the transformation of living patterns after World War II led to new patterns so different from those that came before that historians have given the new model a name: mass consumption. Historians such as Lizbeth Cohen have demonstrated that this growth in consumption and in the middle class that carried it out was fed by the policies and politics of the Cold War, the ideological conflict that followed World War II. Unseen in such a model of society were the feedback loops caused by consumption on such a massive scale. In fact, often one could not even discern the primary force behind such ideal societies: cheap petroleum.

Led by Americans, humans invited petroleum into nearly every aspect of their lives during the late twentieth century. Its affordability during most of this era made reliance seem sensible. However, the status of petroleum never changed: even when its supply made it cheap enough to use it in mundane activities such as manufacturing toothpaste tubes, oil was a finite resource—it would run out. By ignoring this reality, though, the American standard of living became the envy of the world and, therefore, expanded the implications of the ecology of oil as other nations sought to

Figure 6.2. Levittown, New York, in 1957 was a planned community that integrated the automobile into a prefabricated model of suburbia. Such convenient shopping centers became a symbol of American progress during the Cold War. (Library of Congress Prints and Photographs Division, LC-G613-T01-60423-B)

model Americans' behavior. Although the results of this new ecology of crude would prove terribly damaging, the post–World War II era of mass consumption marked a blissful, expansionist time of no questions. As the United States used ideology to fight the Cold War, this consumptive society became an exemplar for nations that yearned for the same standard of living. In short, the view of life on the developed side of the gap drove less-developed nations toward such a goal for themselves.

DEVELOPED SOCIETIES RAISE HUMAN STANDARDS

Following the consumptive patterns defined in the United States but informed by holdover cultural traditions, each developed nation altered basic aspects of the human condition over the course of the twentieth century. In each facet of human life, inexpensive petroleum made these shifts practical and possible to varying degrees as nations sought economic development. These developments brought clear benefits to the human species: lives were saved, people

Figure 6.3. Service stations, such as this one in Miami Beach, Florida, in 1939, represented petroleum companies directly to customers, particularly in the United States. Increasingly, after World War II many companies took these structures very seriously and utilized modernist design and full-service attendants to impress drivers. (Library of Congress Prints and Photographs Division, LC-USF34-051229-D)

fed, and human ideas of time and space utterly transformed. Prosperity followed the innovations that sprung from more widely available petroleum, innovations in transportation, food acquisition and production, the manufacture of artificial forms, and activities in the domestic environment, ranging from housing to chemicals and climate control.

Transportation

Individual transportation was the most obvious revolution of human movement related to the culture of petroleum; however, this one transformation was only a fraction of the total change wrought for human ideas of time and space during the twentieth century. On a larger scale, transportation networks powered by petroleum transformed societies through a trade network of roads used for trucking and innovations enabling air travel. Particularly in the case of air travel, human societies expanded nationally and internationally through a system of connections growing from petroleum products. In each case, initial innovations sparked the gradual construction of complex networks that brought humans access over borders and spatial limits previously unmanageable or impenetrable.

On the ground, long-distance trucking presented a flexibility that railroads could not. Truck transportation proved cost-effective by seizing the petroleum by-product of diesel fuel. Rudolf Diesel developed this fuel and engine design in the late 1870s in hopes of overcoming the inefficiency of other early power systems. Original methods for powering engines applied just 10 percent of innate power supplies to actually moving the vehicle; the diesel compressed air to assist the fuel in raising the engine's temperature and allowed more of the fuel to go toward moving the vehicle. In Diesel's design, fuel is injected into the piston chamber with air, creating an immediate explosion that forces the piston down. Additionally, the fuel needed was different: from the start, fuel for diesel engines allowed flexibility, as gasoline could be used when diluted and mixed with various natural, vegetable oils. When he released his first engine for practical use in 1897, it ran at approximately 75 percent efficiency. It used biodiesel made from peanut oil, which Diesel selected in hopes that it would spur smaller, local industries to supplement the gasoline imported from elsewhere. Stationary diesel engines became popular in industry and shipping by 1900; however, the size and weight of the design continued to limit its usefulness.

These limitations led entrepreneurs to tap diesel engines for different types of transportation tasks, particularly trucking. Diesel-powered trucks hit the road in Germany in the mid-1920s, and Mercedes-Benz released the first automobile with a diesel engine in 1936. As diesels became more popular for trucking, particularly in the United States, oil refiners diminished the use of biofuels and created diesel fuel entirely from fossil fuel residues. Largely due to industry preference, biodiesel receded from major markets for approximately a century. The entirely petroleum-based diesel fuel became the primary fuel for American trucking and industry during the twentieth century. Globally, diesel fuel enabled trucking to assist trade in less-developed nations as well. There, the lack of adequate road development certainly capped trucking's impact, but did not diminish it entirely. Clearly, the implications of long-distance trucking would be felt most in the expansive United States as it began to organize its commercial future around this flexible mode of transportation.

The use of trucks for more than local deliveries expanded after World War I, in which the United States used approximately six hundred thousand trucks. In 1935, the Motor Carrier Act put the federal government squarely behind the future of interstate trucking by expanding the purview of the Interstate Commerce Commission beyond regulating rail and water transportation to include regulating trucking companies involved in interstate commerce. Although there were a variety of rationales for the expansion of interstate highways in the 1950s, their single greatest impact was on the long-haul trucking industry. The interstate highways allowed trucking to expand as an industry in a way seen in no other nation. A culture of trucking took shape around the network of truck stops that became essential to drivers remaining on the road for days and weeks at a time. Access to diesel fuel was now needed in remote portions of the United States through which interstates passed and the truck stop became the essential conduit.

American business wove the trucking network deeply into the nation's commerce through the rest of the twentieth century. In the American countryside, writes historian Shane Hamilton, the expansion of long-haul trucking came "as industrialized agriculture made the practice of farming increasingly peripheral to the economic and social lives of most rural people." Trucking facilitated this transition by tying together more disparate operations and offering drivers a consistent occupation in rural regions.[3] Hamilton continues: "Trucks increasingly replaced trains as the transportation mode of choice for farmers and food processors and retailers—not because trucking was inherently 'better' or less costly than shipping by rail, but because trucks provided the technological flexibility required for the new distribution methods."[4] What began as a political success in road building and subsidies emerged as a system in its own right by the end of the twentieth century. Mastery of such systems of distribution allowed retail innovations that culminated by the 1980s in Wal-Mart. From truck stops to frozen foods, many innovations were required to achieve the Wal-Mart world of efficient distribution; however, at its foundation was the diesel-powered long-distance trucking industry.

Air travel required much more complex innovations, each of which relied on internal combustion engines powered by petroleum products. Although early flying machines were powered by a variety of petroleum derivatives, innovations by Nazi chemists in World War II opened new possibilities through the use of jet fuel. Following the experiments with propeller-based machines begun by the Wright brothers in the 1910s, individual biplanes and pilots squared off in World War I using machine guns and dropping bombs. The era of the Red Baron gave way to stunt fliers known as "barnstormers" who helped to popularize the idea of human flight. By the late 1930s, airlines carried mail and passengers throughout the United States. Flying was expensive and relatively slow; however, Americans who could afford it began taking advantage of its convenience.

World War II helped to commercialize air travel for the United States in a number of ways. Decommissioned military airfields were sold to cities and served as commercial airports, and manufacturers such as Douglas and Boeing remodeled their planes for commercial use, adding pressurized and heated cabins. Jet engines were also added to the mix by World War II. The first jet engine was made in 1931, and by the 1950s large-bodied planes—the Boeing 747, 767, and 777—took to air. Hans von Ohain built a jet engine that flew a plane on August 27, 1939. The engine was powered by gasoline. Englishman Frank Whittle developed his own jet engine, but it was not used to fly a plane until May 14, 1941. Because of a gasoline shortage caused by the war, Whittle's engine used kerosene, which remains the base of modern jet fuels. Today, petroleum is refined into a variety of fuels for air travel, including Jet A and Jet A-1.

Using these sources of power, travel and commerce embraced air travel to link people across the globe in a profoundly new fashion by the 1960s. From Federal Express deliveries to diplomatic missions, air travel became the lifeblood of the global economy. This connectivity can be traced to the Boeing 707, the first jet airliner, which began flying between New York and London in 1959 and cut the time needed to cross the Atlantic Ocean to just six hours. In the United States, strict federal regulation kept fares high until 1978 when airlines were deregulated. Although some airlines, focusing on business travelers, kept rates relatively high, new low-fare carriers (such as Southwest, JetBlue, and AirTran) formed to cater to leisure travelers. In 1975, before deregulation, 205 million people traveled by air each year. This increased to 297 million people in 1980, following deregulation, and soared even higher to 638 million in 2000.[5]

Largely taken for granted by modern humans, these networks for the movement of humans and their goods enabled the borderless era of globalization. Interconnectivity allowed for the expansion of global corporations as well as influential agencies such as the United Nations. The potential implications of this globalization brought serious security issues as well. When airliners fell prey to hijackers or their threats, they demonstrated that developed nations could be accessed by terrorists—small, nonnation actors who wished to leverage their point of view against global powers. In addition, trade and human movement had always created examples of vectors for biological exchange, particularly disease. In the 2008 "bird flu," we see just one example of how complex interconnections moved pathogens to new parts of the world. The expansion of AIDS in the 1980s is also thought to have been exacerbated by the new connections of air travel.

New Agriculture and the Green Revolution

During the first era of industrialization, agriculture in Europe and elsewhere was greatly altered by transportation innovations. In Western Europe and the United States, railroads helped to create an infrastructure for food creation and dispersal. Similarly, steam shipping allowed massive amounts of grain to begin moving by sea throughout the world. And this early phase was just the start of such changes. In the period when agriculture in developed countries derived its energy from fossil fuels "in the form of diesel oil and petrol, rather than fresh hydrocarbons such as hay and oats," writes economic historian Christian Smedshaug, "large areas of land were released."[6] Mechanization, such as tractors and other equipment, allowed larger areas to be farmed, but they also enabled the transfer of land reserved for feeding work animals. The year 1915 marked the high point for the use of draft animals, and by 1920 tractors carried out approximately 10 percent of American agriculture. Just forty years later, tractors carried out 100 percent of American agriculture.[7] Other forces of modern agriculture had allowed industrialized nations to produce significant food surpluses by the late nineteenth century; these were further compounded by the use of petroleum after 1920.[8]

Developed societies, whose origins are often simply explained through their emphasis on industrialization, can in hindsight be seen to have instead consciously emphasized infrastructure development, such as foodways. In the case of the United States, overproduction and drought combined with the Great Depression to create an agricultural crisis in the 1930s. Historian Donald Worster and others have argued that the expansion and practices enabled by mechanized agriculture created an ecological crisis on the Great Plains.[9] In addition, the agricultural crisis stimulated a political response. In the United States and elsewhere, Smedshaug writes, "all countries start industrialization with agriculture as its basis." Even within Europe, he charts a variety of approaches to stabilizing agriculture; however, he notes that a clear pattern

Figure 6.4. Cutting-edge agriculture design emanated from the internal combustion engine—even when it was not particularly impressive. This 1905 image shows the "automobile plow" employed in England. (Library of Congress
Prints and Photographs Division, LC-USZ62-93779)

of history emerges: nations that employed regulation and centralized state
authority industrialized most successfully. "None of today's developed countries industrialized," he writes, "without an active state with national will and
political ability to use a wide range of measures, from import controls and export and import restrictions to prioritizing national players and concentrating
on infrastructure, institutions, education and the important competences."[10]
In the United States, the response to the 1930s crisis created the nucleus of
present-day agricultural politics. Using laws and regulations to assist farming
and also to keep fuel prices low allowed some developed nations to achieve
mastery over the basic human need for nutrition.

Petroleum's role in simplifying and increasing agricultural productivity
may have led it down the path toward emerging as more than a fuel. Systems of trucking for dispersal and mechanized tools such as tractors and

combines, each powered by diesel fuel, transformed humans' food network and, in most cases, significantly reduced food prices. Using petroleum as a fuel, however, was only a portion of the revolution that crude brought to food patterns in the twentieth century. Chemists also played an important role by using petroleum to help expand, simplify, and, at times, enhance the food that appeared in our shopping carts.

Often with petroleum hydrocarbons as a component or active ingredient, chemicals became available to control some of the problems associated with agriculture, including insects and weeds. A variety of chemicals, each derived from or using the energy of petroleum, have been used by farmers to either stimulate growth or control pests. The petrochemical industry emerged to manufacture these products, particularly herbicides and pesticides, during the mid-1900s in massive factories that resembled gigantic laboratories. Although a refinery is needed to make oil into each fuel product, these manufacturers took the chemistry farther and used the oil as the basis for chemicals that became essential to agriculture in developed nations. In most cases, the petrochemical industry also became one of the world's greatest polluters, leaving toxic residue behind wherever such chemicals were manufactured. Most important to twentieth-century agriculture, though, chemists also discovered methods for creating synthetic nitrogen to enhance growing potential—and, of course, petroleum had a role to play in this process!

Although the earth's supply of nitrogen is limited, all life depends on it to serve as the building block from which amino acids, proteins, and nucleic acids are assembled. Plants do not grow without nitrogen, and most of the earth's usable supply could be found stuck to the roots of leguminous plants. Synthetic nitrogen derives from chemists' effort to "fix" it, which is a laboratory process of splitting nitrogen atoms and then joining them to hydrogen in order to create synthetic replicas. Fritz Haber and Carl Bosch created a method for nitrogen fixing that has been largely responsible for the manufacture of synthetic fertilizer.

The Haber-Bosch process combines nitrogen and hydrogen gases under intense heat and pressure. The heat and pressure are supplied by electricity, and the hydrogen is supplied by fossil fuels, normally oil, coal, or natural gas. Journalist Michael Pollan writes: "When human kind acquired the power to fix nitrogen, the basis of soil fertility shifted from a total reliance on the energy of the sun to a new reliance on fossil fuels."[11] The supply of nitrogen fertilizer was quite suddenly nearly boundless, thus liberating humans from the constraints of natural limits and allowing farms (particularly those in the United States) to be managed under industrial principles. Pollan adds: "Fixing nitrogen allowed the food chain to turn from the logic of biology and embrace the logic of Industry. Instead of eating exclusively from the sun, humanity now began to sip petroleum."[12] With this artificial boost, agriculture after 1950 could expand wildly beyond the natural constraints of the land.

Such petrochemical breakthroughs enabled agricultural nations to expand and simplify agriculture, creating a role for modern agricultural corporations throughout the world. In addition, however, these methods and chemicals stimulated one of the first great episodes of international cooperation, known as the "green revolution." Reaching across the gap, agricultural scientists from the developed world during the 1960s shared techniques and hybrid seeds with farmers in less-developed nations. The green revolution brought agricultural technology to many civilizations in which farming was failing for one reason or another, and, therefore, it brought food to starving people in Africa and South America. This revolution in global agriculture began with wheat crops in Mexico and then India before expanding into maize in Africa.[13]

In the process of this assistance, however, many of the techniques and products incorporated these farmers in a model of agriculture much more reliant on petroleum than their previous methods. This was most evident in the use of agricultural chemicals such as industrial fertilizers, the use of which increased sevenfold between 1975 and 2000.[14] Geomorphologist David Montgomery writes that "for the period 1961–2000, there is an almost perfect correlation between global fertilizer use and global grain production."[15]

Figure 6.5. Chemicals made from petroleum-based products are applied to fields in a variety of ways worldwide. Often, farmers utilize crop-duster airplanes, which burn petroleum. (Library of Congress Prints and Photographs Division, LC-USF33-005004-M4)

In many of the nations of Asia, Central America, and South America, the green revolution has been a terrific success in food production—in Asia, for instance, more than three-quarters of the rice grown is from introduced crops. In other areas, such as Africa, it has been less successful.

The separation between developed and undeveloped nations can be seen in the experience of one agricultural chemical, DDT. By the late 1950s, DDT production was nearly five times higher than during the World War II era. In the United States, town and municipal authorities liberally sprayed DDT on American suburbs to eradicate tent caterpillars, gypsy moths, and the beetles that carried Dutch elm disease. It was an important tool in creating the suburban aesthetic of green nature composed of only what we wished. Often, residents would see the plume of spray passing through their neighborhoods and neither shield themselves nor their children and pets from possible effects from overspray. In fact, seeing the spraying rig on a truck or airplane brought relief at what the chemical would do to bothersome insects.

Rachel Carson's famous exposé, *Silent Spring*, published in 1961, highlighted the larger implications of DDT's indiscriminant killing and led the EPA to ban its use in the United States. Today, the United States remains the world's largest producer of DDT as it exports the product for continued use throughout the world—particularly to assist agriculture in less-developed nations. Proponents argue that these products have helped to ease world hunger. In addition, medicines derived at least partly from the petrochemical industry have lowered the costs of pharmaceuticals and allowed organizations such as the Gates Foundation and the United Nations to increase immunization programs worldwide.

The reliance of the entire food network on fossil fuels—part of our ecology of oil—puts humans in a precarious situation as we move forward in the twenty-first century. "For seven thousand years, food empires have expanded as far as transport and topsoil and markets would allow," write Evan Fraser and Andrew Rimas in *Empires of Food*. They continue with the obvious forecast for humans worldwide:

> Every food empire—the network of specialized farms that survive and support urban civilizations through trading—overextends itself. . . . Our agricultural-industrial complex may chug ahead for another generation or two, perhaps sipping a little more cautiously at the oil well, perhaps hammering a few more No Pesticides signs on the edge of soybean fields. But the momentum of the pendulum won't be stilled. Our food system is going to change.[16]

Montgomery adds: "The green revolution's new seeds increased third-world dependence on fertilizers and petroleum. . . . Without cheap fertilizers—and the cheap oil used to make them—this productivity can't be sustained."[17]

The ecology of oil, woven to include essential portions of human life such as foodways, makes such forecasts particularly foreboding.

Flexible Forms: Plastics

In matters of convenience, the ecology of petroleum includes some nonessential but remarkably revolutionary products. In a way similar to the use of petroleum for transportation, the basic integration of petroleum into these other aspects of human life grew from a few basic priorities, including flexibility, planned obsolescence, and disposability. Cheap oil often helped humans to make cheap things, which appealed to mass consumers and helped to fuel broad changes, ranging from product packaging to large, "big box" stores such as Wal-Mart. At other times, cheap oil allowed chemists to cheaply replicate costlier products, usually made from polymers—what we know of as plastics.

These plastics are part of a larger group of petroleum-derived commodities referred to as "synthetics," which might best be considered inexpensive replicas (whether on the level of chemical compounds or the products that these elements are used to create). Most of us know to describe plastic as a "petroleum by-product," but few of us know what role black gold plays in its production. In fact, for its early decades, plastics required no petroleum. The creation of synthetic materials that are related to plastics began in 1907 when a New York chemist named Leo Baekeland developed a liquid material that when cooled hardened into a replica of whatever form one chose. He called this resin material Bakelite. This new material was the first thermoset plastic, which meant that it would not lose the shape that it had taken. In fact, Bakelite would not burn, boil, melt, or dissolve in any commonly available acid or solvent.

In this same general product genre, inventors in the early 1900s developed products such as Rayon and cellophane. Large chemical companies such as DuPont had researchers constantly working in labs to develop any synthetic material that might prove to be useful. In this fashion, DuPont developed nylon during the 1930s, but the company did not make the first pair of stockings until 1939. Many similar innovations also occurred in the 1930s, including polyvinyl chloride (PVC), vinyl Saran wrap, Teflon, and polyethylene. Although each of these items possessed well-known domestic uses, most of them were first used in other products. For instance, during World War II polyethylene was used first as an underwater cable coating and then as a critical insulating material in radar units. By decreasing the weight of radar units, this material made the technology more portable so that it could be placed on planes.

During the 1930s, it became a sign of progress (breaking from the past) to insert these obviously man-made objects of modernity into the most mundane locations in our everyday life. Still, most of these objects were not ubiquitous. Their limited production most often began with coal, from which chemists rent phenol. The process of polymerization resulted in a resin that was formed by condensing phenol and formaldehyde. This resin, then, could be shaped and colored for whatever purpose was desired. With this process, chemists created a string of commercial products continuing from the early Bakelite, including celluloid, which led to acrylic plastics, an array of vinyl compounds, and ultimately to polystyrene.

Historian Jeffrey Meikle notes that these developments meant that by the end of World War II, plastic had become cheaper, less durable, lighter, and increasingly more plentiful. The evolution led to a new category known as thermoplastics that were "driven not so much by market demand as by the pressure of supply, an overabundance of chemical raw materials, waiting to be exploited."[18] The primary substitute for coal, of course, was petroleum, which could create derivatives similar to those from coal. Once again, the key to expansion was cheap oil.

By 1976, more plastic was manufactured, in terms of cubic volume, than all steel, copper, and aluminum combined. In part, the proliferation of plastics stemmed from the idiosyncrasies of production. Relative to other products, plastics are expensive to manufacture in small quantities because of the high fixed costs involved in making the molds and production equipment. Therefore, companies must produce huge quantities to recoup their investment—a situation tailor-made for conspicuous consumption. Today, five resins account for nearly 60 percent of all plastics used by consumers: low-density polyethylene, used in garbage bags; polyvinyl chloride, used in cooking oil bottles; high-density polyethylene, used in milk jugs; polypropylene, used in car battery cases; and polystyrene, used in disposable food containers. With so much plastic in our lives, we have learned that the material has another attribute beyond its flexibility of form: it is remarkably durable. Although its form might break or wear out, the plastic itself endures. In fact, it is almost impossible to dispose of!

While residents of less-developed countries are only now increasing their use of plastics, they are, nonetheless, affected by the tremendous use of plastics on the other side of the gap. Nondegradable plastic packaging is blamed for filling commercial landfills, increasing their operational expense, contaminating the environment, and posing a threat to animal and marine life. Together, this plastic waste accounts for about one-quarter of all municipal solid waste. This is a particularly big problem because of plastic's remarkable durability. By the 1980s, an estimated fifty-two million pounds of packaging were being dumped from commercial fleets into the ocean every year in addition to three hundred million pounds of plastic fishing nets. These trends helped to create one of the most bizarre global symbols of plastics and the era of conspicuous consumption: tidal accumulations of plastic trash in terribly remote locations.

For centuries, oceans have been considered to be so vast that human pollution that was dumped could be absorbed and even processed. By the end of the twentieth century, it was clear that this was no longer the case, and plastics, such as those gathering off Gore Point in the Arctic, became the focus of nonprofit groups. In this instance, a group called the Gulf of Alaska Keeper, or GoAK (pronounced GO-ay-kay), fights to control the massive amount of plastic that accumulates after crossing the Gulf of Alaska or even the Pacific Ocean to arrive there. On nearly any beach it is easy to find the usual cups, bottles, and plastic bags, what the U.S. Environmental Protection Agency (EPA) calls "floatables," those "visible buoyant or semi-buoyant solids"—cotton swabs, condoms, tampon applicators, and dental floss—that people flush into the waste stream.

Chemicals and Climate Control

During the twentieth century, the domestic environment of humans in developed countries became one of the greatest symbols of the gulf between societies. Access to cheap petroleum generated important distinctions in comfort, safety, and health. In the case of homes, developed societies used petroleum-powered transportation to decentralize their living environment into variations of the suburban housing development. Heavy machinery similar to that which transformed agriculture also homogenized topography for use in housing tracts. In each of these homes, prefabricated materials, often enabled by the petrochemical industry, allowed the price of secure housing to drop considerably. All over the world, new housing became accessible to new groups of humans. Within many of these homes, humans lived with comfort and safety previously unknown to most of the species—particularly in hostile climates.

In addition to their use in the manufacture of plastics, petrochemical "feedstocks" are used to produce drugs, detergents, and synthetic fibers. The chemical industry alone uses almost 1.5 million barrels of natural gas liquids and refinery gases a day as feedstocks. These feedstocks are obtained from processing various petroleum fuels and reducing them to their basic chemical elements. These elements become the basic building blocks for the majority of our consumer and industrial chemicals. Chemicals made from a petroleum base are particularly crucial in the operation of technologies used in refrigeration and cooling.

Dichlorodifluoromethane, which became known as Freon, was invented by Thomas Midgley Jr. and coinventor Charles Kettering, using petroleum, to serve as an alternative to the toxic gases that were previously used as refrigerants, such as ammonia, chloromethane, and sulfur dioxide. This breakthrough led to an entire family of related chemicals, with each Freon product designated by a number, including Freon-11, trichlorofluoromethane, and Freon-12, dichlorodifluoromethane, which are coolants, and Freon-113, trichlorotrifluoroethane, which is a cleaning agent. Freons were useful but dangerous from the start: for instance, if its temperature rises higher than 400 degrees Fahrenheit, Freon converts to phosgene gas, commonly known as nerve gas—the agent that gained notoriety in World War I for its sweet smell of cut grass. In this form, the gas caused 90,000 deaths in "the war to end all wars" and 350,000 in World War II (excluding the Nazi use of gas chambers).

Chlorofluorocarbon compounds (CFCs) in general, and Freon in particular, became one of the first foci of the modern environmental era and taught an initial lesson about the problematic existence we had come to in our new ecology of oil. Devra Davis writes of ozone and CFCs—what she calls "free radicals"—in this fashion: "In the lower atmosphere, CFCs are basically inert. . . . But when they float up to the stratosphere, where they are exposed to stronger ultraviolet rays, decomposing molecules of CFCs release atoms of chlorine. Each chlorine atom can destroy tens of thousands of molecules of ozone . . . that serves as a global sun shield."[19] Well before public discourse over the concept of climate change, the ability of the "free radical" CFCs, such as Freon, to create damage that affected every human was profound.

The use of these chemicals, such as DDT, and their production have revealed that despite great advantages, the creation of petrochemicals often comes with serious environmental costs. In the United States, most of this production has been concentrated in the American South; for instance, the locations of the facilities to produce benzene and other petrochemicals have led to charges of environmental justice and racism. Regulation and careful environmental monitoring have managed to somewhat limit the impact of such sites; most often, however, the reaction of the industry has been simply to move the production process overseas to a less regulated site.

Although each of these uses of petroleum presents some deleterious outcomes for human health, the production of petrochemicals, which typically took place near sources of massive quantities of petroleum, seriously affected communities in the United States as well as all over the world. The primary example of the industry's possible outcomes occurred in Bhopal, India; however, the twenty-first century is littered with other sites teetering on the brink of similar cataclysm.

CANCER ALLEYS AND TOXIC CORRIDORS

Consumption creates patterns that, like an animal being hunted in snow, leave tracks connecting it to its source. Ultimately, mass consumption and the tendrils that it extends into the lives of many humans can be traced back through patterns of manufacturing, distribution, and, ultimately, extraction that supplied the raw crude. Because petroleum is the raw material for so many products, its location—or the locations to which it can be easily shipped—often dictates the siting of many other manufacturers. Unfortunately, in most items related to petroleum, such corridors of production also quickly become toxic, leading to disease and other health problems for communities that happen to lie between supplies of petroleum and the market for consumable items.

In the United States, for instance, a "toxic corridor" follows the Mississippi River northward. It is supplemented by petrochemical plants along the Texas coast near Houston and along the shipping channel that connects it to the Gulf of Mexico. In some of these regions, problems of toxic waste and pollution serve as examples of environmental racism, in that as such dangerous industries were sited in areas with political power neither to reject nor to regulate them.

On a global scale, one can trace a similar corridor along the Suez Canal, which opened in 1869. A busy seafaring corridor since the advent of the steamship, the shipping connection serves as a link between Asia and northwestern Europe, particularly the Mediterranean region and northwestern Europe. Although tourism is a primary industry for the lands ringing the Mediterranean Sea, the trade corridor has created surprising concentrations of pollution in sites such as Campo de Gibraltar. The European Pollutant Emission Register has identified this small, bucolic town in the south of Spain next to the overseas UK territory of Gibraltar as one of the most toxic locations in the world.

Because of the many factories that depend on the shipping corridor that passes nearby, industry in the densely populated Campo de Gibraltar emits a wide variety of toxic compounds over the nearby townspeople and environment. The largest firm in this industrial complex is CEPSA S.A., which opened its Gibraltar refinery in 1969. After decades of expansion, the refinery is one of the biggest in Europe, with a production capacity twice that of any other European oil refinery. In addition to refining oil, CEPSA manufactures a variety of petrochemicals, including aviation fuel. CEPSA's refinery in Campo de Gibraltar is also one of the worst polluters in Europe, producing more benzene emissions (forty-three tons per year) than any other site in Spain. Of course, benzene has been linked to a number of serious diseases, including various types of leukemia, respiratory problems, skin problems, and blood disorders. Levels of benzene near the CEPSA refinery have been measured at more than twenty-two times the limit prescribed by the EU directive.[20]

Scientists have blamed Campo de Gibraltar's polluted air for giving the region the highest allergic asthma rate among children and overall mortality rate in Spain—20 percent above the national average.[21] Pollution in the waters of the Mediterranean tends to remain near its discharge source because of relatively weak tidal and current movements. Campo de Gibraltar has been one of many areas impacted by the Mediterranean Action Plan (Med Plan), which was adopted in 1975 with the help of the United Nations Environment Programme. The Med Plan has been widely regarded for successfully raising awareness of pollution in the Mediterranean; however, improvements in environmental quality under the plan have been limited.[22]

The health implications of petroleum processing and manufacturing are felt in many locales worldwide, and often regulation and mitigation are very difficult. In the American South, "Cancer Alley" is the name given to the eighty-five-mile portion of Louisiana that extends from Baton Rouge to New Orleans and was formerly referred to as the "petrochemical corridor." Once many cases of cancer were reported in the small rural communities on both sides of the Mississippi River, the region acquired its foreboding name. The toxic materials released from the numerous petrochemical plants located in cancer alley (more than one hundred industrial facilities in total) are thought to be the smoking gun that makes the state one of the U.S. leaders in deaths from cancer.

There are many examples of accidents in the area, as well as long-term releases of toxic materials that have ruined much of the area's drinking water supply. Mossville, Louisiana, is one representative example. Founded by freed slaves, the town's boom came through the chemical and plastics industries after WWII. In Mossville, companies found little resistance to building factories in close proximity to these disenfranchised black neighborhoods. Today, the town's economy is supported by more than fourteen factories making things like house siding. In these processes, the factories each year release four million pounds of carcinogens, including benzene and vinyl chloride. Today, government researchers find three times the national average of dioxin levels in Mossville residents.[23] After years of complaints to the EPA and the federal government, Mossville agencies now have presented their concerns to the Inter-American Commission on Human Rights, a transborder organization.

Similar issues are made more complicated by international borders along the Amur River, separating Russia and China. An explosion in 2005 destroyed a chemical plant in the Jilin province of eastern China along the

Songhua River and sent slicks of benzene and nitrobenzene downstream and into the Amur River, which flows to Russia. At one time, the benzene level on the Amur rose to 108 times the national safety levels. Russian authorities banned all fishing in the Amur River, and, subsequently, Chinese authorities formally apologized to Russia for the spill and pledged assistance to deal with the consequences. Russia continues to work with China to monitor the impact of such industrial accidents.[24]

CONSUMED BY CRUDE

Each of the benefits or costs of petroleum use requires that petroleum first be extracted. Even in the modern era, the impact of petroleum acquisition carries significant costs for nearby communities. As the consumptive patterns of developed nations demanded greater supply, international corporations followed the supplies into locales that, ironically, had no use for oil. In the case of many less-developed nations, this extractive process has had a severe toll on their communities and cultures.

Ecuador's oil has been harvested since early in the twentieth century. Without a government or local authority to control outside companies, extraction leveled significant swaths of jungle and rainforest along the Amazon River and also led to the installation of the Trans Ecuadorian Oil Pipeline System (known by the Spanish acronym, SOTT). Built in the 1970s and then added to in the first decade of the 2000s, the SOTT system has created additional problems as a result of its lack of technological rigor. First, it leaks, and this constant spillage has contaminated entire stretches of the Amazon on which local populations depend. Second, constructed as inexpensively as possible, the entire pipeline passes above ground, subjecting it to sabotage by angry locals and gangs. Texaco, which led the oil development in Ecuador, over a period of decades haphazardly discharged into the rainforest the oily water residue left from oil production. This practice, in combination with the problems of SOTT, has fouled an entire region known as the Oriente in the Amazon Basin. In the Oriente, this contamination was compounded by Texaco's practice of burning off with no regulation the natural gas emitted by wells. In 1992, Texaco pulled out of Ecuador, leaving the Oriente as a wasteland.

In the 2000s, local activists joined with international lawyers, including Steven Donziger, and celebrity activists to file lawsuits against Chevron (which took over Texaco's work in Ecuador) to pay damages for these ruinous activities. The joint efforts have resulted in one of the most noticeable checks on Big Oil's exploitation of developing nations. Their efforts particularly emphasize the standard practice of these companies to discharge wastewater and waste crude into pits in the jungle that have continued to contaminate water resources—including the Amazon—after the companies left. Made famous in the film *Crude*, the legal case was met by Chevron's defense that the environmental disaster of the Oriente was created by Texaco and the state oil company Petroecuador. Courts ruled in favor of Donziger's lawsuit in 2007 and promised a judgment worth as much as $27 billion. While courts continue to try to make Chevron pay some of this ruling about past contamination, the struggle continues by local activist groups to reap financial gain from oil development while not ruining their living environment.[25]

Similar problems were caused by petroleum development in the African nation of Nigeria. The ecology of this nation exacerbates the implications of oil exploration and development. Extremely dry, Nigeria's soils do not allow extensive agriculture. Petroleum and natural gas deposits are concentrated in large amounts in the Niger Delta and just offshore, which significantly intensifies the impact of spills and pollution. Although there have been a significant number of varied long-term implications of this oil development, the cost to Nigerians might have been most evident in June and July 2001 when 150,000 Nigerian residents of Ogbodo battled a massive petroleum spill from a Shell pipeline. For eighteen days, crude drained into the community's surrounding waterways until Shell finally clamped the pipe on July 12. This was simply one of the most glaring examples of corporate entities such as Shell being allowed unfettered and unregulated opportunity in places such as Nigeria.

The petroleum industry's ethic of extraction can be seen throughout the oil-producing portions of southern Nigeria, where a lack of regulation has allowed Shell and other companies to give little thought to long-term impacts on the lives of residents. As international watchdog organizations have noted, in addition to the large spill in 2001, oil spills routinely pollute groundwater and ruin cropland in a region with shortages of each. Between 1976 and 2001, the government documented 6,817 spills—essentially one per day for twenty-five years. It is suspected, of course, that even more spills have gone undocumented. A lack of interest in updating equipment is primarily to blame. However, in this region in which the crude is seen as a foreign presence and political leadership has been unstable, local residents are also guilty of sabotage and theft. In a land of extremely limited opportunity, these activities demonstrate that Nigerians feel little ownership over the industry. Oil development is resented, and, therefore, such activities are seen to impact only distant corporations.[26]

In Nigeria, residents had never been able to view their petroleum reserves as a national treasure. Starting in 1906, British businessman John Simon Bergheim acquired a monopoly on the supply. For the next six years, officials in the Colonial Office protected Bergheim's monopoly over prospecting rights, rewrote mining legislation at his request creating the Southern Nigerian Mining Regulation (Oil Ordinance) of 1907, and provided the Nigeria Bitumen Corporation with a loan to support its search for petroleum. By 1912, the corporation had sunk about fifteen wells in southern Nigeria, east from the Lekki lagoon toward the Niger Delta. Skipping a few decades, developers returned in 1937 when an Anglo-Dutch consortium, Shell D'Arcy, came to Nigeria and had the whole country as one concession. Between 1938 and 1939, the company drilled seven boreholes, and then development lapsed again until 1951. Shell's big strike came in 1956 at Oloibiri, and an American company, Tenneco, moved in by 1960 when Nigeria attained its independence from Britain.

Once Nigeria was opened to all outsiders, within the first five years of independence, more than nine international oil companies had become active, namely: Shell-BP, Mobil, Tenneco, Texaco, Gulf (now Chevron), Safrap (now Elf), Agip, Philip, and Esso. These international corporations were joined in the late 1960s by Japan Petroleum, Occidental, Deminex, Union Oil, Niger Petroleum, and Niger Oil Resources. This era of oil development resulted in the formation of the Nigerian National Oil Corporation (NNOC), the predecessor of the Nigerian National Petroleum Corporation (NNPC), and the admission of Nigeria into OPEC, the Organization of the Petroleum Exporting Countries, in July 1971. In each case, the Nigerian government entered into agreements with these international corporations and kept a portion of the oil profits; the primary difficulty came from the lack of stability and democratic representation within the government. In 1986, the Nigerian government established a Memorandum of Understanding (MOU) that guaranteed a margin of two dollars per barrel to the producing companies in exchange for certain exploration and enhanced recovery commitments. With this legal structure, the nation was treated much as the oil camps of previous generations: Nigerians received almost none of the financial benefits of development and were left, for the most part, with only the residual impacts of oil development.[27]

Isaac Asume Osuoka, director of Social Action, Nigeria, believes that callousness toward the people of the delta stems from their economic irrelevance. "With all the oil money coming in, the state doesn't need taxes from people. Rather than being a resource for the state, the people are impediments. There is no incentive anymore for the government to build schools or hospitals." "I can say this," Osuoka said firmly. "Nigeria was a much better place without oil." When groups such as Osuoka's have demanded action, multinational corporations have resisted. The political structure of Nigeria provides residents little ability to demand action or recompense.[28]

The lack of Nigerian ownership over the industry may be most evident at Oloibiri, where the oil development largely began. The original wellhead hasn't produced oil for decades and it sits abandoned and unattended. In 2001, a plaque was added to serve as the foundation stone for the Oloibiri Oil and Gas Research Institute, which was to be a government-funded museum and library. The plaque remains the only evidence of this idea. The town, which had swelled to a population of ten thousand during its oil boom, now has fewer than one thousand residents. Instead of a monument, this site stands as a symbol of the incongruity of Nigeria's approach to oil development. Of course, the industry brings in revenue: it is estimated that the Nigerian National Petroleum Corporation owns 55 to 60 percent of multinational oil operations onshore and, through these projects, brings in approximately $60 billion annually.[29] Most experts agree that the problem is in Nigeria's leadership. In recent decades, although the government has evolved from a military dictatorship to a democracy (the latest attempt at civil governance began in 1999), little effort is made to disperse any of this revenue to Nigerians. In one report, a Western diplomat referred to "the institutionalized looting of national wealth." The head of Nigeria's anticorruption agency estimated that in 2003, 70 percent of oil revenues—more than $14 billion—was stolen or wasted.[30]

For obvious reasons, many Nigerians have become disenchanted with the government's ability to exert any control over oil development. In the nation's fractured political structure, some warlords have stepped forward in recent years to act almost as "Robin Hood" heroes, leading attacks on facilities and pipelines owned by Royal Dutch/Shell, Chevron, and others. Dukabou Asari, for instance, has led such actions and siphoned away oil supplies to put crude in the hands of the general public. In one instance, the situation got even more complex as the government responded by hiring groups such as Asari's to protect the oil infrastructure. At the very least, the confusing ownership, development, and protection system creates a morass in which each group operates against the others, and the only clear result is that the public receives neither benefit nor oil.[31]

In theory, there is a system for dispersing Nigeria's oil wealth: the federal government retains roughly half and gives out the rest each month, on a sliding scale, to the thirty-six state governments. The core oil producers—Rivers, Delta, Bayelsa, and Akwa Ibom—receive the most. Even in these regions, however, little of this wealth trickles down to most Nigerians. Yet the oil continues to flow out of regions such as Bonny Island, where oceangoing tankers line up in Cawthorne Channel awaiting their fill that they will then disperse throughout the globe. In nations such as Nigeria, the extraction of crude has not benefited citizens' everyday life—they see neither a "Futurama" world of roads nor one of disposable plastics. However, they are burdened with many of the costs of the extraction that benefits developed societies.

In each of these nations exploited by oil development, on top of environmental despoliation and social disarray we see examples of what economists refer to as the "Dutch disease." In a boom economy created for oil extraction, foreign products initially become cheaper to buy with the strengthened local currency, and domestic products that are desired by foreign workers become more expensive. This disruption to the local economy is one of the residual effects that remains when the oil development diminishes. In some developed nations that host oil development, such as Norway, economists have attempted to sterilize the local economy by investing oil money in foreign stocks and bonds so that the local economy can be allowed to remain relatively unchanged. Weathering boom in this sustainable fashion, however, takes centralized control and planning; in both Ecuador and Nigeria we see examples of developing nations with no ability to manage their relationship with crude. By default, then, their crude reality becomes one of extraction—of resources, economic potential, and regional culture.

CONCLUSION: THERE WILL BE SPILLS

As with any energy source, petroleum is not entirely an industrial product; at each of its stages of development—harvest, processing, distribution, and use—it becomes enmeshed in social processes. For crude, its more insidious implications have been appreciated for many years. Most often, voices such as Ida Tarbell and Rachel Carson refused to allow the standardizing ethical impulse of Big Oil to seep from the industrial barracks to infect human and ecological communities. They demanded that the value of petroleum's harvest and use never overwhelm basic expectations of fairness and health. With the social good that derives from widespread petroleum use, boosterlike networks of support often fed growing patterns of consumption. However, there were exceptions.

American scholar John Ise may have been the first public critic to fully grasp the potential difficulties of this ideology that emerged between the world wars when the American and international models of development merged. In *The United States Oil Policy* and other writings of the late 1920s, the University of Kansas economics professor described the history of the petroleum industry as a moral disaster. Where Tarbell at least celebrated the early, wildcat phase of development, Ise echoed Rockefeller in castigating the wastefulness of the early years. As Big Oil emerged to eliminate a great deal of the waste, Ise lamented the emerging structure as "a gigantic system of wrong" because of its continued emphasis of the boom-and-bust cycle. As a "natural monopoly," petroleum in Ise's mind demanded public regulation.

A major portion of this culture of oil, in Ise's mind, derived from consumers who contributed to the wastefulness by employing crude for "unimportant purposes" such as use in automobiles, a mindless extravagance being used by "fat-bellied bankers and bourgeoisie . . . by gay boys and girls in questionable joy rides . . . by smart alecks who find here an exceptionally flashy and effective way of flaunting their wealth before those not so fortunate as themselves."[32] In contrast to such frivolity and the ideology of Big Oil, Ise argued for a bona fide model of petroleum conservation. Cheap oil had to go, and, whenever possible, the United States needed to keep its reserves in the ground and import whatever oil was required. Of course, such an extreme perspective contradicted the entire spirit of the industry and, to some degree, that of the entire, and expanding, nation. Held at bay for a generation, such a view of conspicuous consumption as sinister reemerged at the close of the twentieth century.

As petroleum-based industries extended throughout the globe, the movement of petroleum products became a critical portion of the global economy. Although great improvements were made in the technology used to move petroleum from its source to wherever it was needed, that movement had its own impact, most often symbolized by oil spills. Unlike the small-scale but persistent spills seen in production locations such as Nigeria, hundreds of spills occurred as tankers passed distant waters to deliver their crude. From the well-known wreck of the *Exxon Valdez* in 1989 to the 2010 wreck of the Chinese-registered *Shen Neng 1* (carrying coal but spilling oil) into the coral reef off of Australia, ocean spills became a hallmark of humans' life with petroleum.

Even before the petroleum arrives at the tanker, of course, spills are already a scourge of the industry. The most famous example might be BP's 2010 platform collapse and well leak in the Gulf of Mexico. In such a case, an international corporation's activities cause tremendous damage to national interests where the development takes place. As ensuing events demonstrate, when such a nation is the United States, the event plays out in a media spotlight that could eventually bankrupt one of the world's largest corporations. Most often, however, these spills and accidents—which are an undeniable part of the process of providing crude—play out in nations without the United States' ability to grab international attention. Whether the events take place in Nigeria or India, the awareness of the human costs of our petroleum habit soon wanes. The reason, of course, is that we desperately need petroleum for our everyday life. Humans in Western nations simply must acquire it from somewhere.

Spilled oil will eventually break down in the ocean. Transformed into synthetic products, such as a rubber duck, for instance, the materials' durability long outlasts the products' usefulness. Donovan Hohn recently proved this fact dramatically by following thousands of bath toys that had been lost at sea. His book, *Moby-Duck*, tells the story of a massive container ship—a "floating warehouse"—that departed Hong Kong in 1992 only to lose two columns of containers stacked six high into the Pacific Ocean. As water flooded one container, it soaked the cardboard boxes inside and discharged thousands of little packages onto the sea. It was the case, Hohn notes,

> that every package comprised a plastic shell and a cardboard back; that every shell housed four hollow plastic animals—a red beaver, a blue turtle, a green frog, and a yellow duck—each about three inches long; and that printed on the cardboard in colorful letters in a bubbly, childlike font were the following words: THE FIRST YEARS. FLOATEES. THEY FLOAT IN TUB OR POOL. PLAY & DISCOVER. MADE IN CHINA. DISHWASHER SAFE.[33]

Through his effort to track down as many as possible of the 28,800 plastic Floatees lost at sea, Hohn creates a parable of conspicuous consumption, because, simply, he accomplishes his goal: he finds many of the plastic ducks and other animals spread throughout the corners of Earth's oceans—even years later.

When Hohn traces how his plastic duck came to be, he finds that Floatees were no longer in production, the company that produced them having been sold for $136.8 million in 2004. He is able to trace their manufacture to Po Sing plastics factory in Dongguan, China. When he travels to the industrial town in the Pearl River Delta, Hohn witnesses the zinc-alloy, die-cast mold machine that can produce one hundred thousand toys, three or four per minute, before it wears out. The factory worker estimates that a set of four plastic animals would wholesale for around eighty cents with materials to make them costing approximately half of that. Often, he explains, the packaging is "more expensive to make than the product."[34]

An engaging, epic quest turns monstrous when we see his tale as only one small example of the durability and enduring impact of the products of conspicuous consumption. In the quest of the rubber Floatee, Hohn learns that between 60 and 95 percent of marine debris is made of plastic. In addition to plastic floating animals, this debris includes the "floatables" that are contained in the 850 billion gallons of untreated sewage and storm runoff.

"We have allowed oil to become," as Jeremy Rifken points out, "vital to virtually everything we do."[35] When our ecology of petroleum is viewed through the natural systems with which it intersects and interacts, it is unsustainable and poisonous. Even if a spill never occurs and products can be used to their desired end, many humans now see that the ubiquity of petroleum in our lives possesses dramatic costs. In the case of synthetic replication—plastics—for instance, lower product prices have fueled overconsumption and waste. We made our ability and need to replace what we already had—a defining characteristic of life in all developed societies in the late twentieth century—sound like an innovation by calling it "planned obsolescence."

In *Made to Break*, cultural historian Giles Slade writes:

> Deliberate obsolescence in all its forms—technological, psychological, or planned—is a uniquely American invention. Not only did we invent disposable products, ranging from diapers to cameras to contact lenses, but we invented the very concept of disposability itself, as a necessary precursor to our rejection of tradition and our promotion of progress and change.[36]

Not only did we create inexpensive, easily replaced products from cheap petroleum, we humans in developed nations made a society that wished—and, in fact, needed—to replace these items again and again and again. Our need for petroleum to manufacture these products became an endless loop; the commodity, however, as we knew from its earliest use, was not going to be continuously available.

Chapter Seven

To Have and Have Not

Business began on September 23, 2008, but it was anything but "as usual." Opening a new office functions on a literal level, which requires buying desks, copiers, and paper clips; in some cases, though, it also functions on a symbolic level. In the case of Shell Oil's office opening on this day in Baghdad, Iraq, it functioned on a series of symbolic levels. For instance, although its intention was to conduct business, its location needed to be kept secret. If its location was revealed, the office would likely be attacked by Al Qaida or other enemies in the unstable, American-occupied nation. Therefore, it was a symbol of the precarious occupation undertaken by the United States five years earlier.

However, the opening of the Shell office also served as a symbol of the reintroduction of foreign oil companies following a thirty-two-year absence. During this time, Iraq had been ruled by a dictator, Saddam Hussein, who had nationalized the oil supply; he had taken the reserves as property of the federal government and made their development one of the government's essential duties. Hussein was a precursor of what today we refer to as "petrodictators," a group of world leaders who use their nations' oil supplies to finance their regimes and to buoy their international standing. In addition, Shell's office suggests a reality about the U.S. invasion that the administration of George W. Bush had long denied: petroleum had been a serious consideration in its 2003 invasion of Iraq.

Throughout 2008, announcements regarding Iraq had belied the host of other rationales offered for the American-led invasion. Thanks to the United States–led toppling of Hussein, no-bid contracts were acquired by American oil firms to develop the Iraqi fields. Exemplified by the opening of Shell's office, these agreements marked the return of these companies to Iraq following the nationalization of its petroleum production by Saddam

Hussein. Although Hussein's demise included myriad other issues ranging from WMDs to reported attempts to assassinate the first President Bush, the Western world cared about him because of Iraq's oil. More precisely, shifts in the world petroleum supply and in Middle Eastern geopolitics demanded increased involvement in the region by nations from all over the world. The various rationales for war presented to the American public shared a common theme: the conflict would be brief because of Iraqis' ability to immediately create revenue from selling their crude—to the United States, added the unstated implication.

That petroleum was an issue of national security would have never occurred to the American public in 1950, even though World War II had made political leaders acutely aware of its strategic importance; however, today the concept is so common that most Americans find it impossible to recall a day when the United States controlled the bulk of the world's petroleum supply. Indeed, a new world order has evolved that is organized by the power emanating from crude: some must have it but do not possess sufficient reserves themselves, and others possess it but do not need it for themselves. In this twenty-first-century era of haves and have-nots, political scientist Michael Klare writes that the United States and other developed nations now exist in an era of "resource wars," which he describes in this fashion:

> For the American military establishment, this concern has particular resonance: while the military can do little to promote trade or enhance financial stability, it *can* play a key role in protecting resource supplies. Resources are tangible assets that can be exposed to risk by political turmoil and conflict abroad—and so, it is argued, they require physical protection. While diplomacy and economic sanctions can be effective in promoting other economic goals, only military power can ensure the continued flow of oil and other critical materials from (or through) distant areas in times of war and crisis. As their unique contribution to the nation's economic security, therefore, the armed forces have systematically bolstered their capacity to protect the international flow of essential materials.[1]

Economists have also parceled the concept of resource wars into categories of new and old warfare. By doing so, they follow the logic of this chapter to argue that oil and war have been linked since the start of the twentieth century as oil "was considered a key strategic commodity and security." Economists Mary Kaldor, Terry Lynn Karl, and Yahia Said then go on to explain that in new oil wars, the government connection has been eroded. "New wars," they write, "are associated with weak and sometimes ungovernable states where non-oil tax revenue is falling, political legitimacy is declining and the monopoly of organized violence is being eroded. In such wars, the massive rents from petroleum are used in myriad ways to finance violence and to foster a predatory political economy."[2] As a "rentier war," conflict over oil is based only on crude's remarkable value. Interested parties express little or no interest in long-term development of the region or resource. In addition, they often care little about the global nature of the commodity—except that it will bring them revenue. Often, they work with global oil corporations in an unfettered and unregulated arrangement that is seen as a major threat to the stability of crude as a commodity. This chapter will trace the growing intricacy of petroleum after 1970 that has set the context for this era of new oil wars.

The necessity of a stable supply of petroleum for U.S. national security emerged in the second half of the twentieth century and then intensified. As American petroleum reserves were depleted and increasing consumption left the nation no choice but to increase imports, the United States was drawn into the Middle East petroleum vortex that had involved the great colonial powers for more than a century. Although Saudi Arabia remained the strongest American friend in the region, conflict with Iraq emerged as the most significant demonstration of the geopolitical concept of resource wars. With the erosion or retreat of colonial authority, many nations suddenly faced power vacuums that were seized by a variety of leaders. The late twentieth century saw many leaders of the developed world attempting to find diplomatic or military methods for managing relations with such individuals. These efforts grew more intense when the nations were of strategic importance because of their location or the resources that they possessed. In this fashion the postcolonial era saw nations categorized by a petroleum measuring stick: have or have-not. Of course, the suddenly independent nations of the Middle East fell into the "have" category.

Possessing oil, however, did not result in an automatic economic shift within a nation. As journalist Peter Maass writes in *Crude World:* "One of the ironies of oil-rich countries is that most are not rich, that their oil brings trouble rather than prosperity."[3] In Nigeria, government ministers clash with military generals, and civilians are entirely ignored in the effort to ease access to the nation's oil reserves. Ecuador's lack of concern over the behavior of oil developers contaminated a tributary of the Amazon River on which all life in the region depends. And, in nations ranging from Russia to Venezuela to Guinea, government officials have used oil to consolidate political power and undergird their presence on the world stage.

The events in Iraq of the twenty-first century were set in motion by the embargo of the 1970s, which was directed toward the United States but carried with it a dramatic effect on European powers, particularly France and Britain. As a result, the petroleum-desperate United States expanded its relations with Saudi Arabia and Kuwait. In addition, the primary concessions that had begun in Persia in 1901 and tied the region to Europe had expired.

A bold new day of American geopolitics in the region had begun with the leadership of the Shah of Iran in the late twentieth century. In addition, from the 1970s forward, a nation such as Iraq was not simply left to British trade and development. In fact, Iraq, under the command of Hussein, remained a largely autonomous wild card in the region. After supplying nations caused petroleum disruption in the last decades of the century, it became apparent that ensuring control and supply could be used as a rationale for warfare. Competition for the remaining petroleum reserves focused the attention of many nations on the Middle East, which holds approximately two-thirds of the known supply. During the second decade of the twenty-first century, Dubai, one of the United Arab Emirates, grew from the desert much like a mirage and ascended to power in the region.

By early 2010, the primary purpose behind the 2008 opening of the Shell office emerged, as the Anglo-Dutch company and the Malaysian state-run oil company Petronas received a twenty-year deal to develop Iraq's largest oil field, Majnoon. In addition, on January 14, 2010, the headline in the *New York Times* read: "U.S. Companies Race to Take Advantage of Iraqi Oil Bonanza." The familiar large American oil-field supply companies (including Halliburton, Baker Hughes, Weatherford International, and others) sought, in the words of the *Times*, "to revive the country's stagnant petroleum industry, as Iraq seeks to establish itself as a rival to Saudi Arabia as the world's top oil producer."[4] Were these elements of Big Oil simply stepping into a vacuum in order to help all concerned by stabilizing Iraq's immense oil wealth? Or had this always been the intention of the U.S. decision makers? Did they make war for oil? An affirmative response coheres with the general shift of the developed world toward a more complex culture of petroleum.

Behind this and other similar initiatives is the pressing need for crude—and not just for transportation. Nations without road and rail infrastructure—as well as infrastructure needed to grow, store, and process grain and other foodstuffs—also find it difficult to feed all of their citizens. In the twenty-first century, four nations produce almost two-thirds of the world's total wheat, rice, and feed grain, which require petroleum-intensive agriculture. China and the United States account for approximately 20 percent each, while the European Union and India produce 14 and 10 percent, respectively. Growing populations will demand even greater production, which in turn requires more petroleum.[5] Complicating the situation further, in the new world order many developed nations are serving as food exporters. For instance, neocolonial arrangements are being formed between nations—China with Saudi Arabia, Libya with Ukraine, and India with Kazakhstan—to provide food crops to nations without the ability to produce their own. In this fashion, nations on the other side of the development gap artificially leap it—skipping the costly development of infrastructure—on the value of commodities such as petroleum, creating a remarkably complex world.

MANIPULATING SCARCITY

In the twenty-first century, the value of crude is well-known, and nations possessing it openly leverage its value in order to benefit themselves. This point in the geopolitical structure of the world differs significantly from that of a century earlier when global corporations and the nations behind them bullied and dominated nations possessing petroleum. The 1970s are key to this transition; then, automobile lines at gas stations in the United States and Europe functioned as one indicator of massive changes in global affairs after World War II.

"Decolonization" refers to this era when many additional nations, loosed from colonial authority, became autonomous, responsible for their own development and governance. Although the Cold War added a new version of quasi-colonial authority as the American and Soviet diplomats vied to spread their ideology and to squelch that of their opposing superpower, overall, nations in Africa and particularly the Middle East could begin to pursue their own futures. Even if they lacked the internal political infrastructure to do so, they each sought to expand what power they did possess. In this new, unfettered political environment, the use and management of every resource took on strategic importance, and, therefore, it follows that the administration of the world's most sought-after commodity reflected these changes most acutely. Simply, when petroleum supplies stuttered, there was no safety net to catch American and European consumers—no federal method for offsetting the temporary glitches in supply.

From the stranglehold of Western powers and the large petroleum corporations that dominate them, oil grew into a tradable, ultravolatile commodity. Yergin writes that this new era in world oil demonstrated that "oil was now clearly too important to be left to the oil men."[6] As political leaders in oil nations assessed how best to leverage power for their nations from their supply of crude, it took little time for them to also realize the merit of joining forces with similarly endowed nations. Joining forces would allow oil-producing nations to control supply and prices and, finally, to gain a competitive advantage in negotiations with transnational corporations.

This was the essential goal in September 1960 when nations formed the Organization of the Petroleum Exporting Countries (OPEC) in Iraq. Its formation was precipitated by changes in the oil market after World War II and driven by the new status of many of these less-developed nations. Lacking exploration skills, production technology, refining capacity, and distribution networks, oil-producing countries were unable to challenge the dominance of the oil companies prior to World War II.[7] OPEC allowed oil-producing nations to hold sway against powerful oil corporations that had dominated them in the previous era of oil exploration. It was one of the first large-scale, international political groups framed around a single resource—a cartel. OPEC's founding members in 1960 were Iran, Iraq, Kuwait, Saudi Arabia, and Venezuela. Eight other countries joined later: Qatar (1961), Indonesia (1962), Libya (1962), United Arab Emirates (1967), Algeria (1969), Nigeria (1971), Ecuador (1973), and Gabon (1975). (Ecuador and Gabon withdrew from the organization in 1992 and 1994, respectively.)

Across differences of location, climate, religion, and political structure, these nations had the common concern of oil. To varying degrees, though, they also shared small size and a lack of political influence on the world scene. Bound together, OPEC's purpose was obvious: to manage supplies of crude on the market in order to maintain high prices and, thereby, to leverage the profits of member nations. In short, they sought to exploit and leverage the culture of petroleum that pumped through nations such as the United States and to take advantage of the emerging geopolitical situation: the increasing scarcity of petroleum supplies in the face of its necessity in developed nations.

It seems ironic today to talk about oil producers—whether corporations or nations—needing to manipulate markets in order to keep the price of petroleum profitable; yet, as we noted above, major oil companies colluded among themselves and with national powers through tools such as colonialism from the 1920s to the 1960s to prevent prices (and profits) from falling. As these corporations' influence waned, other methods were employed. One of the most significant difficulties was that as prices fell, domestic producers simply could no longer compete. Moreover, during the 1950s the Eisenhower administration concluded (as the Japanese had prior to World War II) that dependence on foreign oil placed the United States' national security in jeopardy. The United States responded by implementing import quotas, which were intended to keep domestic prices artificially high and to represent a net transfer of wealth from American oil consumers to American oil producers. By 1970, the world price of oil was $1.30 per barrel and the domestic price of oil was $3.18.[8]

OPEC AND THE "OIL WEAPON"

OPEC's ability to manipulate prices did not fully become a reality until Egyptian leader Anwar Sadat urged members to "unsheath the oil weapon" in early 1973. The primary rationale for this action was politics. Israel's military aggression outraged its Arab neighbors throughout the late 1960s. Israel's attack on Egypt in 1967 resulted in an earlier embargo, which proved unsuccessful because of an oversupply of crude on the world market. In October 1973, U.S. President Richard Nixon agreed to provide more military jets to Israel after a surprise attack on the nation by Egypt and Syria. On October 19, the Arab states in OPEC (Arab Oil Exporting Countries, OAPEC) elected to cut off oil exports to the United States and to the Netherlands.

In petroleum circles, the embargo is often referred to as the "First Oil Shock." As such, it combines new market features of the early 1970s: first, production restraints that were ultimately supplemented by an additional 5 percent cutback each month, and, second, a total ban on oil exports to the United States and the Netherlands and eventually also to Portugal, South Africa, and Rhodesia. Factoring in production increases elsewhere, the net loss of supplies in December 1973 was 4.4 million barrels per day, which accounts for approximately 9 percent of the total oil available previously.[9] Although these numbers told of a genuine shortfall in the overall supply, the fickle petroleum market accentuated the embargo's importance by inserting a good bit of uncertainty and panic. American consumers felt the impact most because they had grown so completely accustomed to a culture defined by petroleum abundance.

In order to provide oil to consumers, brokers began bidding for existing stores of petroleum. In November 1973, per-barrel prices had risen from around $5 to more than $16. Foreshadowing patterns of the twenty-first century, consuming nations bid against each other in order to ensure sufficient petroleum supplies. Retail gasoline prices in the United States spiked by more than 40 percent. Although high costs were extremely disconcerting, there were also temporary outages of supply. American consumers, previously content to drive their cars until gas gauges neared empty, now lined up for a few-gallon ration whenever it was available. One journalist described the scene near New York City in this fashion:

> Anxious motorists overwhelmed gasoline stations in the metropolitan [New York] area yesterday, with many stations running out of supplies early in the day, while dealers hoped incoming deliveries under February allocations would restore calm by mid-week.
>
> In Brooklyn, Murray Cohen, an owner of the AYS Service Station at Avenue Z and East 17th Street, said he had imposed a $3 maximum for each car's purchases, only to find that most people needed only 75 cents' worth to fill up. One man, he said, waited in line for an hour and could use only 35 cents' worth.
>
> In Washington, William E. Simon, director of the Federal Energy Office, who had asked drivers not to buy more than 10 gallons at a time, yesterday issued an appeal to them to stay away from stations unless they bought at least $3 worth. . . . "Panic buying isn't helping the situation."[10]

Figure 7.1.   At various times during the 1970s gas crisis, Americans and other consumers throughout the globe dealt with temporary scarcity. A shortage created largely by international political disagreements brought lines to many gas stations. (Library of Congress Prints and Photographs Division, LC-DIG-ppmsca-03433)

Many American states implemented a system of gas purchasing on either even or odd days, based on the car's license plate number.

As the nation most defined by the new era of petroleum consumption, the United States had the rudest awakening during this period of false scarcity. Intermittently, U.S. motorists throughout 1973 and 1974 needed to wait in line for one hour, two hours, or more—often, ironically, with their engines running the entire time. In other regions, the worst harbinger became signs that read: "Sorry, No Gas Today." Expressway speeds were cut to fifty miles per hour from sixty or seventy. Some tolls were suspended for drivers who carpooled in urban areas. Even if communities did not implement rationing plans, the American culture of petroleum was altered (at least temporarily) by plans being leaked to the public. For instance, in the New York City region the Federal Energy Office estimated that residents eighteen years of age and older could expect to receive books of vouchers for thirty-seven gallons per month.[11]

By the end of 1973, in fact, gas lines were plentiful throughout the United States and Europe. Supplies of petroleum were least disturbed on the West Coast, but by February even California had adopted rationing based on odd and even days. Gas station operators were subjected to mistreatment, violence, and even death threats and attacks. Drivers also reacted with venom to other drivers attempting to cut into gas lines. At the root of such anger, of course, was the cruel reality that the events of humans' everyday lives—kids going to school, adults going to work or shopping, goods moving in every direction, and even cutting grass—might be constrained, that humans in developed societies such as the United States were finding their choices limited. Nothing could seem more discordant to the ideals of expansive consumption. For these reasons, the implications of the 1970s crisis were diverse and transformative, particularly for the nation most dependent on oil imports.

CONFRONTING AMERICAN CONSUMPTION

While the embargo had economic implications, it had begun as a political act by OAPEC nations, and, therefore, Nixon dealt with it in a variety of ways, including international political negotiation. These negotiations were based on the emergent geopolitical organization of the world, even if they actually had little to do with the trade of black gold. Negotiations heated up on a number of fronts, including between Israel and its Arab neighbors, between the United States and its allies, and between the oil-consuming nations and the Arab oil exporters. There was a new urgency to the interconnection of trade networks, and establishing a discourse that demonstrated mutual respect became a priority for all concerned. Convincing Arab exporters that negotiations would not begin while the embargo was still in effect, the Nixon administration leveraged the restoration of production in March 1974. However, staring into the face of petroleum scarcity stirred many American politicians to consider new options for reforming American patterns of consumption. For a brief time, some American consumers were also willing to admit that their culture of mass consumption might be unsustainable.

Behind the scenes, the embargo and supply difficulties considerably shifted internal relations in the Middle East. In *Oil Kings*, historian Andrew Scott Cooper demonstrates how the Shah of Iran worked separately with Nixon to confront OPEC's power structure and production limits. "With a vast supply of petrodollars and U.S. weapons pouring in," writes Cooper, "there seemed to be nothing to stop the empire of Iran and its Shahanshah from dominating not only the Persian Gulf and the land bridges into Central Asia, but even . . . down along Africa's east coast."[12] Trading arms and flexing quotas in the early 1970s, the relationship between the United States and Iran actually destabilized the Shah's power in the region and in his own nation. When, after 1975, the United States increased oil imports from Saudi Arabia, the Shah's standing was undercut further, and he was left largely unprotected.

The problem of petroleum imports became even more complex when, at the end of the decade, just as some Americans might have begun to think problems with the petroleum supply were a thing of the past, relations with Iran took a turn for the worse. When Iranians took Americans hostage in 1979, U.S. President Jimmy Carter placed an embargo on the importation of Iranian oil into the United States and froze Iranian assets. The Second Oil Shock followed, only to be exacerbated in 1980 when the Iran-Iraq War abruptly removed almost four million barrels of oil each day from the world market—15 percent of total OPEC output and 8 percent of free world demand.

For many activists, politicians, and planners in the United States and many developed nations, the 1970s seemed to emerge as a hinge that would lead them away from their dangerous dependence on petroleum now largely imported from other nations. For many consumers, things had clearly changed in the consumptive nature of American life. In particular, the American idea of energy use—in its broadest sense—was brought under new scrutiny. This impact could be seen most clearly in the Oval Office of Carter, a trained nuclear engineer. Carter was moved to consider deeply the ways that American society insatiably consumed energy. He reflected on revolutionary new ideas such as that put forward by economist Amory Lovins in a 1976 *Foreign Affairs* article entitled "Soft Energy Paths." In his subsequent book, Lovins contrasted the "hard energy path," as forecast at that time by most electrical utilities, and the "soft energy path," as advocated by Lovins and other utility critics. He writes:

> The energy problem, according to conventional wisdom, is how to increase energy supplies . . . to meet projected demands. . . . But how much energy we use to accomplish our social goals could instead be considered a measure less of our success than of our failure. . . . [A] soft [energy] path simultaneously offers jobs for the unemployed, capital for businesspeople, environmental protection for conservationists, enhanced national security for the military, opportunities for small business to innovate and for big business to recycle itself, exciting technologies for the secular, a rebirth of spiritual values for the religious, traditional virtues for the old, radical reforms for the young, world order and equity for globalists, energy independence for isolationists. . . . Thus, though present policy is consistent with the perceived short-term interests of a few powerful institutions, a soft path is consistent with far more strands of convergent social change at the grass roots.[13]

In addition to promoting coal and nuclear power, Carter took the ethic of energy conservation directly to the American people.[14] His administration would be remembered for events such as the Iranian hostage crisis; however, when he controlled the agenda he steered American discourse to issues of energy. In a 1977 speech, Carter urged the nation:

Tonight I want to have an unpleasant talk with you about a problem unprecedented in our history. With the exception of preventing war, this is the greatest challenge our country will face during our lifetimes. The energy crisis has not yet overwhelmed us, but it will if we do not act quickly.

It is a problem we will not solve in the next few years, and it is likely to get progressively worse through the rest of this century.

We must not be selfish or timid if we hope to have a decent world for our children and grandchildren.

We simply must balance our demand for energy with our rapidly shrinking resources. By acting now, we can control our future instead of letting the future control us. . . .

Our decision about energy will test the character of the American people and the ability of the President and the Congress to govern. This difficult effort will be the "moral equivalent of war"—except that we will be uniting our efforts to build and not destroy.[15]

In a risky political move, Carter attempted to steer Americans down a path less trodden—in fact, a path requiring severe difficulty and radical social and cultural transition. The postwar ideals of "Futurama" and muscle cars, he argued, needed to change, and Americans needed to prioritize resource management inspired by the concepts of restraint and conservation.

It was a lonely argument to make in the United States during the late 1970s, when the vast majority of Americans knew little of environmental perspectives. He described an ethic opposed to the conspicuous consumption that lay at the foundation of the American ecology of oil. Although he offered a clear vision of our limited future based on increasingly scarce extracted energy resources, by the 1980s many Americans were returning to business as usual—or worse. In this reaction to the 1970s oil crisis, however, Americans were an exception among developed nations. In many other nations, the hinge effect of the 1970s brought an intellectual end to any illusions of conspicuous consumption organized around the wasteful use of petroleum. Instead, it marked a paradigm shift toward new ideas about energy that were focused on renewable sources.

In some other developed nations, centralized authority—including forms of socialism—became a tool for more quickly implementing the lessons of the 1970s in the form of taxes, mass transit development, and diversification of energy supplies. The reaction to the 1970s hinge created a clear gap within the developed nations, separating those that institutionalized the transition of the 1970s (particularly the European Union) and the one that regressed (the United States)—creating a new, more sinister variation on the idea of haves and have-nots within the developed nations. Within the next few decades, overreliance on imported crude would define a new era of international relations and even provide rationales for waging war.

THE ERA OF HOARDING: STRATEGIC PETROLEUM RESERVE

Possibly the most obvious response to scarcity was feigning control through the creation of a tool for stockpiling petroleum supplies. Conceived in the 1970s, the U.S. Strategic Petroleum Reserve (SPR) is the world's largest supply of emergency crude oil. Although the American people of the late twentieth century did not necessarily prioritize conserving fuel, SPR demonstrates that a clear lesson had been learned among the nation's strategic planners. From the American perspective, this lesson was best kept from the public and from other nations. Particularly in relation to SPR, it was to the American advantage not to alert others of the drastic measures on which it was about to embark.[16]

Faced with the obvious reality that it required petroleum acquired from elsewhere, the United States made its acquisition a matter of national security while largely hiding the actual logic from American consumers. There was, as yet, no national discussion of "peak oil," although the creation of SPR was largely an admission of petroleum's finite supply. As such a commodity, petroleum should be hoarded in times of peace and safety so that the nation was best prepared for the scarcity that might arrive when the equilibrium was disturbed for some reason.

Although such a reserve had been considered since the 1940s, the embargo by OPEC in 1973 and 1974 demonstrated the need for American leaders to possess a reserve in order to offset disruptions in supply, whether caused by political or natural occurrences. President Ford signed the Energy Policy and Conservation Act (EPCA) on December 22, 1975, which declared it to be U.S. policy to establish a reserve of up to one billion barrels of petroleum. The Gulf of Mexico region offered easy access to petroleum shipping and refinery lanes as well as the necessary geological infrastructure: underground salt domes. Brought up to the earth's surface in Saudi Arabia or elsewhere, the crude oil was then pumped back into the ground beneath American soil.

The domes had been selected over a few earlier alternatives that were discussed, including a flotilla of tankers and large rubber bags in aboveground locations. Once the caverns were selected, they were readied through a technique called "solution mining" in which water was pushed through the domes and then sucked out until a significant hole underground had been hollowed. Through salt engineering, though, the caverns became watertight (or oiltight). The salt wraps itself around the oil like plastic, so the caverns don't leak. During the next twenty years, the federal government spent $37 billion to construct and fill the SPR.

In April 1977, the government acquired several existing salt caverns to serve as the first storage sites (it estimated that five hundred such caverns existed). Construction of the first surface facilities began in June 1977, and in July administrators began to fill them with oil. Although filling continued over the next decades, the public truly only heard of the SPR when a president considered allowing a withdrawal under the authority of the EPCA. In the event of an energy emergency, SPR oil would be distributed by competitive sale. The SPR has been used under these circumstances only twice (during Operation Desert Storm in 1991 and after Hurricane Katrina in 2005).

Today, the SPR has grown to approximately 700 million barrels, and plans are in place to increase it to 1.5 billion barrels. Its proponents argue that it is a significant deterrent to oil-import cutoffs and a key tool of foreign policy. They argue that in an era of declining petroleum production, the SPR has allowed the United States to overcome its "energy impotence." Would the SPR be as effective if each nation had its own, though? We may need to find out: by 2006, those declaring some version of their own strategic petroleum reserves included each nation in the European Union (this was a requirement of the directive establishing the twenty-seven-nation union), China, Israel, Jordan, Singapore, South Korea, Taiwan, Thailand, Japan, and South Africa; and nations developing reserves include India, Russia, Iran, Australia, New Zealand, and the Philippines.

Figure 7.2. In regions such as Iraq, petroleum brought together Western interests with regional and local power. (Library of Congress Prints and Photographs Division, LC-DIG-matpc-13159)

Figure 7.3. Developing wells in locations such as the Iraqi desert required the construction of work camps by Western oil companies. (Library of Congress Prints and Photographs Division, LC-DIG-matpc-13161)

According to the United States Energy Information Administration, approximately 4.1 billion barrels of oil are held in strategic reserves, of which 1.4 billion is government-controlled. The remainder is held by private industry. Currently, the U.S. reserve is the world's largest and is contained at two sites in Texas (Bryan Mound, located near Freeport, and Big Hill, near Winnie), two sites in Louisiana (West Hackberry, near Lake Charles, and Bayou Choctaw, near Baton Rouge), and a final site being added at Richton, Mississippi. Although this development is unbelievably profitable for oil producers, it represents the competitive marketplace created by true scarcity. This is not the false scarcity of the 1973 embargo; instead, this scarcity, derived from the concept of "peak oil," brings with it an air of finality. In this revolutionary new logic, as the scientific reality of petroleum supplies comes in line with the culture of consumption, each user races to be the first to acquire the scarce resource on which its society depends.

PETRODICTATORS AND SOCIALISTS
LEVERAGE GROWING SCARCITY

In an era of petroleum hoarding, the nations possessing crude—the "haves"—obviously experienced a significant increase in their global stature. The term "petrodictator" has been attached to a variety of leaders in locations ranging from Azerbaijan to Venezuela. Each leader or group uses the power of the petroleum commodity to his own advantage and to raise the international stature of his nation. Although part of the landscape that holds "new oil wars," these leaders are not only using their oil for its rentier value. Defining the form, Saddam Hussein, the Iraqi leader from 1979 to 2003, pressed the advantage of petroleum wealth more than any other (Iraq had nationalized its oil industry in 1972). In the end, most observers would claim that he overplayed his petroleum advantage; petrodictators who followed have learned from his example how to preside over the commodity in this new era of resource wars.

In his boldest move, of course, Hussein sought to function as the enforcer of OPEC's interest in limiting production and, thereby, managing the global price. Making its own determination to appease the United States, Kuwait consistently overshot its production caps during the 1980s. Although this willingness enhanced the nation's relations with Western powers, OPEC leaders grew increasingly frustrated with its rogue production. In Iraq, Hussein rose to dictatorial power in 1979 and began building the region's largest military. First used in 1979 to invade Iran, in 1990 Hussein, with an additional eye toward Kuwait's access to the Persian Gulf, decided to be OPEC's enforcer, and the Iraqi army invaded Kuwait. As Hussein increased his oil reserves by 20 percent overnight, the world looked on and imagined the consequences if his campaign continued into the lightly armed Saudi Arabia and United Arab Emirates—which would then provide him with control of approximately half of the world's proven petroleum reserves. With their hand forced by a continued need for petroleum, the United States and allies "drew a line in the sand."

The ensuing months were marked by efforts to use the United Nations to arrive at a nonmilitary diffusion to the situation. This was abandoned, ultimately, on January 17, 1991, when a massive multinational force authorized by the UN and led by the United States descended on the Persian Gulf with the goal to return Hussein and his army to Iraq. Most of the fighting lasted just hours as Hussein's army suffered grave defeat at the hands of the world's most advanced military technology. In fact, the war itself symbolized the gap between developed and less-developed nations as Hussein's army—dominant within the Middle East and Africa—appeared primitive and hopelessly overmatched. This, however, did not mean that his forces could not exert great damage on the real source of the conflict: before retreating, Hussein's army set afire approximately eight hundred Kuwaiti oil wells, creating a modern environmental disaster.

Allowed to retreat to Baghdad, Hussein remained in power until another American president—another George Bush—seized the moment in 2003 to commit a largely American force to dislodging the dictator. The logic of the war in 2003 was tied to the attacks on American soil on September 11, 2001. Action against leaders such as Hussein, President George W. Bush argued, fell into a new strategy of preemptive warfare that was designed to head off future attacks or conflicts. Critics immediately claimed it was a resource war designed to open Iraq's petroleum reserves to unfettered use and development by the United States. For the purpose of our consideration, hindsight demonstrates that, at the very least, access to crude was one of the fringe benefits to unseating Hussein. The instability that ensued after Hussein's fall, capture, and death thwarted hopes for immediate development of Iraqi oil; however, by 2010, Iraq's new petroleum order was clear.

The next-most-obvious petrodictator is Venezuela's Hugo Chavez, who learned from Hussein's model. A great admirer of Cuba's Fidel Castro, Chavez swept to political leadership in 1998 and, ever since, has sought to use his nation's enormous oil reserves to leverage international standing for himself and Venezuela. Internally, Chavez promised "revolutionary" social policies and constantly labeled the "predatory oligarchs" of the establishment as corrupt servants of international capital. Internationally, Chavez employed what he refers to as "oil diplomacy." Venezuela has "a strong oil card to play on the geopolitical stage," he explained. "It is a card that we are going to play with toughness against the toughest country in the world, the United States."[17] In OPEC, Chavez has fought to keep prices high and has even publicly questioned whether or not barrel prices should still be measured on the basis of the American dollar. Whether speaking at the United Nations to demonize the United States or threatening to sell Venezuela's oil only directly to underprivileged populations in the United States, Chavez's international standing—whatever it might actually be—is based on his nation's vast supply of crude.

Russia has followed a different political model in recent years; however, petroleum has emerged as a major structuring agent for its base of national power following the fall of Communism. Oil production is no longer financed by the state budget, but now instead is supported by selling the output to other nations. In at least one region—West Siberia—just as the Communist government fell and Russia emerged as an independent region, the former Soviet Ministry of Oil petitioned Moscow to form a joint stock company known as

Lukoil.[18] Other petroleum resources were divided among workers and private companies in very complex and unclear arrangements during the early days of Russia's independence. Historian John D. Grace writes: "By the beginning of 1995, of the roughly three dozen original Soviet-era producers in Russia, over 20 were still wholly in state hands and 13 were listed as private companies. . . . The most important of these were Lukoil, Yukos, Surgutneftegaz, Slavneft, Sidanco, Kominift, Eastern Oil and Onako." In the Volga-Ural basin, Grace noted two additional companies that remained under the control of local governments: Tatarstan and Bashkortostan.[19] As a few Russians took control of the nation's banking system, these oligarchs soon became major players in the new oil companies—particularly Lukoil.

By the early twenty-first century, Lukoil used Western oil and gas corporations as its model. It took over smaller companies and diversified into international operations beyond exploration and production, including refining, marketing, and manufacturing petrochemicals. In 2002, Lukoil became the first Russian oil company to list its shares on a Western exchange (in London).[20] Lukoil became an active player in Colombia and Iraq and also took over many of the major pipeline projects near the Caspian Sea. New trading arrangements were formed with Asian nations, particularly Japan and China, and poised Lukoil to take advantage of some of the world's fastest-growing oil markets. Whether the companies are truly independent or not, thanks to their rapid success the new Russia stands as a leader in the production and distribution of oil today.

Petrodictators have often managed to maintain control of their nations for fairly lengthy regimes. There is growing evidence, however, that a lopsided emphasis on petroleum development by dictatorial powers does not end well. Regardless, petroleum supplies have emerged as the single most significant equalizer for nations on the less-developed side of the gap discussed above.

Other nations have used a state-owned or socialist model to emphasize oil development that supports infrastructural development. In developing the North Sea supply of oil, for instance, a group of European nations have carried out a joint initiative. The United Kingdom, Denmark, Norway, Germany, and the Netherlands formed joint tax and licensing regimes to develop the difficult North Sea offshore supply after 1968. In Norway, for instance, the state-owned Statoli corporation has helped the nation become the world's third-largest oil exporter and eighth-largest producer. Choosing not to join OPEC, Norway instead established the Petroleum Fund of Norway in 1990 to collect profits from sales and licensing fees. One of the largest public funds in the world, this fund is largely held to ensure the nation's economic stability when oil supplies diminish. Particularly because Norway's population stands at less than five million, critics in recent years have questioned whether or not it is necessary to create such a large savings fund. Recently, many critics have called for the fund to be used more for internal improvements and national needs.

CONFLICT AND MODERNIZATION IN DEVELOPING AFRICA

Decolonization brought changes to a number of nations, whether or not they possessed valuable resources such as petroleum. In the case of many African nations, the decades after World War II witnessed a great expansion of agricultural capabilities. In many of the nations of Asia, Central America, and South America, the green revolution has been a terrific success in food production. In other areas, such as Africa, it has been less successful.

Petroleum played a role in this agricultural shift, and some of these nations acquired the trappings of modern life seen in more developed societies. In most cases, however, African nations have found this productivity difficult to sustain. For this and other reasons, the initial modernization of many African nations after the colonial era has given way to destabilization and conflict. The revolution in agricultural productivity has, at least at times, resulted in conflict and even the destruction of nations.

Darfur, which is located in the African nation of Sudan, provides the preeminent example of how such destabilization might exacerbate existing ethnic or economic divisions. Arab nomads with livestock are pitted against African farmers who practice more sedentary plant cultivation. As the expanding population has resulted in ecological crisis and desertification, each group blames the other. In desperation, each group in Darfur fights the other for survival, quite literally: the nomads expand southward searching for new grazing land, and the farmers move northward to find arable land. The bloody atrocities of the conflict grow from ethnic differences; however, the stress of development and sustainability creates the pressure that ignites the conflict.

In Equatorial Guinea, the difficulties are quite different. In a manner similar to that of the petrodictators discussed above, President Teodoro Obiang has used new petroleum discoveries to his political advantage; however, his country receives little benefit. Particularly in less-developed nations, oil wealth can be stolen by a corrupt leader who accepts bribes or negotiates lucrative side deals to direct exploration and production contracts. Oil discoveries in the 1990s propelled Equatorial Guinea into prominence, and by the twenty-first century the nation was the third-leading producer of petroleum in sub-Saharan Africa. In short, Obiang's relationship with the developed world—particularly the United States—has done little to close the gap for his nation, even though he personally has reaped millions.

One of the last African nations to become independent in the 1960s, Equatorial Guinea, which is dispersed over a series of islands, had little to offer industrialists. Driven by the quest to achieve a maximum profit margin, oil companies create harvest and production infrastructure in places such as Equatorial Guinea entirely off the grid, using only imported materials and labor. Applying the ethic behind earlier boomtowns, Marathon and other oil production companies moved easily into less-developed environments and created the setting that they required for oil production. In Equatorial Guinea, the company built a concrete plant, for instance, that could be dismantled and moved elsewhere when the oil had played out. Asian workers at oil production plants lived in trailers that had been imported from abroad. And each of the company's facilities was joined by its own satellite communication network reaching directly back to headquarters in Houston, Texas. The work of oil producers was made simpler in nations such as Equatorial Guinea as leaders there made sure that there would be no dispute or discussion over plans for access and development of oil reserves.

More problematic from a legal and ethical standpoint is the fact that Equatorial Guinea's citizens have also been insulated from the proceeds of the harvesting of its oil reserves. Journalist Peter Maass writes that oil "not only offers itself as a treasure to be stolen; it can become a political amulet that protects thieves from abandonment or punishment."[21] Obiang lived opulently on the proceeds from oil development, and, additionally, he set up accounts at the Riggs Bank in Washington, D.C., to provide an easier way for the American companies with whom he was working to deposit funds. The arrangement worked well enough to process nearly $1 billion in payments from oil companies, which were content not to concern themselves with what happened to the funds afterward. After being alerted to the arrangement, the U.S. Senate investigated and released the report "Money Laundering and Foreign Corruption: Enforcement and Effectiveness of the Patriot Act, Case Study Involving Riggs Bank."[22] Although there had been great oil wealth to be had in Equatorial Guinea, internal politics limited its value for the nation.

For African nations, crude has often only meant an extractive enterprise; proceeds have done little to close the development gap while the crude is drained and used to help other nations prosper. In the case of Equatorial Guinea, China is now extracting most of its oil, as Obiang continues to profit.[23]

WARRING FOR PETROLEUM ACCESS

From the perspective of developed nations on the other side of the gap, the use of petroleum supplies as a political weapon demanded an increasingly active culture of engagement. At his inauguration as U.S. president in 1989, George H. W. Bush seemed to speak directly to the Middle East and to petrodictators when he said: "They got a President of the United States that came out of the oil and gas industry, that knows it and knows it well." Bush's worldview teamed with his business experience to make him one of the first Western leaders who clearly—and openly—believed in the strategic importance of U.S. influence in the OPEC-dominated Middle East, which was now responsible for producing two-thirds of the world's oil.

At this historic juncture, OPEC was wrestling with the idea of fixing petroleum prices for the good of all its members, but, because of their own economic needs, many individual nations were unwilling to limit production. When Saddam Hussein invaded Kuwait in 1990, Bush orchestrated the joint action by United Nation forces to stop his progress and, ultimately, to force Iraqi forces out of their neighboring nation. As Iraqi forces fled Kuwait, they lit on fire many of the nation's oil wells. This act of terrorism created an environmental hazard and debilitated Kuwait's immediate ability to produce oil. Most damaging, though, was Hussein's miscalculation that presented the United States with a military presence in the world's key oil region. Bush accomplished his goal of creating a mutually dependent relationship between Persian Gulf nations and the United States. However, this did not necessarily mean that price stability would last. The late 1990s brought more problems related to underproduction. The production imbalance led to the tripling of gasoline prices in 1999 and 2000. As Kaldor, Karl, and Said trace the roots of the twenty-first-century war in Iraq, they argue that the United States sought to fight an "old war" about oil by using the commodity to facilitate the decision to go to war. The conflict, it was argued, would be paid for and largely absorbed by Iraq's oil revenues.[24]

In a twist of historical fate, the presidential election of 2000 brought George W. Bush, son of the previous president, into office. Although Iraq's leader Hussein and Middle Eastern oil supplies were priorities of the younger Bush, oil prices remained somewhat low. Energy security, though, emerged in the public sphere following the attacks of September 11, 2001. Although unrelated to Hussein, these attacks became a leveraging point with which President Bush could make unseating the Iraqi leader a mission of the American military, using two rationales: first, Hussein's unreliability and possible dangerousness was compounded by his control of such significant oil reserves, and, second, if an invasion was carried out, revenue from petroleum sales would help quickly stabilize the new Iraq and decrease the financial resources necessary from the United States or any other occupying nation. Both of these arguments for war derived from the importance of petroleum.

Had the 2003 American-led invasion been about oil supplies? Wound tightly into our ecology of oil, developed nations required a steady supply of crude. And, clearly, the need to preserve energy security abroad had steadily increased during the twentieth century. Until the end of World War II, domestic supplies allowed Americans to watch European powers colonize and develop Middle Eastern supplies; the end of the war, though, brought the same realization to American foreign policy makers. The world that emerged in the twenty-first century clearly factored geopolitics into nearly every diplomatic interaction. Protected from this reality by more than half a century of disinformation, American consumers clearly became the last to comprehend the implications of our dependency. History may show that the invasion, occupation, and support for rebuilding Iraq had crude at its core. Clearly, however, this war was a leading symbol of a new world petroleum order organized according to the haves and have-nots and generated by various efforts to compensate for each nation's particular standing in the petroleum organization.

To make the new petroleum order even more clear, in 2004 Nancy Birdsall and Arvind Subramanian published "Saving Iraq from Its Oil" in the influential journal *Foreign Affairs*. The article sought to advise the United States and occupying nations how they might best make Iraq's petroleum a beneficial resource for developing a new nation. This argument was based on a simple yet remarkable main idea. They write of petroleum's "resource curse" in this fashion: "Oil riches are far from the blessing they are often assumed to be. In fact, countries often end up poor precisely because they are oil rich. Oil and mineral wealth can be bad for growth and bad for democracy, since they tend

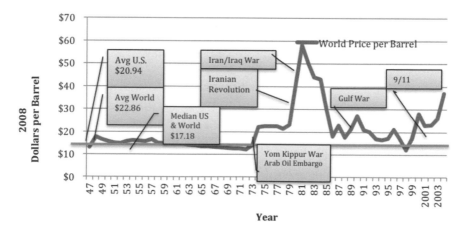

Figure 7.4. Crude Oil Prices and Events in Middle East, in 2008 dollars (Data from U.S. Energy Information Administration)

to impede the development of institutions and values critical to open, market-based economies and political freedom."[25] The bitter irony of the Iraq War, of course, is that despite its origins, it became a new oil war in which nonstate actors took an active role in fomenting dissent and complicating American occupation of the country. In the process, these activities by terrorists neutralized the ability of profits from crude to assist the settlement of a new Iraq.

CONCLUSION: DUBAI AND HUMAN MIGRATIONS FOR CRUDE

Symbols can be very important to entire societies. For instance, the events of September 11, 2001, demonstrated that for some in less-developed nations, made to feel powerless by a lack of opportunity and access to developing their nation's resources, two identical office towers, known as the World Trade Center in New York City, marked the point at which—in some small or potentially significant way—the gap could be breached. Although the loss of thousands of American lives that day has resulted in expanded military activity by the United States as well as an intensified culture of domestic security, the world's skyline tells us that the gap has very likely not closed; however, the centers of power may have begun to shift.

Erupting into the sky with much more symbolism than utility, the Burj Khalifa opened for business in Dubai in early 2010. A symbol of an emerging world order, Burj Khalifa is a rocket-shaped edifice that soars 828 meters, or 2,717 feet. It is the world's tallest structure, with views that can reach one hundred kilometers (approximately sixty miles). At a cost estimated at $1.5 billion, the Burj took five years to build, is more than 160 floors high, and has comfortably surpassed the previous record holder in Taipei. If the 1970s oil crisis marks the point where developed nations were forced to acknowledge their need for oil from less-developed nations, Burj Khalifa marks the permanent institutionalization of this crude reality.

Dubai, the city over which the Burj towers, emerged in the first decade of the twenty-first century as a global phenomenon. It is one of the seven emirates of the United Arab Emirates (UAE), located south of the Persian Gulf on the Arabian Peninsula. The Dubai Municipality is sometimes called "Dubai state" to distinguish it from the emirate. Although the city grew with the petroleum industry at the close of the twentieth century, at the start of the twenty-first Dubai positioned itself as the economic center for an emerging global economy. Focused on organizing the financial development of projects in the Middle East and Southeast Asia, the city also functions as an oasis for the diverse workforce that began to operate within the Persian Gulf.

The increasing importance of crude was not only noticeable in political leadership at the dawn of the twenty-first century. Harvesting crude, wherever it occurred, also created patterns of worker migration from neighboring regions. In the Persian Gulf region, population shifts connected to petroleum have become a defining characteristic. One of the most significant labor influxes to the Persian Gulf since 1990 has been from Kerala, India. In 1998, for instance, nearly 1.4 million Keralans emigrated from India, approximately 95 percent of whom were destined for Arab countries of the Middle East. Nearly 40 percent of this total immigrated to Saudi Arabia and 30 percent to the UAE.

In the Middle East, generations of workers have moved with the oil industry. Facing low-paying jobs or unemployment at home, for decades many have worked abroad as laborers, taxi drivers, or food preparers, wiring money to their families or returning with it on occasional visits. Recent years have seen an increase in the number of professional workers, particularly those coming from nations such as Egypt. Whereas in the past, engineers and other professionals would take their training and find employment in Europe or the United States, they are finding increasing opportunities closer to home. Egypt has an estimated 5 million workers abroad, including 1.5 million based in the Persian Gulf region. Remittances from those in the United States, Europe, and the Persian Gulf are a key source of foreign currency for Egypt. Egyptians sent home $8.56 billion in remittances in the 2007–2008 fiscal year, up from $6.32 billion a year earlier.

Much of this work is focused on a new city that has taken shape in the region: both the work of international economic trading that takes place in it and the work of constructing the physical monument in which much of it will take place. Blending World Trade Center with Las Vegas decadence, Dubai now focuses around the Burj, with its mix of nightclubs, mosques, luxury suites, and boardrooms. In the Burj, one finds the extravagant splendor of the world's first Armani hotel, the world's highest swimming pool (on the 76th floor), the highest mosque (on the 158th floor), and fifty-four elevators that can hit speeds of sixty-five kilometers per hour (40 mph). For the more than twelve thousand people who occupy its six million square feet, the Burj is an oasis from the desert that surrounds it as well as from the overwhelming poverty of the majority of the UAE public.

To make the irony more acute, a global economic slowdown in 2008 made Dubai and the Burj appear more as a symbol than a genuine accomplishment. The city's real estate market collapsed, and the Burj project was rocked just as it neared completion. At this point, the building was named Burj Dubai. To save the project and ensure its 2010 completion, the neighboring kingdom of Abu Dhabi propped up its financing. "Dubai not only has the world's tallest building, but has also made what looks like the most expensive naming rights deal in history," said Jim Krane, author of *City of Gold: Dubai and the Dream of Capitalism*. "Renaming the Burj Dubai after Sheikh Khalifa of Abu Dhabi—if not an explicit quid pro quo—is a down-payment on Dubai's gratitude for its neighbor's $10 billion bailout [in 2010]."[26]

Economic observers have little doubt that the economy will recover, and when it does it will still be organized by certain basic global realities. Chief among these, of course, is the increasing need for petroleum emanating through the Burj.

INFRASTRUCTURE
NYMEX and the Commodity of Crude

"If the United States celebrated economic milestones the way we celebrate military and political ones," writes business journalist Lisa Margonelli in *Oil on the Brain*, "we'd all get a holiday on March 30 to honor the day in 1983 when crude oil futures first began trading, making all of us participants in the giant world market of petroleum."* With this change in the pricing of petroleum, prices were no longer set in "backroom deals" between wealthy petroleum tycoons and political leaders. Now, information flowed more freely and prices fluctuated as oil was bought and sold on the spot market. The price might still be a fiction—based on suppositions and subjective observations—but now its volatility was compounded because traders' whims could be reflected immediately in the markets.

The process of opening the market had begun with the 1978 creation of a heating oil exchange, which was loosely based on the type of exchanges used by growers of food crops such as potatoes. This had been one of the primary purposes for the New York Mercantile Exchange (NYMEX) since it opened in 1872. An important part of such trading is the exchanging of futures contracts, which, in the case of oil, are certificates representing one thousand barrels of oil to be delivered on a specific day between one month and six years in the future.† In short, they are a bet on the price for that oil at a particular moment in the future. Futures buying helps refiners and producers to better manage their budgets and to hedge against any dramatic drops in price.

This abstract system borders on the bizarre because NYMEX contracts actually only concern one kind of oil: West Texas Intermediate delivered by pipeline to Cushing, Oklahoma. The global index is determined, however, from this one point, and therefore from that point emanates the price of crude being bought and sold all over the globe—in total, 161 kinds of crude oil (including both OPEC and non-OPEC). Worse, this price is determined on the commodities trading floor by crowds of traders who shout, wave cards, and, generally, react to the day's news. The crude pit, in Margonelli's words, "is an intoxicating mix of operative drama and Super Bowl spectacle." Using the description of Robert Weiner of George Washington University and Resources for the Future, she writes:

> One criticism of the oil market is that it encourages speculation, which possibly drives up the price of oil. "People in the oil industry say that speculation is bad," says . . . Weiner . . . "but the market needs speculators. They're like grease. They lubricate the system by taking sides of the deals. Without speculators, there would be no NYMEX because buyers and sellers wouldn't have anyone to sell to and buy from."‡

Developed as a reaction to the 1970s oil crisis, futures trading at NYMEX has shaken the power structure of crude. Power has not necessarily moved away from leaders of oil-producing countries nor been wrested from the heads of the world's massive

---

* Lisa Margonelli, *Oil on the Brain: Petroleum's Long, Strange Trip to Your Tank* (New York: Doubleday, 2007), 120.

† Margonelli, *Oil on the Brain*, 122.

‡ Margonelli, *Oil on the Brain*, 129–31.

oil corporations. Instead, crude oil as a commodity has permitted power to be shared with additional actors: futures traders and the investors that they represent.

At the very least, these structural changes have increased the volatility of oil prices today. Therefore, in the twenty-first century, when frustrated consumers shake their heads and ask, "How do they come up with these gas prices, anyway?" the most accurate response might be a simple shrug.

Part IV

LIVING WITH LIMITS
AND ENERGY TRANSITIONS,
1980–PRESENT

INFRASTRUCTURE
Climate Change Reveals a New World Order

While some politicians and media pundits debate whether or not climate change is actually occurring, the coverage of glaciers worldwide has been reduced by approximately 20 percent and some entire landmasses have been lost to rising seas. From the halls of the Bella Center in Copenhagen to mangrove forests on islands off India in the Bay of Bengal, humans have been forced to adapt to climate change—it is changing the way we live and the future that we can hope for.

New Moore Island has been embroiled in controversy since it emerged from the Bay of Bengal after a cyclone at about the time of the 1973 Arab Oil Embargo. The island, which stood 1.3 miles long and 1.1 miles wide, became contested terrain as both India and Bangladesh (which called the island South Talpatti) laid claim to it. As the political wrestling took place during the 1990s, scientists noted that the island was shrinking as part of the larger, 81-square-mile reduction in land mass witnessed in the Bay of Bengal's Sunderbans mud flats during the past forty years. The Bay of Bengal will likely be "ground zero" for the impacts of climate change, which is a particularly cruel reality because of the poverty in which most island villages exist. A UN panel predicted that if seas rise by the 3.3 feet that has been forecasted, 17 percent of Bangladesh will disappear by 2050, which would displace approximately 20 million of the nation's 150 million people. In the case of New Moore Island, however, Sugata Hazra, director of Jadavpur University's School of Oceanographic Studies in Calcutta, commented: "What these two countries could not achieve from years of talking has been resolved by global warming."* The controversial island may well cease to exist.

In another example, Ifalik, part of the Federated States of Micronesia (FSM), a remote belt of six hundred islands in the tropical western Pacific, saw extreme high tides in late 2008 that damaged homes, eroded coastlines, and inundated crops. One local resident, Pekaicheng, knew just whom to blame: "The big countries are contaminating the whole universe," he says, "and it's getting us before it gets them." According to NASA satellite data, sea levels in the tropical western Pacific rose about 4 inches (10 centimeters) between 1993 and 2008, which is a faster rate than most other locations on the planet and far outpaces the global average of 1.7 inches (4.5 centimeters). A report released on November 24, 2008, by a group of leading climate researchers states that seas could rise as much as 3.5 to 6.5 feet (1 to 2 meters) by the end of the century. FSM won't necessarily be off the map, but the map will have changed dramatically.†

This sort of outcome has led international agencies to begin to prepare residents of island communities for what they see as an inevitable outcome. In the publication *Surviving Climate Change in Small Islands—A Guidebook*, the Tyndall Centre instructs readers that small islands need to prepare for this inevitable rise in sea

---

* Mark Mangier, "India-Bangladesh Dispute Is Moot after Island Sinks," *Seattle Times*, March 25, 2010, seattletimes.nwsource.com/html/nationworld/2011432281_island25.html.

† Justin Nobel, "A Tiny Pacific Island Faces Climate Change," *Time*, December 14, 2009, www.time.com/time/specials/packages/article/0,28804,1929071_1929070_1947456,00. html#ixzz0lA3rQ9Fj.

level.‡ In response, some island nations have decided not to wait for their homes to be lost. Kivalina, an Inupiat Eskimo village of four hundred people perched on a barrier island north of the Arctic Circle, is accusing two dozen fuel and utility companies of helping to cause the climate change that it says is accelerating the island's erosion. The village wants the companies, including ExxonMobil and Shell Oil, to pay the costs of relocating to the mainland, which could amount to as much as $400 million. The case is one of three major lawsuits filed by environmental groups, private lawyers, and state officials around the United States against big producers of heat-trapping gases.

Generally, these legal cases rely on the common-law doctrine of nuisance, the same concept that allows neighbors to sue one another over disturbances such as noises and odors that interfere with other individuals' ability to use or enjoy their own property. Initially, few observers placed the impacts of climate change in this category, and such legal cases were referred to as frivolous. Now, however, international insurance companies compare such suits to those that led companies in industries such as lead and asbestos to declare bankruptcy. Could Big Oil be next?

---

‡ Emma L. Tompkins et al., *Surviving Climate Change in Small Islands—A Guidebook* (Norwich, U.K.: Tyndall Centre for Climate Change Research, University of East Anglia, 2005), available at www.tyndall.ac.uk/sites/default/files/surviving.pdf.

Chapter Eight

"Peak Oil," Climate Change, and Petroleum under Siege

The small speedboats wove in and out of the massive wake left behind the *Maran Centaurus*. Massive oil tankers like the *Maran Centaurus* had been the great breakthrough when Samuel and others created the much larger version of the skiffs that had carried the world's first commercial crude down Oil Creek in Pennsylvania. Increasing the efficiency of these conveyors of crude smoothed over the problem of oil's dispersed occurrence and made petroleum accessible to consuming nations anywhere with minimal variation in price. Today, though, the massive haulers of crude have come to represent something different, something that functions as a symbol of the crude realities surrounding humans' relationship with oil: they are a symbol of "the Gap" discussed by Marks in the introduction, and, as such, just like the vessels in the Age of Sail far from home and without the defenses of the nation whose flag they fly, these tankers are a target. The International Maritime Bureau reported that in 2009 and 2010, sea attacks worldwide surged 39 percent to approximately 406 cases. They report that Somali pirates were responsible for 217 of the global attacks and had seized 47 vessels, a growing number of which were oil tankers.

On this day, November 29, 2009, the speedboats burst upon the *Maran Centaurus*, a Greek-flagged tanker holding two million gallons of crude valued at $150 million, approximately 800 miles (1,300 kilometers) off the Somali coast. Overseeing this cache and the massive vessel holding it is a crew of only fifteen to thirty seamen, from all over the world and with little if any military training. Ships such as *Maran Centaurus* are low-lying fruit waiting to be picked by these bands of modern-day pirates, nationless actors emanating from tribes in Somalia. It is a terrorist act against the oil establishment and all the nations that rely on it. The instability of these critical shipping lanes is yet another reason that nations depending on imported oil face a greater impetus than ever before to break out of the dependence that defines their ecology of oil; nevertheless, nations with an interest in industrializing—particularly India and China—still maintain that expanding petroleum use is a necessary part of their development. Early 2010, for instance, saw China displace the United States as the world's largest market for new automobiles.

Simultaneously, a nation such as Saudi Arabia, the world's leading supplier of oil, shapes a national development strategy based on alternative energies. Far from environmentally conscious, the Saudi royal family, instead, may know the value of their oil reserves better than anyone. As global supplies diminish, their reserves are simply too valuable on the global market to waste them on domestic consumption. And, in fact, while China pursues access to global oil supplies, it simultaneously prioritizes infrastructural development that will soon position it as the world's leader in alternative energy technology. Similarly, the energy scene of the second decade of the twenty-first century in many developed nations—including the United States—emphasizes alternative energy sources to a degree never seen previously. Some observers of the energy situation claim that humans are undergoing an "energy transition" away from their reliance on fossil fuels, including petroleum.

No longer a culture seeing oil as a resource delivering great new opportunity and possibility, as during the twentieth century, our twenty-first-century culture of oil is a grudging—almost apologetic—one. Simply, we wish it were not so. The culture of oil has become incredibly complicated as nations possessing petroleum leverage their position and those needing it require great fortune or military force. And now scientists have acquired convincing data that each of us—every human on earth—is imperiled by the use of petroleum by developed nations. Undaunted, the industrial apparatus of Big Oil crashes forward toward future scarcity that it selectively elects not to discuss; all the while consumers and consuming nations gnash their figurative teeth and attempt to stimulate a transition toward a more complicated but sustainable energy future.

These larger concerns clarify the plight of *Maran Centaurus* and other tankers under siege as an example of humans' current energy transition. When, once again, the European Union (EU) and Maran Tanker Management Inc. paid a reported $5.5 million ransom, the ship and crew were released unscathed. Merely marking an increased cost of doing business—such as paying a toll—such payments resemble the act of swatting a pesky fly. No pesticide or larger strategy is cost-effective to minimize this momentary glitch. On the horizon, though, is a time when such shipments would be less crucial. The ecology of oil is embroiled in a significant moment of transition in these early decades of the twenty-first century.

HUBBERT'S PEAK AND THE REALITY OF OIL SUPPLIES

Writing generally about consumptive patterns, historian William Cronon described the capitalist model that grew in the New England colonies of North America when he wrote: "The people of plenty were a people of waste."[1] The reality of petroleum has always been that it will run out, even when suppliers tried to convince us otherwise, whether at Spindletop in Texas, in Bahrain, or in Saudi Arabia. Today, acceptance of this reality is referred to as "peak oil."

Based on the general theories of petroleum geologist M. King Hubbert, "peak oil" ran contrary to the culture of petroleum in nations such as the United States during the twentieth century. When Hubbert, who was working for Shell, first forecast in 1949 the brevity of the petroleum age, his employer and many professionals called him the latest in a century's worth of "Chicken Littles"—skeptics predicting the impending end of petroleum supplies. In 1956, Hubbert put a point on his argument by focusing on the American domestic reserves, which he forecast would peak within thirty to thirty-five years and then slowly decline. His professional standing did not change until his forecast proved accurate, when American production reached its peak in 1970. His theory became known as "Hubbert's Peak," and geophysicists set out to apply his calculations to the known global supplies. Kenneth Deffeyes, for instance, reports that this global peak occurred in the first decade of the twenty-first century.[2]

In the intervening years, petroleum geology changed dramatically. Seismic mapping now made it possible to map quite accurately the petroleum reserves that lay untapped beneath the earth's crust. With this additional technology, estimates of reserves—and theories such as Hubbert's—gained considerable credibility. Within this accepted paradigm, the primary variability became how increased competition, particularly as India and China industrialized, might make the supply's demise come even more rapidly than forecast. Although it remains nearly impossible for geologists to focus on a specific date and some critics continue to quibble with Hubbert's computations, by the early twenty-first century energy forecasters began to change the culture of petroleum to reflect an awareness of petroleum's impending decline in supply. Large international oil companies began to diversify their efforts somewhat, particularly in the public sector. For instance, in 2001 British Petroleum (BP) actually changed its official name to BP and its slogan to "Beyond Petroleum."

Whether or not the industry for which Hubbert worked openly adopts his theory, the corporate culture of Big Oil has radically changed in the twenty-first century. The prudence of relying on endless supplies of crude has been called into question by geological reality. Much of humans' contemporary culture of oil grows from a general acceptance of the concept of "peak oil,"

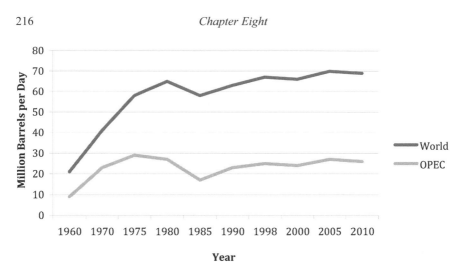

Figure 8.1. World Crude Oil Production (Data from U.S. Energy Information Administration)

whether the supply lasts thirty or fifty additional years. We live, however, in a moment of reconfiguration as we reconsider what role petroleum needs to play in the future of developed societies.

A glimpse of this future came in the early twenty-first century when prices of crude oil destabilized. Although there were a host of geopolitical, weather, and economic explanations for the spike in prices during 2007 and 2008, the outcome was unthinkably high prices for this essential commodity. From the

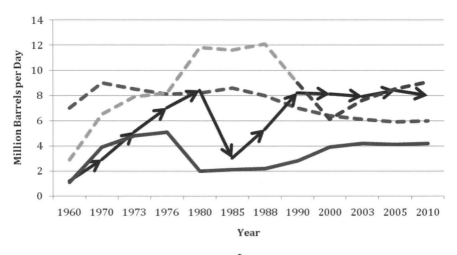

Figure 8.2. Leading Crude Oil Producers (Data from U.S. Energy Information Administration)

mid-1980s to September 2003, the inflation-adjusted price of a barrel of crude oil on NYMEX was generally less than $25 per barrel. Then, during 2004, the price rose above $40, and then to $50. A series of events led the price to exceed $60 by August 11, 2005, and then briefly to exceed $75 in the middle of 2006. Prices then dropped back to $60 per barrel by the early part of 2007 before rising steeply again to $92 per barrel by October 2007. These record prices, then, were repeatedly shattered throughout the spring of 2008 until prices reached $147.02 per barrel on July 11, 2008. Some analysts predicted $300 per barrel oil by 2013. Although this could still happen, per barrel prices spent most of 2010 and 2011 between $70 and $90 per barrel. With the looming scarcity of peak oil and increased consumption worldwide, most analysts agree that prices will only go up from their current point.

During these years of price spikes in the first decade of the twenty-first century, consumers received another reason to growl about Big Oil as the major oil companies garnered the largest profits in the business history of the world. Between 2004 and 2007, the profits of the super-majors—ExxonMobil, Total, Shell, BP, Chevron, and ConocoPhillips—totaled $494.8 billion. Higher prices, it seemed clear, primarily resulted in more profits for these companies. This reality set the stage for consumers to feel a severe new level of frustration toward Big Oil in the twenty-first century.

GRASPING THE IMPLICATIONS OF FOSSIL FUEL USE

This dramatic new reality has gained additional logic from scientific findings about petroleum that reach beyond issues of supply. For most of the twentieth century, scientists worked to quantify the outcomes of burning all fossil fuels, particularly petroleum. By the second half of the century, many humans in developed societies found that they had a villain living among them: the internal combustion engine (ICE). In its earliest version, this reimaging of the ICE had little to do with the growing scarcity of petroleum supplies; instead, critics emphasized the inevitable outcome of burning petroleum in car engines: emissions and air pollution. Prior to the public understanding of concepts such as greenhouse gases and climate change, air pollution was acknowledged to be unpleasant and, very likely, unhealthy.

Air pollution, generated by industrialization in general, has been documented to possess health effects for humans since the early 1900s. The connection between smog and auto exhaust is credited to Arie Haagen-Smit, a German researcher at the California Institute of Technology. During the 1950s, in order to bring his findings to the public, Haagen-Smit fought off the savage criticism of the auto manufacturers, who claimed that a well-tuned vehicle had no such adverse effects on the air.[3] Severe smog episodes in California kept the issue in the public arena and helped to make it one of the primary issues for the nascent American environmental movement. The seminal event in the emergence of modern environmentalism, Earth Day 1970, contained many activities that related to air pollution.

As scientists in the late 1960s began to understand the complexities of air pollution, it became increasingly apparent that, in addition to producing specific toxic emissions such as lead, the internal combustion engine was a primary contributor to air pollution and smog. Emissions from the United States' nearly two hundred million cars and trucks account for about half of all air pollution and more than 80 percent of air pollution in cities. In the United States, federal legislation began in 1965 with the Motor Vehicle and Air Pollution Act, which was followed in 1970 by the Clean Air Act. In 1975, a California act required that vehicle exhaust systems be modified prior to the muffler to include a catalytic converter. Costing approximately $300, early converters ran the exhaust through a canister of pellets or honeycomb made of either stainless steel or ceramic. The converters offered a profound, cost-effective way of refashioning the existing fleet of American vehicles to accommodate new expectations for lower auto emissions.

In addition, the scientific scrutiny of auto emissions proceeded on one additional, much more specific front. Air testing on emissions and the smog that they created also revealed a now undeniable result of auto use: lead poisoning. The willingness to tolerate lead additives in gasoline had persisted from the 1920s. In the 1970s, though, auto manufacturers were faced with a dramatic change in the public's expectations regarding lead. In January 1971, EPA's first administrator, William D. Ruckelshaus, declared that "an extensive body of information exists which indicates that the addition of alkyl lead to gasoline . . . results in lead particles that pose a threat to public health." Following California's lead with catalytic converters, U.S. automakers responded to the EPA's lead phase-down timetable by equipping new cars (starting in 1975) with pollution-reducing catalytic converters designed to run only on unleaded fuel. With the fleet largely converted, Congress finally banned the use of leaded gasoline in the United States in 1989.

For most scientific observers, the root of each of these environmental problems—as well as others such as acid rain—was the burning of fossil fuels, which released massive amounts of carbon (in the form of carbon monoxide and carbon dioxide) into the earth's atmosphere. The transportation sector alone is responsible for about one-third of the total production of carbon dioxide in the United States. And, of course, the internal combustion engine is a primary contributor. Not only is smog unpleasant and unhealthy, it may actually be contributing to the ruination of the entire planet.[4]

Some scientists went even further. They argued that the burning of fossil fuels had broadened humans' environmental impact so severely that a new geological epoch should be named: the anthropocene. Chemist Paul Crutzen argued in a 2002 article in *Nature* that humans have become a geologic agent comparable to erosion and eruptions, and accordingly "it seems to us more than appropriate to emphasize the central role of mankind in geology and ecology by proposing to use the term 'anthropocene' for the current geological epoch."[5] In this paradigm, the human—particularly its high-energy-use versions—had become immoral, exploiters of the earth's finite resources. Now, there also appeared to be evidence that our dependence would affect the lives of every human and other living thing on earth.

PETROLEUM USE AND CLIMATE CHANGE

The scientific understanding of climate change emerged as an international undertaking at the end of the twentieth century. In 1985, the Vienna Convention for the Protection of the Ozone Layer argued that ozone depletion demanded action or it would lead to numerous health problems (such as skin cancer) brought on by exposure to UV radiation, which would eventually cost society substantial sums. Two years later, in 1987, the Vienna framework was given teeth in the Montreal Protocol. The protocol specified formal emission restrictions and led twenty nations (including the United States) to sign on. This remarkable international agreement provided climate scientists, politicians, and members of the general public who were increasingly concerned about global warming with a model for action. As a consensus took shape in the science behind global warming, the call for action increased.[6]

In the United States, a number of scientific reviews sounded increasingly strong warnings to policy makers. Arguably, the rise of global warming as a national and international political issue exemplifies the ever-greater development of public knowledge and democracy—simply, the public was much more aware of basic ecological principles than at any time in the past. By the late 1980s, as the result of increased awareness of environmental problems, greater reporting in the media, and responsiveness of the political system, global warming was on the cusp of receiving a place in the public consciousness and was ready to take off—should something happen to demand action.

The year 1988 came as if on cue. First, the heat waves and droughts of the American summer of 1988, especially in the central and eastern states, made a great deal of news in magazines, newspapers, and TV programs. The National Climatic Data Center (of NOAA) estimated that there were about $40 billion in economic losses and five thousand to ten thousand deaths. At the start of this difficult summer, in late June, NASA scientist James Hansen gave testimony to Congress in which he said that it was virtually certain that human activity was responsible for the global warming trends and that this might bring more storms, floods, and heat waves in the future. Hansen made the now-famous remark: "It's time to stop waffling . . . and say that the greenhouse effect is here and is affecting our climate now."[7] Polls indicated that, over the next year, public awareness of global warming rose considerably. However, the United States possessed political and cultural baggage that would not allow it to lead global action on this issue.

Primary leadership on climate change action came from the United Kingdom, which possessed a particularly strong interest in the issue because, as a relatively small nation geographically, it stood to lose a great deal from climate change. For one thing, its temperate climate was dependent on the Gulf Stream, which was potentially endangered by global warming. In 1988, the conservative Prime Minister Margaret Thatcher (who had a degree in chemistry from Oxford University) became the first major politician to embrace global warming as an important issue. After being briefed on the science of global warming by her adviser Crispin Tickell, Thatcher brought the issue to the attention of the nation's scientists in a major speech to the Royal Society.[8]

In 1988, rising scientific interest and political concern about global warming gave rise to the foundation of an international agency, the Intergovernmental Panel on Climate Change (IPCC), by the World Meteorological Organization and the United Nations. The IPCC's task was to organize the work of an international group of scientists to produce periodic reports summarizing the best knowledge on the world's climate in order to help political leaders make policy decisions. U.S. President Ronald Reagan was strongly in favor of forming the body. Through a series of reports starting in 1990, the IPCC began a decade-long process of attempting to explain the implications of climate change to the world community. Throughout the 1990s and into the twenty-first century, the consensus on anthropogenic global warming continued to deepen. A remarkable new reason for relying less on petroleum was emerging before humans' eyes at the dawn of the twenty-first century.

From these scientific understandings, a steady push grew for international mitigation of the factors thought to contribute to climate change. In 1997, the UN organized the Conference on Climate Change in Kyoto, Japan, which ultimately resulted in the Kyoto Protocol, fully ratified in 2005. Moving the policy and scientific reality to the mainstream, Al Gore and film producer Laurie David created *An Inconvenient Truth* to serve as a counterbalance to the misinformation about global warming that they felt was being sent to the public through popular and political culture. By designing a film that would receive a large release and by teaming it with other media outlets, including a book authored by Gore, Gore and David brought new energy and awareness to the issue, which culminated with an Emmy Award and a Nobel Peace Prize in 2007 for Gore and the IPCC. As one of the primary contributors to potentially damaging emissions, the burning of petroleum swiftly became part of a new equation. Although a sweeping shift from ICE has not yet taken place, climate change offered a new logic to fuel global interest in an energy transition away from petroleum's use, particularly for transportation.

BREAKING THE PETROLEUM
PARADIGM IN TRANSPORTATION

Particularly in the United States, where the ICE was an ingrained portion of our basic infrastructure, breaking the habit has proven challenging and—at best—protracted. Policy historian Richard Andrews writes that the 1973 embargo initiated three types of U.S. policy changes related to energy: first, there was an increased emphasis on tapping domestic supplies or energy; second, there was a new recognition that energy conservation was an essential element of any solution; and third, electric utility companies were forced to accept and pay fair wholesale rates for electricity created by any producer. Each initiative became a component of the energy transition that unfolded; however, the most intractable part of energy consumption for Americans was obviously personal transportation.

In particular, the gas crisis moved some Americans to take another look at the electric vehicle, which had remained alive—but barely—throughout the twentieth century. Without governmental support and despite the contrary efforts of larger companies after World War II, independent manufacturers continued to experiment with creating an electric vehicle that could be operated cheaply and travel farther on a charge. The problems were similar to those faced by Edison and earlier tinkerers: reducing battery weight and increasing range of travel. Some of these companies were already in the auto business, including Kish Industries of Lansing, Michigan, a tooling supplier. In 1961, it advertised the Nu-Klea Starlite, an electric vehicle with a clear, bubble roof. Priced at $3,950 without a radio or a heater, the car's mailing advertisements promised "a well designed body and chassis using lead acid batteries to supply the motive energy, a serviceable range of 40 miles with speeds on the order of 40 miles an hour." By 1965, another letter from Nu-Klea told a different story: "We did a great deal of work on the electric car and spent a large amount of money to complete it, then ran out of funds, so it has been temporarily shelved."[9] The Nu-Klea was not heard from again.

As part of the political initiatives described above by Andrews, in 1976 the U.S. Congress passed legislation supporting research on electric and hybrid vehicles. Focused around a demonstration program of seventy-five hundred vehicles, the legislation was resisted by industry from the start. Battery technology was considered to be so lacking that even the demonstration fleet was unlikely. Developing this specific technology was the emphasis of the legislation in its final rendition. Historian David Kirsch argues that this contributed significantly to the initiative's failure: "Rather than considering the electric vehicle as part of the automotive transportation system and not necessarily a direct competitor of the gasoline car, the 1976 act sponsored a series of potentially valuable drop-in innovations." Such innovations would allow electric technology to catch up to gasoline, writes Kirsch. However, "given that the internal combustion engine had a sixty-year head start, the federal program was doomed to fail."[10]

One test did take place in the United States, though. California combined clean air legislation with electric technology to create the only bona fide initiative of the late twentieth century. The California Air Resources Board (CARB) helped to stimulate CALSTART, a state-funded nonprofit consortium that functioned as the technical incubator for America's efforts to develop alternative-fuel automobiles during the 1990s. Focusing its efforts on the project that became known as the EV, this consortium faced auto manufacturers' onslaught almost single-handedly. Working in cooperation with General Motors (GM), CALSTART ran the EV-1 pilot project, which has been immortalized in the film *Who Killed the Electric Car*. After a highly successful run in the late 1990s, the project was cancelled as GM shifted from experiments with electric vehicles to purchase the Hummer line and create the large, heavy SUVs that would most appeal to one segment of American consumers.

Americans, it seemed, could not break the cycle themselves. Therefore, the entrenchment of American manufacturers in internal combustion engines, which will go down in the annals of business history as one of the worst strategic decisions, made hybrids entirely the domain of Japanese manufacturers. One of the first sources of evidence that a serious energy change was under way was the shift in type of automobiles demanded by U.S. consumers starting in 2005 and reaching a fever pitch by 2008. The prolonged increase in gasoline prices to the $4-per-gallon range irreparably altered the American auto marketplace and demonstrated just how much influence consumers could have on the auto industry. Toyota and Honda led the way by making hybrid vehicles widely available. In addition, as Americans' love affair with large vehicles gave way to economic judgment, drivers chose smaller vehicles. American manufacturers were left very near complete ruin because of their emphasis on manufacturing larger vehicles, including SUVs and full-size pickup trucks. A swift market shift was then followed in 2008–2009 by a more widespread, international economic collapse, leaving almost all American vehicle manufacturers with little choice but to file for bankruptcy or request assistance from the federal government.

In the case of America's Big Three—those companies that delivered ten-thousand-pound large vehicles for middle-class consumers for most of the 1990s—entire plants dedicated to manufacturing SUVs and trucks were shut down or shifted to making smaller cars. The biggest losers in the market were the big pickups and SUVs that Ford and its domestic rivals, General Motors and Chrysler, relied on for much of their profits. "We saw a real change in the industry demand in pickups and S.U.V.'s in the first two weeks of May [2008]," Ford's chief executive, Alan R. Mulally, said. "It seems to us we reached a tipping point."[11] In 2007, pickups had accounted for about 14 percent of the overall U.S. market, but in the following year this segment decreased to 9 percent. Mulally said the striking shift by consumers from trucks and SUVs into smaller cars and crossovers now appears to be "structural in nature" rather than a short-term reaction to gas prices. "We needed to act now," he said.

Ford had few designs on the table for such vehicles. In order to get vehicles to consumers as quickly as possible, Ford transformed a Mexican large truck plant to make the European-designed Fiesta small car for North America from early 2010. The Cuautitlán facility near Mexico City was converted from producing F-Series pickups for Mexico—future supplies will be imported from the United States—to producing small cars for all of North America. "Ford is absolutely committed to leveraging our global assets to accelerate the shift to more fuel-efficient small cars and powertrain technologies that people really want and value," said Ford's Mulally. "Customers responded very positively after seeing both the sedan and hatchback versions of the Verve small car concept [at motor shows]," noted Mark Fields, Ford's president of operations

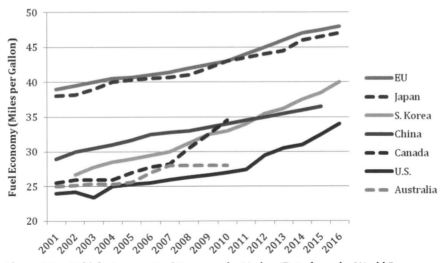

Figure 8.3. Vehicle Average Fuel Economy by Nation (Data from the World Resources Institute)

in the Americas. "We know the market is headed toward more small cars and crossovers. With our product and manufacturing flexibility, we will be able to offer both models and add production capacity."[12]

This is in contrast to Toyota and Honda, which already had manufacturing facilities for very efficient vehicles like the Fit and Yaris, as well as the Prius and Civic hybrids. Prior to 2006, the Fit and Yaris had been manufactured for many years but had never been sold in the United States. All Honda and Toyota had to do was make minor modifications and begin shipping them to the United States beginning in 2006, as well as boost their production of hybrids to meet the increasing demand. Once again, the flexibility of international manufacturers gave them a strong competitive advantage over American carmakers.

Today, American automakers now need to be concerned with a global marketplace and, therefore, the tastes of international consumers. Globally, small car sales are expected to grow from 23 million in 2002 to an estimated 38 million in 2012. Driving the growth in the North American market is a group of young people aged thirteen to twenty-eight years—dubbed "millennials." Today, this group numbers approximately one billion worldwide and will represent 28 percent of the total U.S. population by 2010. These consumers, who have grown up entirely in a world of high-priced gasoline, realize that alternatives are a must. Over the summer of 2008, which saw gasoline prices remain over $4 per gallon, the Big Three U.S. automakers—General Motors, Ford Motor Company, and the Chrysler Group unit that was sold by DaimlerChrysler—reported a 19 percent decline in sales in July compared to a year earlier, while most overseas automakers had single-digit declines or even modest gains during the same period. This decline left the domestic brands with only 48.1 percent of U.S. sales, down 4 percentage points from a year earlier and less than the previous low, set in June 2008, of 50.2 percent. As a group, Asian brands posted a 5.6 percent drop in U.S. sales, but that was enough to capture 44.6 percent of total U.S. sales.[13] The European brands sales were off only 2.4 percent, good enough for 7.3 percent of the market.

In addition to shrinking the types of vehicles composing its fleet, American manufacturers also stepped up efforts to create commercially available hybrids and alternative-fuel vehicles. First in 2006 and again in 2008, Honda and Toyota were being forced to employ waiting lists for their commercially available hybrids. Each American company advertised hybrid models, but few of them actually made it to the road. Instead, GM and Ford each strategically elected to develop plug-in, all-electric vehicles to be available commercially by 2010. (They turned out to be available in only limited quantities in 2011.) American manufacturers also made their fleet appear more "green" by selling vehicles able to use more biofuels. The "flex fuel" label demarcated vehicles that had only been modestly adjusted from the standard internal combustion engine.

Therefore, the American manufacturers already handled the transition with a bit of awkwardness. The larger economic collapse of 2008 and 2009 took a bad situation for American manufacturers and made it grave. Only Ford survived without government assistance, and the entire American industry retooled. Instead of complete collapse, the American auto industry used the federal government to remake itself and to recalibrate its priorities to cohere more with a new era. Although the sector continues to trail some international companies, American auto companies now have a clear trajectory in common with Toyota and Honda—as they try to better mimic the international manufacturers' willingness to adjust and even to redefine modes of transport away from the ICE.

MODELING ALTERNATIVES ON THE GLOBAL STAGE

Today, the transportation sector is wide open for new possibilities. Although Toyota broke through the frontier of reliable hybrid vehicles, its safety problems uncovered throughout 2010 broke its juggernaut on the automobile market. New technologies are being developed by new manufacturers all over the world in what promises to be a dynamic new era in human movement, somewhat similar to that witnessed a century ago. One of the most significant differences in this era of innovation, though, is its truly global nature. The development of early autos was a transnational undertaking; however, it was entirely driven by European and American inventors. Today's manufacturers are often much more than inventors, and the markets that they seek to develop extend through Southeast Asia to emphasize India and China.

In one of the most remarkable experiments, over the last few decades Brazil's leaders have used their quasi-dictatorial control to impose some of the most radical alterations in the transportation sector. In 2007, after securing enough fuel crops in production, Brazil committed itself almost entirely to the use of biofuels for transportation. Thirty years prior, the nation, which had imported 75 percent of its oil, reacted to the 1970s oil crisis by setting out to use ethanol made from sugarcane to liberate itself from imported oil. When the OPEC oil embargo crippled the nation's economy, Brazil's dictator at the time heavily subsidized and financed new ethanol plants. In addition, he directed the state-owned oil company, Petrobras, to install ethanol tanks and pumps around the country. With his centralized political control, he offered tax incentives to Brazilian carmakers to encourage them to crank out cars designed to burn straight ethanol. When democracy was restored after 1985, Brazil's centralized initiatives provided a head start for an energy transition.

The conversion of Brazil's transportation sector has established it as an example for other nations. By the mid-1980s, nearly all the cars sold in Brazil ran exclusively on *álcool*, or ethanol. Just a decade later, the ethanol industry had become self-sufficient and no longer required government subsidies. "Today," writes journalist Joel K. Bourne Jr., "nearly 85 percent of cars sold in Brazil are flex: small, sporty designs that zip around the lumbering, diesel-belching trucks in São Paulo." The Brazilian vehicles do not rely on corn-based ethanol, which uses only the kernel and requires the use of enzymes to break down starches and begin the fermentation process. Instead, Brazil's method uses the entire sugarcane stalk, which is already 20 percent sugar and begins fermenting almost as soon as it is cut from the field. Industry leaders estimate that sugar-based ethanol creates from 55 to 90 percent less carbon dioxide than gasoline.[14]

The ability of China to so strictly control its path towards industrialization, of course, relies on strict centralized authority. For instance, in a second example, China, expediting its movement toward industrialization in the second decade of the twenty-first century, has become one of the world's largest consumers of fossil fuels; however, it does so while also emphasizing renewable sources in both energy production and transportation. Thus, when the global recession shrank petroleum demand worldwide, China swept past the United States to become the largest importer of oil from Saudi Arabia.[15] In addition to constructing refineries in China specifically to process Saudi crude, China is constructing two refineries in Saudi Arabia for this purpose. China's rapid energy growth, however, is based mainly in coal, which supplies almost 80 percent of the nation's energy. As part of its centrally controlled drive toward industrialization, though, China has designed a low-carbon path decreasing its energy intensity— energy used per unit of economic output—by 20 percent by 2011. It leads the world in installed solar hot-water heating capacity and will soon be the world leader in wind power capacity. Nuclear power and carbon capture technology will also be important in the future, as China strives to balance economic development, resource constraints, and environmental sustainability.

The centerpiece of this low-carbon industrialization strategy is China's Energy Conservation Law, which was formed in 1997. Updating the law in October 2007, the National People's Congress made it one of few in the world requiring practical implementation to promote comprehensive energy conservation and providing the legal basis for long-term resource conservation in China. The Energy Conservation Law now reads:

> Conservation of resources is one of China's basic national policies. The national energy development strategy is to implement both energy conservation and energy development simultaneously, while putting energy conservation first. . . . The State Council and local people's governments above the county level should integrate energy conservation into the national/local economic and social development plan and the annual development plan, and should coordinate the

preparation and implementation of specific annual and long-term energy conservation plans. . . . Energy conservation target obligation and assessment will be implemented by the state, and the completion of energy conservation goals will be used as appraisal factors for local governments and for all parties responsible. . . . The state implements industrial policies that are conducive to energy conservation and environmental protection, policies limiting the development of high energy-consuming and high polluting industries, and policies promoting the development of industries that conserve energy and protect the environment.[16]

In addition to decreasing per capita GDP energy consumption by 20 percent, the plan seeks to decrease sulfur dioxide and other emissions by 10 percent in order to tackle air and water pollution. In 2008, forty-six new standards were enacted in the law, including twenty-two for energy consumption limits per unit produced, eleven for the end-use energy efficiency of relevant products, five for economical fuel use indicators in the transportation sector, and eight basic standards for energy efficiency metering, computing, and so forth. China also announced fuel economy standards for automobiles, covering all varieties of vehicles, which are more stringent than those in the international community. In total, China has established nearly two hundred energy efficiency standards.

As a result, in addition to being the world's most rapidly industrializing economy, China is the world's fastest-growing user of renewable sources of power. The original target of 30 gigawatts of wind power development by 2020, established in the current national program, will certainly be exceeded. China will become the world leader in wind power capacity in the near future, with the potential for several hundred gigawatts in the long run. The nation also possesses the world's largest hydroelectric power system. By 2020, about 300 gigawatts of hydropower will be exploited, and in the longer term hydropower capacity may reach 400 gigawatts or more, with 70 gigawatts produced by small hydro plants. China has also become the world leader in the manufacture of solar photovoltaic (PV) cells. Nationwide, China uses more than 120 million square meters of solar heat collectors, displacing about 20 million tons of coal. The central government has invested 2 billion yuan to purchase PV power systems for remote and poor towns and villages to provide basic power access where the grid is not accessible. Solar power is also being used in many public buildings and facilities, including the Olympic village in Beijing.[17]

As for transportation, China offers carmakers one of the greatest opportunities of the twenty-first century. In new vehicle acquisition China passed the United States in 2010 to become the world's largest market for new cars, and, therefore, the American manufacturer Ford is making sure to cater to its unique needs. In a 2010 *New York Times* article titled "In China, Back to Henry's Way," Keith Bradsher and Vikas Bajaj argue that the company's new emphasis on small, inexpensive models (and its scaling back on large, luxury models) is a return to the company's roots. Ford's rise in Asian sales follows the 2010 decision by General Motors (GM)—which still sells more vehicles in Asia—to focus on the European market and allow its Chinese partner, Shanghai Automotive, to take over its operation in China and India. It is clearly a time of significant change in the world's transportation business. And we have not yet discussed possibly the world's most innovative manufacturer of all.

As another indicator of a new era of industrial development, India houses one of the fastest-growing internal combustion engine–powered vehicle manufacturers, Tata Motors. India's market possibilities have been identified by other manufacturers, including Honda, which established centers in India in 2006 with a goal of producing and selling a total of 150,000 units per year by 2010. Instead, Honda has sold nearly double this expectation. The growth of this market is one of the driving forces behind India's own manufacturer, Tata, which already has auto manufacturing and assembly plants in Jamshedpur, Pantnagar, Lucknow, Ahmedabad, and Pune in India, as well as in Argentina, South Africa, and Thailand. A manufacturer of buses, trucks, and trains, Tata has in recent years diversified its auto division in a number of important ways: First, in 2008, as the American manufacturers collapsed and sought to sell off specific brands, Tata purchased Rover and Jaguar from Ford. Second, Tata has set out to make the world's cheapest car: the Tata Nano, priced at 100,000 rupees (US $2,500)—Tata Nano Europa has been developed for sale in developed economies and hit markets in 2010, while the normal Nano hit markets in South Africa, Kenya, and other countries in Asia and Africa by late 2009. And, third, rechargeable battery versions of each model were released in 2010.

Tata is creating a new model for manufacturers as, from an early stage, it operates as a truly international corporation. Release of Tata's electric versions will first occur through its UK subsidiary to markets in Finland. Its production and assembly operations now occur in several other countries, including South Korea, Thailand, South Africa, and Argentina, with expansion planned in Turkey, Indonesia, and countries in Eastern Europe. Tata also is developing joint venture assembly operations in Kenya, Bangladesh, Ukraine, Russia, and Senegal and has sales dealerships in twenty-six countries across four continents. Clearly, Tata is poised for international growth, but its primary consumer base remains in the Indian subcontinent, primarily in India, Bangladesh, Bhutan, Sri Lanka, and Nepal, though it has a growing consumer base in Italy, Spain, and South Africa. Tata's home, India, has doubled the amount of roadways over the last decade, and the World Bank is currently financing the expansion of rural roads. Tata has positioned itself to take advantage of this expansive moment much as Ford did a century ago.

As global transportation patterns move forward on so many fronts, it is also important to note a revealing look backward—at the Hummer, the heaviest consumer vehicle ever manufactured. The Hummer, the consumer cartoon of the military Humvee, was a symbol from the beginning. Purchased by GM at the start of the twenty-first century, the Hummer brand demonstrated a moment of unapologetic clarity for an American manufacturer: instead of efficiency or new models of powering transportation, GM offered American consumers a device that appealed only to their passions for raw power (at mpg levels in the high single digits).

Although all car companies wish to make profits, few others made a determination as brash as GM's. Following the economic collapse of 2008 and 2009, when GM required a government bailout to avoid bankruptcy, Hummer became a symbol of what had gone wrong for American manufacturers; however, it did not lose its consumer cache—at least not initially. As GM sold off its smaller brands, Hummer received interest from Sichuan Tengzhong Heavy Industrial Machines of China, which offered a price of $160 million. One stumbling block was reported to be the Chinese government, which was pursuing a national mandate for small, efficient vehicles. Sichuan argued that it could easily make a lighter, more efficient version of the brand; by February 2010, though, the deal was dead, the brand defunct, and its assembly-line factories closed.[18]

In this new era of personal transportation, manufacturers prioritized flexibility of form and power. Most importantly, though, companies prioritized the flexibility needed to extend their products in a global market, both in terms of the business of manufacturing and distribution, as well as the actual product that was being created. After decades of aesthetic decadence, the automobile had once again become a utilitarian device for the movement of humans all over the globe.

FULLY ACCOUNTING FOR ENERGY PRODUCTION AND ICE

The maturation of climate change from the status of a scientific concept to that of a global problem demanding mitigation has spurred interest in the construction of energy pricing that will account for the outcomes—particularly pollution—attached to burning all fossil fuels, but particularly petroleum. Although humans have just begun to envision possible scenarios, technologies, and policies that may mitigate the effects of climate change, policy initiatives are taking shape in the second decade of the twenty-first century that will likely impact transportation patterns and particularly the use of the internal combustion engine (ICE). Different nations have pursued a variety of economic models that place a value on the carbon generated by gas-powered internal combustion engines. However, thus far, these approaches follow a few general themes or ideas.

Most importantly, emissions from burning fossil fuels such as petroleum are now being factored into commodity costs through "carbon accounting." Informal arrangements for "carbon offsets" are one example; however, much more sweeping examples are now being considered. With the full accounting of fossil fuel energy sources and their impacts on human health, the environment, and climate change, alternative energy sources have become mainstream. This full accounting of the price of fossil fuels can be done in a variety of ways:

- Ideally, the producer of a certain type of energy should be required to pay for its production and all detrimental effects to society and the environment. When this is done, the producer would then pass this cost along to the consumer. The consumer would then be able to reap the financial benefit if they were to choose a low energy-existence life. Even without complete production-side accounting, the government plays an important role in energy accounting by providing incentives to those who use renewable energy and purchase products that consume less energy. These incentives are nearly always financial in nature, so they don't provide for cleaner air or environment.
- Another way for the government to promote a full accounting of energy production is to establish a carbon tax or carbon-trading scheme. The emission of carbon dioxide is the leading cause of global climate change and will have an impact of massive proportions in future generations. By enacting a carbon tax, the government doesn't stop the emission of carbon dioxide and the accompanying climate change, but it does make those emissions more expensive. The producer of energy that emits carbon dioxide then must pass this cost along to the consumer. This is similar to production-side accounting and encourages the use of energy producers who don't emit carbon dioxide.
- A third way for the government to be involved is to pass laws to prevent the emission or release of harmful pollutants. This is sometimes called a "command and control" structure by those opposed to it. With this legal requirement, an energy producer must take necessary steps at whatever costs to prevent the harmful pollution. This cost is then passed on to the consumer. This is production-side accounting. If this were done, it would not be necessary for renewable incentives or carbon taxes to be provided. However, this type of legal requirement to prevent harmful pollution has proven very difficult to enact and enforce.[19]

In practice, governments of developed nations employ a mix of these accounting schemes, and they have had the effect of making alternative energy production cost-competitive. As more of these schemes are employed to account for additional harmful pollution from the use of fossil fuels, alternative energy will continue to become more cost-effective, and perhaps petroleum and other fossil fuels will become cost-prohibitive.

CONCLUSION: THE LAST GASP FOR OLD HABITS?

In the twenty-first century, our ecology of oil is obviously in flux; however, that doesn't mean that all of the details of our crude reality are receding—hardly! *New York Times* columnist Thomas Friedman could not disguise his perception of the scene before him in his September 14, 2008, column titled "Making America Stupid," even though he asked readers to imagine the reaction of observers from Russia, Iran, and Venezuela as Rudy Giuliani led the Republican National Convention in the chant "Drill, baby, drill!" "I'll tell you what they would have been doing," Friedman offers,

> the Russian, Iranian and Venezuelan observers would have been up out of their seats, exchanging high-fives and joining in the chant louder than anyone in the hall—"Yes! Yes! Drill, America, drill!"—because an America that is focused first and foremost on drilling for oil is an America more focused on feeding its oil habit than kicking it.[20]

The 2008 presidential election in the United States, with the Republican motto ringing throughout the land, clearly had a dimension of a referendum on energy consumption. In truth, the reliance on petroleum served as one of many symbols of a previous era as change seemed to unfold on many fronts in the other direction. However, it can't be overstated that the United States, the greatest of all energy consumers, voted for a different, uncertain direction later in 2008. The election of Barack Obama was an acknowledgment by a majority of Americans that an energy transition swirled about us and that it required the United States to change from business as usual.

The Obama administration has led many initiatives that are founded on a new energy paradigm—particularly one that acknowledges the implications of climate change. Efforts that began with the "Cash for Clunkers" program to trade in old vehicles for more fuel-efficient ones now are part of a debate over how best to establish a carbon economy that quantifies the pollutants created by burning fossil fuels. And, very quickly, Obama's EPA declared CO_2 a pollutant, like other greenhouse gases. Under the leadership of Steven Chu, a Nobel Prize–winning physics professor, Obama's Department of Energy has taken a diversified view of the nation's energy future.

As the United States attempts to move away from a century of energy decadence, developing nations seek their own opportunities with their accompanying challenges. In China, for instance, approximately 2,000 new vehicles hit the road each day, contributing to overwhelming traffic and air pollution. In 2010, Beijing counted 700,000 new registered vehicles, up from 550,000 in 2009, 376,000 in 2008, and 252,000 in 2007. Although there have been efforts to develop mass transit and bike routes, as China's middle class grows (estimated to reach 45 percent of the overall population by 2020) the desire for vehicles is expected only to grow. "Fifteen years ago," said Wang Li Mei, secretary general of the China Road Transport Association, "hardly anyone could afford a car. Today, everyone can. History just evolved in its own way. Each day we're getting more cars, and each week, we're building more roads."[21] In China, road-building efforts can't keep up with this remarkable growth.

An obvious image of humans' energy transition is emerging. While nations throughout the globe pursue a new, more sustainable strategy for industrial growth, at present the most direct path to industrialization remains fossil fuels. Thanks to the United States and other nations with a continuing reliance on fossil fuels, shipments of crude such as that on board *Maran Centaurus* will continue to be a symbol for nations on either side of the economic gap. If the pattern of shifting away from petroleum continues and combines with the pressures of peak oil and climate change, though, such tankers may become a symbol of a different gap: that separating autonomous nations, in control of their own energy futures, and the others who compete for a dwindling supply of finite petroleum. Such a future would seem destined to lead to more and more aggressive wars and conflict regarding oil supplies—clearly, a crude reality of the most dire sort.

PORTRAIT OF ADDICTION: U.S. PETROLEUM USE

As the world's greatest consumer of petroleum, the United States merits special consideration as we chart humans' relationship with crude. Figures 8.4 through 8.9 capture historical patterns in the raw numbers.

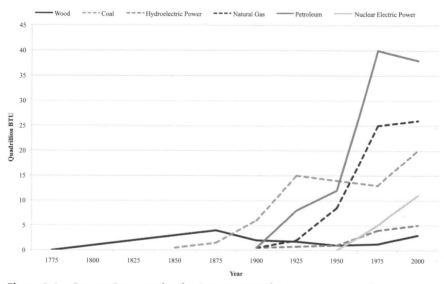

Figure 8.4. Energy Consumption by Source (Data from U.S. Energy Information Administration)

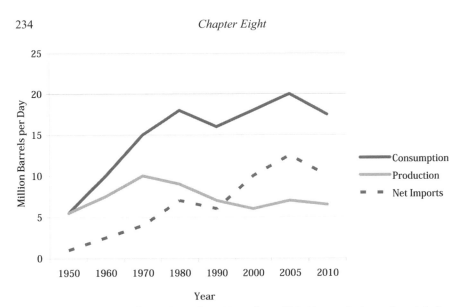

Figure 8.5.   U.S. Petroleum Overview (Data from U.S. Energy Information Administration)

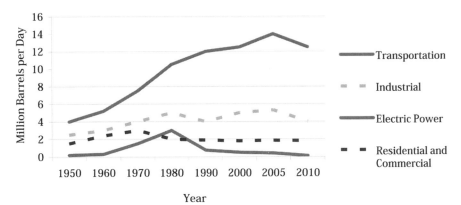

Figure 8.6.   U.S. Petroleum Consumption by Sector (Data from U.S. Energy Information Administration)

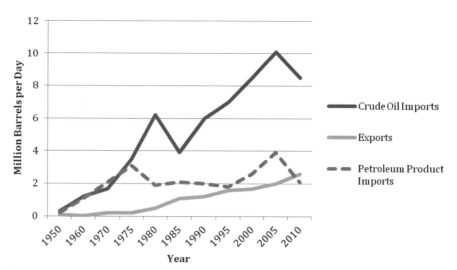

Figure 8.7.   U.S. Petroleum Trade (Data from U.S. Energy Information Administration)

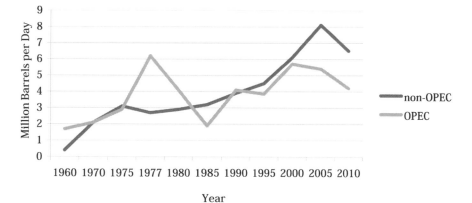

Figure 8.8.   U.S. Petroleum Imports from OPEC and Non-OPEC Countries (Data from U.S. Energy Information Administration)

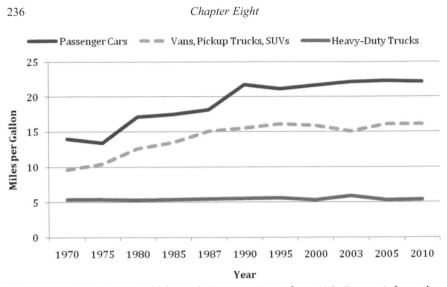

Figure 8.9. U.S. Motor Vehicle Fuel Economy (Data from U.S. Energy Information Administration)

Epilogue

Resource Curse:
Time for an Oil Change?

The headlines spanning a mere two months of the second decade of the twenty-first century would have made a lesser industry quake:

- Save Energy, Save Our Troops: Simple Efficiency Steps Would Mean Fewer Risky Expensive Fuel Convoys
- Dutch Lawmakers Want Answers from Shell on Oil Pollution in Nigeria
- Russia Embraces Arctic Drilling
- Chevron Is Ordered to Pay $9 Billion by Ecuador Judge: Company Found Liable for Amazon Damage
- Libyan Oil Pays Poorer African Neighbors for Allegiance to Qaddafi
- Oil Prices Skyrocket on Middle-Eastern Unrest
- Oil Keeps Flowing Despite Unrest, but High Prices Jangle Nerves Worldwide
- Iran Threatens to Block Strait of Hormuz—Global Energy Flow at Risk
- EU Agrees to Freeze Imports of Crude from Iran

Reports of Big Oil's demise, which, of course, grow out of preparing for a future without it, are at present greatly exaggerated; instead, these headlines and many others present an industry ascendant. Each of the primary trends of the twentieth century charted in the previous pages has extended and focused in the early years of the twenty-first: humans' ecology of oil has only grown more complicated, with the culture of petroleum winding deeply into social patterns across the globe, politics and diplomacy between nations, economic patterns of sustained growth and development worldwide, and the definition and consideration of global policies based on the findings of large-scale scientific inquiry. Yet, regardless of power and influence, a paradigm shift has clearly occurred—Big Oil has been found out. But will it matter? Is the crude reality, in fact, that the human system now relies so completely on oil that the species will not continue without it?

**Figure E.1.   Gas stations, found around the world and in countries producing no petro-
leum themselves, connected citizens to an ecology of petroleum. (Library of Congress
Prints and Photographs Division, LC-DIG-highsm-06278)**

In the twenty-first century, many historic moments possess a clear, oily
subtext. A counternarrative has even gained support that entirely turns on its
head the previous, progressive view of development that guided petroleum in
the twentieth century. In the twenty-first century, writers such as Peter Maass
and scholars including Terry Lynn Karl posit the "oil curse" theory that urges
nations possessing oil reserves to learn from the recent past—to look at the
leaders and societies that petroleum development left in its wake over the last
fifty years. "Petrodollars," they write, "actually sever the very link between
people and their government that is the essence of popular control."[1] Maass
writes in *Crude World*: "There is too much corruption-inducing, economy-
deforming, conflict-enhancing, fate-altering value locked up in natural
resources like oil."[2] Economist Karl adds: "As long as petroleum fulfills a
fundamental need and yields a profit for powerful state and private interests,
governments will choose to exploit it—and consider themselves fortunate."[3]
From Coal-Oil Johnny to Jeb Clampett and now to leaders such as Presidents
Hugo Chavez and Teodoro Obiang, people all around the world—and their
entire nations—have been corrupted by oil.

    Karl argues, though, that this curse is not "inevitable": "There is nothing
inescapable about the future repercussions of petroleum or any other commodity."[4] In some cases these cautionary tales have encouraged leaders to pursue

development of petroleum much more carefully. However, there is no disputing that many less-developed nations with petroleum reserves are poised to become the future characters in this exploitative legacy of extraction, and African nations are next in line. For instance, the 2011 vote for independence in South Sudan has roots in oil. The complex political division between South Sudan and North Sudan, many observers argue, is rooted in the oil curse and whether or not oil revenues will be shared among the members of the public or remain concentrated among political elites in cahoots with global oil corporations.

The newly recognized State of South Sudan is home to oil and what comes with it. For instance, it is estimated that approximately twenty-four thousand Chinese live in Sudan, where China has invested some $15 billion, all of it in service of the 300,000-odd barrels of oil the China National Petroleum Corporation produces each day in the petroleum-rich southern province of Abyei, whose oil is shipped 930 miles north to Port Sudan.[5] The vote for independence gave the south control of almost 80 percent of Sudan's current oil production of 490,000 barrels a day, which is third-largest in sub-Saharan Africa. However, most of the refineries are located in North Sudan; moreover, the State of South Sudan is landlocked and the only pipeline to the sea runs through North Sudan. The regional balance of power—complete with the vested interest of China, the major importer of Sudanese oil—twists in the twenty-first-century culture of petroleum.

Will this lead to the emergence of a new petrodictator or the outbreak of civil war? Can the political outcomes be trusted when outside interests, such as China, hold such an obvious stake in the commodity's future? Obviously, petroleum is only becoming more integral to regional and international political stakes.

Some scholars have even exploded the paradigm of the "oil curse" to suggest that consuming nations—even if they have achieved incredible standards of living—will suffer the impact of the curse as they attempt to acquire sufficient crude when global supplies fade.[6] In this theory, nations such as the United States will find themselves at a competitive disadvantage in coming decades because of their crude habit. At the very least, acquiring the necessary petroleum supplies will become more costly, both economically and politically, as scarcity increases.

When yet another U.S. president stood before the world's greatest petroleum glutton in 2011 to discuss energy conservation, his discussion possessed a profoundly new, holistic view of energy. After describing escalating gasoline prices in the spring of 2011, President Barack Obama explained:

> But here's the thing—we've been down this road before. Remember, it was just three years ago that gas prices topped $4 a gallon. Working folks haven't forgotten that. It hit a lot of people pretty hard. But it was also the height of

political season, so you had a lot of slogans and gimmicks and outraged politicians waving three-point-plans for two-dollar gas—when none of it would really do anything to solve the problem. Imagine that in Washington.

The truth is, of course, that all these gimmicks didn't make a bit of difference. When gas prices finally fell, it was mostly because the global recession led to less demand for oil. Now that the economy is recovering, demand is back up. Add the turmoil in the Middle East, and it's not surprising oil prices are higher. And every time the price of a barrel of oil on the world market rises by $10, a gallon of gas goes up by about 25 cents. . . .

So here's the bottom line—there are no quick fixes. And we will keep on being a victim to shifts in the oil market until we get serious about a long-term policy for secure, affordable energy.

We've known about the dangers of our oil dependence for decades. Presidents and politicians of every stripe have promised energy independence, but that promise has so far gone unmet. I've pledged to reduce America's dependence on oil too, and I'm proud of the historic progress we've made over the last two years towards that goal. But we've also run into the same political gridlock and inertia that's held us back for decades.

That has to change.

We cannot keep going from shock to trance on the issue of energy security, rushing to propose action when gas prices rise, then hitting the snooze button when they fall again. The United States of America cannot afford to bet our long-term prosperity and security on a resource that will eventually run out. Not anymore. Not when the cost to our economy, our country, and our planet is so high. Not when your generation needs us to get this right.

It is time to do what we can to secure our energy future.

So today, I'm setting a new goal: one that is reasonable, achievable, and necessary. When I was elected to this office, America imported 11 million barrels of oil a day. By a little more than a decade from now, we will have cut that by one-third.

After emerging over the course of the twentieth century, the strategic significance of crude oil is no longer a secret. Solutions, also, are no longer a secret. And the greatest guzzlers of crude may face the most difficult travails as humans transition to sustainable forms of energy.

This book has traced a trajectory toward globalization and the reorganization of the world economy around necessary resources, which is best exemplified by petroleum. The narrative curve, then, points to an obvious conclusion to our story of global competition for petroleum as the developed nations are joined in a fierce search for remaining petroleum reserves by industrializing nations such as India and China. In fact, with a view focused on energy transition and informed by the implications of humans' culture of petroleum in the twentieth century, the strategic advantage for the future clearly slips away from developed nations and, instead, shifts to those with flexible, developing economies—unencumbered by our crude reality.

Chronology of Petroleum
in World History

450 BCE	Herodotus described oil pits near Babylon.
325 BCE	Alexander the Great used flaming torches of petroleum products to scare his enemies.
ca. 100 CE	Plutarch described oil bubbling from the ground near Kirkuk in present-day Iraq.
347 CE	Chinese reported to have drilled holes in ground using bamboo to extract oil.
Eighth c. CE	Baku people used ground impregnated with oil for heating because of absence of wood.
Ninth c. CE	Arabian traveler Baladzori (Al-Belazuri Ahmed) described in "The Conquest of the Countries" that political and economic life on Absheron had been long connected with oil.
Tenth c. CE	Arabian traveler Abu-Dulaf visited and described Absheron's oil sources; he noted that there were two major sources—black oil and white oil. White oil was exported to Iran, Iraq, and India as a valuable article.
Twelfth c. CE	A unique medicinal oil from the Naftalan (Azerbaijan region) was used for curing various health problems. It was carried in wineskins through the territory of modern Georgia to the Black Sea shores and from there to other countries of the world.

1273   Marco Polo recorded visiting the Persian city of Baku, on the shores of the Caspian Sea in modern Azerbaijan. He saw oil being collected from seeps for use in medicine and lighting.

1849   Abraham Gesner developed a method for distilling kerosene from crude oil.

1858   First oil well was drilled in North America at Oil Springs in Ontario, Canada.

1859   Col. Edwin Drake struck oil 69 feet below the surface of the ground in Titusville, Pennsylvania.

1861   First recorded shipping of oil between countries—from Pennsylvania to London on the sailing ship *Elizabeth Watts*.

1862   De Rochas of France patented the four-stroke engine.

1863   John D. Rockefeller founded an oil-refining company in Cleveland.

1877   Rockefeller controlled 90 percent of American refining.

1878   First oil drilling took place at Lake Maracaibo, Venezuela.

1879   Thomas Edison invented the electric lightbulb.

1882   Standard Oil Trust formed.

1885   Oil discovered in Sumatra by Royal Dutch.

1892   Standard Oil Company of Ohio broken up by federal regulators.

1895   Internal combustion engine invented.

1896   Henry Ford's first motor car was built.

1901   Spindletop gusher blew out on January 10, 1901, near Beaumont in East Texas. It was drilled by Captain Anthony Lucas and heralded the birth of the Texas oil industry: Gulf and Texaco.

1902   Ida Tarbell began campaign against the monopoly and questionable practices of the Standard Oil Trust; she published a series of articles in *McClure's* magazine (1902–1904).

1903   Wright brothers take first powered flight.

1905   Baku oil fields set on fire during Russian Revolution.

1906   Federal government filed suit against Standard Oil under the Antitrust Act.

1907   Shell (British) and Royal Dutch merged to form Royal Dutch/Shell.

1908   Oil discovered in Persia; Anglo-Persian Oil Company formed (later becomes British Petroleum).

1910   First oil discovery in Mexico at Tampico on the Gulf Coast.
       U.S. Congress authorized legislation to set aside land as Naval Petroleum Reserves.

1911   Breakup of Standard Oil Trust ordered by U.S. Supreme Court.

1921   First experiment using seismic waves to image the earth's subsurface—at Vines Branch in south central Oklahoma by William Haseman, Clarence Karcher, Irvine Perrine, and Daniel Ohern.

1924   Teapot Dome scandal

1930   East Texas oil field discovered by "Dad" Joiner.

1931   Conrad and Marcel Schlumberger successfully identified the presence of oil in a formation by measuring resistivity.

1932   Oil discovered in Bahrain.

1933   Saudi Arabia granted oil concessions to Standard of California, which became California Arabian Standard Oil Company (Casoc).

The Texas Company introduced the first submersible drilling barge, which was used in the estuaries near Lake Pelto, Louisiana.

1934   The first floating drilling rig reported in the Caspian Sea.

1938   Mexico nationalized foreign oil companies; all assets placed under the control of Pemex.

Oil discovered in Kuwait and Saudi Arabia.

1942   Japan invaded Indonesia for access to its oil reserves.

1944   Casoc became Aramco (Arabian American Oil Company).

1947   Kerr McGee brought in the first producing oil well on the Outer Continental Shelf off Louisiana.

1948   Ghawar Field—the largest conventional oil field in the world (about eighty billion barrels)—discovered in Saudi Arabia.

1950   Aramco made agreement with Saudi Arabia.

1951   Anglo Iranian Oil Company nationalized.

1954   Anglo-Persian Oil Company renamed British Petroleum.

1960   OPEC (Organization of Petroleum Exporting Countries) founded in Baghdad; members included Saudi Arabia, Venezuela, Kuwait, Iraq, and Iran.

1967   Great Canadian Oil Sands Ltd. (later Suncor) began production of tar sands north of Fort McMurray, Alberta, Canada—first commercial production of the largest oil resource in the world.

1968   Oil discovered on the North Slope of Alaska.

1969   Santa Barbara oil spill occurred six miles offshore from Summerland, California; created major backlash against oil industry.

Oil discovered in North Sea.

1971   OPEC countries began nationalizing oil assets; Libya nationalized BP concession.

U.S. oil production peaked.

1972   Iraq nationalized Iraq Petroleum Concession.

1973   Iran nationalized oil assets.
Saudi government acquired a 25 percent interest in Aramco.
Yom Kippur War: Egypt and Syria attacked Israel.
Arab placed oil embargo on oil exports to the United States for siding with Israel in the Yom Kippur War; oil prices rise from $2.90 to $11.65.

1974   **March:** Arab oil embargo on oil exports to the United States lifted.

1975   Venezuelan oil industry nationalized.
First oil production from North Sea.
Strategic Petroleum Reserve (SPR) authorized in the United States to store an emergency supply of oil in salt domes.

1977   Alaska oil pipeline completed.

1980   Saudis bought out the balance of Aramco from U.S. oil companies.

1989   Exxon Valdez ran aground in Prince William Sound, Alaska.

1990   Iraq invaded Kuwait; UN embargo placed on Iraq.

1991   Gulf War began, combat operations known as Operation Desert Storm; Kuwait oil fields set alight.

1997   Kyoto Agreement proposed to limit greenhouse gases.

1998   BP announced plans to acquire Amoco for $48.2 billion.
Exxon decided to acquire Mobil for $75.4 billion.

1999   Atlantic Richfield (Arco) acquired by BP Amoco.

2001   **September 11:** Terrorist attacks on the United States.

2002   Conoco and Phillips merged to form ConocoPhillips.

2003   **March 19–20:** U.S.-led invasion of Iraq began; sought to overthrow Saddam Hussein and prevent the spread of weapons of mass destruction.

2005   **March 23:** Explosion at BP's Texas City Refinery killed 15 people and injured 170 others.
April 4: Chevron-Texaco offered to buy Unocal Corp. for $16.4 billion.
August: Chevron Corp. acquisition of Unocal Corp. finalized.
September: The 1,770 km long Baku-Tbilisi-Jeyhan (BTJ or BTC) oil pipeline began operation at the Sangachal Oil Terminal in Baku. It is the second-longest oil pipeline in the world after Russia's Druzhba.

2006   **September:** Russia exerted nationalistic pressures on multinational oil companies—Shell, Exxon, and ConocoPhillips.
December 18: Statoil and Norsk Hydro merged to create a $92.3 billion enterprise.
December 22: Gazprom bought half of the Sakhalin-2 project from Shell and partners for $7.45 billion, part of continuing Russian efforts to have more control over their industry.

2007   **March 27:** Venezuela finalized deal with China National Petroleum Corp. to export more oil to China instead of to the United States.
May 1: Venezuela nationalized part of oil industry by taking over operating control of oil fields operated by ConocoPhillips, Chevron, ExxonMobil, BP, Statoil, and Total.

2008   **July 11:** Crude oil hit a record high of more than $147.27 per barrel on continued concern over supplies and the weak U.S. dollar.
November 18: Saudi supertanker hijacked off Somalia.

2010   **April 20:** Deepwater Horizon rig explosion and fire occurred while drilling BP's Macondo exploration well in the Gulf of Mexico; eleven workers were killed and there was concern about a major environmental catastrophe along the Gulf Coast.

The chronology is adapted from www.geohelp.net/world.html.

Chronology of Spills

The following list includes major oil spills since 1967.

1967   **March 18, Cornwall, England:** *Torrey Canyon* ran aground, spilling 38 million gallons of crude oil off the Scilly Islands.

1976   **December 15, Buzzards Bay, Massachusetts:** *Argo Merchant* ran aground and broke apart southeast of Nantucket Island, spilling its entire cargo of 7.7 million gallons of fuel oil.

1977   **April, North Sea:** Blowout of well in Ekofisk oil field leaked 81 million gallons.

1978   **March 16, off Portsall, France:** Wrecked supertanker *Amoco Cadiz* spilled 68 million gallons, causing widespread environmental damage over one hundred miles of the Brittany coast.

1979   **June 3, Gulf of Mexico:** Exploratory oil well Ixtoc 1 blew out, spilling an estimated 140 million gallons of crude oil into the open sea.
July 19, Tobago: The *Atlantic Empress* and the *Aegean Captain* collided, spilling 46 million gallons of crude. While being towed, the *Atlantic Empress* spilled an additional 41 million gallons off Barbados on August 2.

1980   **March 30, Stavanger, Norway:** A floating hotel in the North Sea collapsed, killing 123 oil workers.

1983   **February 4, Persian Gulf, Iran:** Nowruz Field platform spilled 80 million gallons of oil.
August 6, Cape Town, South Africa: The Spanish tanker *Castillo de Bellver* caught fire, spilling 78 million gallons of oil off the coast.

1988   **July 6, North Sea off Scotland:** An explosion and fire killed 166 workers on Occidental Petroleum's *Piper Alpha* rig in the North Sea; there were 64 survivors. It was the world's worst offshore oil disaster.

November 10, Saint John's, Newfoundland: *Odyssey* spilled 43 million gallons of oil.

1989   **March 24, Prince William Sound, Alaska:** The tanker *Exxon Valdez* hit an undersea reef and spilled more than 10 million gallons of oil into the water, causing the worst oil spill in U.S. history.

December 19, off Las Palmas, the Canary Islands: An explosion in an Iranian supertanker, the *Kharg-5*, caused 19 million gallons of crude oil to spill into the Atlantic Ocean about four hundred miles north of Las Palmas, forming an oil slick covering one hundred square miles.

1990   **June 8, off Galveston, Texas:** *Mega Borg* released 5.1 million gallons of oil some sixty nautical miles south-southeast of Galveston as a result of an explosion and subsequent fire in the pump room.

1991   **January 23–27, southern Kuwait:** During the Persian Gulf War, Iraq deliberately released between 240 and 460 million gallons of crude oil into the Persian Gulf from tankers ten miles off Kuwait. The spill had little military significance. On January 27, U.S. warplanes bombed pipe systems to stop the flow of oil.

April 11, Genoa, Italy: *Haven* spilled 42 million gallons of oil in Genoa port.

May 28, Angola: *ABT Summer* exploded and leaked 15 million to 78 million gallons of oil off the coast of Angola.

1992   **March 2, Fergana Valley, Uzbekistan:** An oil well spilled 88 million gallons of oil.

1993   **August 10, Tampa Bay, Florida:** Three ships collided: the barge *Bouchard B155*, the freighter *Balsa 37*, and the barge *Ocean 255*. The *Bouchard* spilled an estimated 336,000 gallons of No. 6 fuel oil into Tampa Bay.

1994   **September 8, Russia:** A dam built to contain oil burst and spilled oil into a Kolva River tributary. The U.S. Energy Department estimated the spill at 2 million barrels. The Russian state-owned oil company claimed that the spill was only 102,000 barrels.

1996   **February 15, off the Welsh coast:** The supertanker *Sea Empress* ran aground at port of Milford Haven, Wales; spewed out 70,000 tons of crude oil; and created a twenty-five-mile slick.

1999   **December 12, French Atlantic coast:** Maltese-registered tanker *Erika* broke apart and sank off Brittany, spilling 3 million gallons of heavy oil into the sea.

2000   **January 18, off Rio de Janeiro:** A ruptured pipeline owned by the government oil company, Petrobras, spewed 343,200 gallons of heavy oil into Guanabara Bay.

November 28, Mississippi River south of New Orleans: The oil tanker *Westchester* lost power and ran aground near Port Sulphur, Louisiana, dumping 567,000 gallons of crude oil into the lower Mississippi River. The spill was largest in U.S. waters since the *Exxon Valdez* disaster in March 1989.

2002   **November 13, Spain:** *Prestige* suffered a damaged hull and was towed to sea and sank. Much of the 20 million gallons of oil remains underwater.

2003   **July 28, Pakistan:** The *Tasman Spirit*, a tanker, ran aground near the Karachi port and eventually cracked into two pieces. One of its four oil tanks burst open, leaking 28,000 tons of crude oil into the sea.

2004   **December 7, Unalaska, Aleutian Islands, Alaska:** A major storm pushed the MV *Selendang Ayu* up onto a rocky shore, breaking it in two. Most of the 337,000 gallons of oil that were released were driven onto the shoreline of Makushin and Skan Bays.

2005   **August and September, New Orleans, Louisiana:** The Coast Guard estimated that more than 7 million gallons of oil were spilled during Hurricane Katrina from various sources, including pipelines, storage tanks, and industrial plants.

2006   **June 19, Calcasieu River, Louisiana:** An estimated 71,000 barrels of waste oil were released from a tank at the CITGO Refinery on the Calcasieu River during a violent rainstorm.
            July 15, Beirut, Lebanon: The Israeli navy bomb the Jieh coast power station, and between 3 million and 10 million gallons of oil leak into the sea, affecting nearly one hundred miles of coastline.
            August 11, Guimaras Island, Philippines: A tanker carrying 530,000 gallons of oil sank off the coast of the Philippines, putting the country's fishing and tourism industries at great risk.

2007   **December 7, South Korea:** An oil spill caused environmental disaster, destroying beaches, coating birds and oysters with oil, and driving away tourists with its stench. The *Hebei Spirit* collided with a steel wire connecting a tugboat and barge five miles off South Korea's west coast, spilling 2.8 million gallons of crude oil.

2008   **July 25, New Orleans, Louisiana:** A sixty-one-foot barge, carrying 419,000 gallons of heavy fuel, collided with a six-hundred-foot tanker ship in the Mississippi River near New Orleans. Hundreds of thousands of gallons of fuel leaked from the barge, causing a halt to all river traffic while cleanup efforts commenced to limit the environmental fallout on local wildlife.

2009   **March 11, Queensland, Australia:** During Cyclone Hamish, unsecured cargo aboard the container ship MV *Pacific Adventurer* came loose on deck and caused the release of 52,000 gallons of heavy fuel and 620 tons of ammonium nitrate, a fertilizer, into the Coral Sea. About sixty kilometers of the Sunshine Coast were covered in oil, prompting the closure of half of the area's beaches.

2010   **January 23, Port Arthur, Texas:** The oil tanker *Eagle Otome* and a barge collided in the Sabine-Neches Waterway, causing the release of about 462,000 gallons of crude oil. Environmental damage was minimal as about 46,000 gallons were recovered and 175,000 gallons were dispersed or evaporated, according to the U.S. Coast Guard.

April 24, Gulf of Mexico: The *Deepwater Horizon,* a semisubmersible drilling rig, sank on April 22 after an April 20 explosion on the vessel. Eleven people died in the blast. When the rig sank, the riser—the five-thousand-foot-long pipe that connects the wellhead to the rig—became detached and began leaking oil. In addition, U.S. Coast Guard investigators discovered a leak in the wellhead itself. As much as 60,000 barrels of oil per day were leaking into the water, threatening wildlife along the Louisiana coast. Oil reached the Louisiana shore on April 30, affecting about 125 miles of coast. By early June, oil had also reached Florida, Alabama, and Mississippi. It was the largest oil spill in U.S. history.

Timeline of oil spills adapted from "Oil Spills and Disasters," Infoplease .com, www.infoplease.com/ipa/A0001451.html#ixzz1Vzdncj9i.

Notes

PROLOGUE

1. "US General: Afghan Civilians Wounded at Bomb Site," *Associated Press*, September 6, 2009.

2. When he wrote "The Tragedy of the Commons" in 1968, ecologist Garrett Hardin was not speaking of oil; however, he was using the original Greek meaning of the term "tragedy" that applies very effectively to the reality of our relationship with crude. Garrett Hardin, "The Tragedy of the Commons," *Science* 162 (1968): 1243–48.

3. U.S. Energy Information Administration, *Annual Energy Review 2009:* Petroleum, Figure 5.1. Available at 205.254.135.24/totalenergy/data/annual/index.cfm.

INTRODUCTION: BEGINNING AS BLACK GOO

1. Alfred Crosby, *Children of the Sun: A History of Mankind's Unappeasable Appetite for Energy* (New York: Norton, 2006), 60–62.

2. Sonia Shah, *Crude: The Story of Oil* (New York: Seven Stories Press, 2004), xiii.

3. Shah, *Crude*, xv.

4. Shah, *Crude*, xvi.

5. Shah, *Crude*, 59.

6. Shah, *Crude*, 110.

7. John R. McNeill, *Something New under the Sun: An Environmental History of the Twentieth-Century World* (New York: Norton, 2000), 298.

8. Robert Marks, *Origins of the Modern World: A Global and Ecological Narrative*, 2nd ed. (Lanham, Md.: Rowman and Littlefield, 2007), 2–6.

9. McNeill, *Something New under the Sun*, 10.

10. McNeill, *Something New under the Sun*, 14–55.

11. McNeill, *Something New under the Sun*, 14–15.

CHAPTER 1. FROM BLACK GOO TO BLACK GOLD

1. Karen A. Selsor et al., "Late Prehistoric Petroleum Collection in Pennsylvania," *American Antiquity* 65, no. 4 (Oct. 2000): 780–81.

2. Selsor et al., "Late Prehistoric Petroleum," 782–83.

3. Sonia Shah, *Crude: The Story of Oil* (New York: Seven Stories Press, 2004), xxi.

4. R. J. Forbes, *Studies in Early Petroleum History*, vol. 1 (Westport, CT: Hyperion, 1958), 6–8.

5. Forbes, *Studies in Early Petroleum*, 1:28–30.

6. Forbes, *Studies in Early Petroleum*, 1:9.

7. J. H. Thomson and Sir Boverton Redwood, *Handbook on Petroleum for Inspectors under the Petroleum Acts* (London: Charles Griffin, 1901), 5–6.

8. Forbes, *Studies in Early Petroleum*, 1:46.

9. Georgius Agricola, *The Textbook of Minerology* (Basel, 1546), 73.

10. Carl J. Wendt and Ann Cyphers, "How the Olmec Used Bitumen in Ancient Mesoamerica," *Journal of Anthropological Archaeology* 27, no. 2 (2008): 175–91.

11. David T. Day, *A Handbook of the Petroleum Industry* (New York: John Wiley & Sons, 1922), online at www.archive.org/stream/handbookofpetrol01dayduoft/handbookofpetrol01dayduoft_djvu.txt.

12. Brian Black, *Petrolia: The Landscape of America's First Oil Boom* (Baltimore: Johns Hopkins University Press, 2003), 23.

13. Black, *Petrolia,* 40–45.

14. Paul Lucier, *Scientists and Swindlers: Consulting on Oil and Coal in America, 1820–1890* (Baltimore: Johns Hopkins University Press, 2009), 146.

15. Lucier, *Scientists and Swindlers*, 151.

16. Lucier, *Scientists and Swindlers*, 152.

17. Lucier, *Scientists and Swindlers*, 185.

18. Lucier, *Scientists and Swindlers*, 200.

19. Lucier, *Scientists and Swindlers*, 211.

20. Lance E. Davis, Robert E. Gallman, and Karin Gleiter, *In Pursuit of Leviathan: Technology, Institutions, Productivity, and Profits in American Whaling, 1816–1906* (Chicago: University of Chicago Press, 1997), 29–31.

21. Elmo Hohman, *The American Whaleman: A Study of Life and Labor in the Whaling Industry* (Clifton, N.J.: Augustus M. Kelley Publisher, 1972), 234.

22. John Bockstoce, *Whales, Ice, and Men: The History of Whaling in the Western Arctic* (Seattle: University of Washington Press, 1995), 125. Bockstoce uses Waddell's personal journal and *Shenandoah*'s log to re-create this series of events.

23. The final chapter in this episode played out when the United States claimed that the total cost of the ships destroyed by *Shenandoah* was $14 million and that Britain should be held responsible because of its involvement in the construction and launch of the Confederate vessels. An international tribunal agreed and awarded recompense of $15.5 million in gold. Paul H. Giddens, "Derricks and Sabers," *Petroleum Today,* Summer 1961, 12–13.

24. Harold Williamson, Arnold Daum et al., *The American Petroleum Industry*, vol. 1 (Evanston, Ill.: Northwestern University Press, 1963), 89–92.

25. *Oil City Register*, November 24, 1864.

26. Lease, Thomas Holmden to James Faulkner Jr., Venango County Deed Book Z, 19, recorded May 2, 1864.

27. *Titusville Morning Herald*, August 16, 1864; *Pithole City Directory*, 1865–1866, 6.

28. Paul Sabin, *Crude Politics: The California Oil Market, 1900–1940* (Berkeley: University of California Press, 2005), 2.

29. Sabin, *Crude Politics,* 18.

30. Judith Walker Linsley, Ellen Walker Rienstra, and Jo Ann Stiles, *Giant under the Hill: A History of the Spindletop Oil Discovery at Beaumont, Texas, in 1901* (Austin: Texas State Historical Society, 2002), 73.

31. Linsley et al., *Giant under the Hill*, 114.

CHAPTER 2. CROSSING BORDERS TO INCREASE SUPPLY

1. Ron Chernow, *Titan: The Life of John D. Rockefeller, Sr.* (New York: Random House, 1998), 130.

2. Chernow, *Titan*, 132.

3. Chernow, *Titan*, 137.

4. Daniel Yergin, *The Prize: The Epic Quest for Oil, Money, and Power* (New York: Free Press, 1993), 117–19.

5. Yergin, *The Prize*, 56.

6. Steve LeVine, *The Oil and the Glory: The Pursuit of Empire and Fortune on the Caspian Sea* (New York: Random House, 2007), ix.

7. LeVine, *The Oil and the Glory*, 16–24.

8. LeVine, *The Oil and the Glory,* 68.

9. LeVine, *The Oil and the Glory*, 122–23.

10. Arash Khazeni, *Tribes and Empire on the Margins of Nineteenth-Century Iran* (Seattle: University of Washington Press, 2009), 112.

11. William Engdahl, *A Century of War: Anglo-American Oil Politics and the New World Order* (London: Pluto Press, 2004), 23–27.

12. Engdahl, *A Century of War*, 38–42.

13. John D. Grace, *Russian Oil Supply: Performance and Prospects* (London: Oxford University Press, 2005), 6.

14. LeVine, *The Oil and the Glory*, 19.

15. LeVine, *The Oil and the Glory*, 30.

16. Although its two million barrels provided only a modest footnote to U.S. and Russian production (185 and 65 million barrels respectively).

17. Alison Frank, *Oil Empire: Visions of Prosperity in Austrian Galicia* (Cambridge: Harvard University Press, 2005), 152.

18. Frank, *Oil Empire*, 18.

19. Frank, *Oil Empire*, 174.

20. Frank, *Oil Empire*, 21.

21. Engdahl, *A Century of War,* 38.

22. Myrna Santiago, *The Ecology of Oil: Environment, Labor, and the Mexican Revolution, 1900–1938* (New York: Cambridge University Press, 2006), 7.

23. Santiago, *The Ecology of Oil*, 8.

24. Yergin, *The Prize*, 150. See also John H. Maurer, "Fuel and the Battle Fleet," *Naval War College Review* 34 (November–December 1981): 60–77.

25. Santiago, *The Ecology of Oil*, 156.

26. Santiago, *The Ecology of Oil*, 163.

27. Peter Shulman, "Science Can Never Demobilize," *History and Technology* 19, no. 4 (2003): 371.

28. Shulman, "Science Can Never Demobilize," 371.

29. Shulman, "Science Can Never Demobilize," 372.

30. Shulman, "Science Can Never Demobilize," 375.

31. Shulman, "Science Can Never Demobilize," 375.

32. Winston Churchill, House of Commons, June 17, 1914.

33. John Ise, *The United States Oil Policy* (New Haven, Conn.: Yale University Press, 1926), 489–90.

CHAPTER 3. MODELING BIG OIL

1. Judith Walker Linsley, Ellen Walker Rienstra, and Jo Ann Stiles, *Giant under the Hill: A History of the Spindletop Oil Discovery at Beaumont, Texas, in 1901* (Austin: Texas State Historical Society, 2002), 162.

2. Roger M. Olien and Diana Davids Olien, *Oil and Ideology: The Cultural Creation of the American Petroleum Industry* (Chapel Hill: University of North Carolina Press, 1999), 4.

3. For Lloyd, railroads were the original exploiters, and petroleum interests such as Standard had exploited them further. He writes: "It is the railroads that have bred the millionaires who are now buying newspapers, and getting up corners in wheat, corn, and cotton, and are making railroad consolidations that stretch across the continent." Olien and Olien, *Oil and Ideology*, 67.

4. Olien and Olien, *Oil and Ideology*, 92–97.

5. Daniel Yergin, *The Prize: The Epic Quest for Oil, Money, and Power* (New York: Free Press, 1993), 104–8; Ron Chernow, *Titan: The Life of John D. Rockefeller, Sr.* (New York: Random House, 1998), 440–45.

6. Chernow, *Titan*, 451.

7. Olien and Olien, *Oil and Ideology*, 92–97.

8. Chernow, *Titan*, 112.

9. Chernow, *Titan*, 112.

10. David S. Painter, *Oil and the American Century* (Baltimore: Johns Hopkins University Press, 1986), 3.

11. Yergin, *The Prize*, 238.

12. Yergin, *The Prize*, 239–40.

13. Leonardo Maugeri, *The Age of Oil: The Mythology, History, and Future of the World's Most Controversial Resource* (New York: Praeger, 2006), 24.

14. Maugeri, *The Age of Oil*, 25.

15. Maugeri, *The Age of Oil*, 25.

16. Maugeri, *The Age of Oil*, 41–42.

17. Maugeri, *The Age of Oil*, 43.

18. Maugeri, *The Age of Oil*, 45.

19. Olien and Olien, *Oil and Ideology*, 119–27.

20. Maugeri, *The Age of Oil*, 45.

21. Myrna Santiago, *The Ecology of Oil: Environment, Labor, and the Mexican Revolution, 1900–1938* (New York: Cambridge University Press, 2006), 149.

22. Santiago, *The Ecology of Oil*, 150–51.

23. Santiago, *The Ecology of Oil*, 153.

24. Santiago, *The Ecology of Oil*, 162.

25. Santiago, *The Ecology of Oil*, 161.

26. Yergin, *The Prize*, 156.

27. Robert Vitalis, *America's Kingdom: Mythmaking on the Saudi Oil Frontier* (Stanford, Calif.: Stanford University Press, 2007), 55.

28. Vitalis, *America's Kingdom*, 60.

29. Vitalis, *America's Kingdom*, 60.

30. Vitalis, *America's Kingdom*, 94–95.

31. Vitalis, *America's Kingdom*, 266–68.

32. Alexis Madrigal, "The Legend of Coal Oil Johnny, America's Great Forgotten Parable," *Atlantic*, October 18, 2010, at www.theatlantic.com/technology/archive/2010/10/the-legend-of-coal-oil-johnny-americas-great-forgotten-parable/64475/.

33. *Beverly Hillbillies*.

CHAPTER 4. THE CULTURE OF PETROLEUM: HITTING THE ROAD

1. J. B. Jackson, *Discovering the Vernacular Landscape* (New Haven, Conn.: Yale University Press, 1988), 22.

2. Edwin Black, *Internal Combustion: How Corporations and Governments Addicted the World to Oil and Derailed the Alternatives* (New York: St. Martin's Press, 2006), 37.

3. Clay McShane and Joel Tarr, *The Horse in the City: Living Machines in the Nineteenth Century* (Baltimore: Johns Hopkins University Press, 2009), 35.

4. McShane and Tarr, *The Horse in the City*, 35.

5. Black, *Internal Combustion*, 39.

6. McShane and Tarr, *The Horse in the City*, 15–16.

7. Rudi Volti, *Cars and Culture: The Life Story of a Technology* (Baltimore: Johns Hopkins University Press, 2004), 19.

8. Black, *Internal Combustion*, 40–46.

9. Black, *Internal Combustion*, 51.

10. Black, *Internal Combustion*, 51–52.

11. David A. Kirsch, *The Electric Vehicle and the Burden of History* (New Brunswick, N.J.: Rutgers University Press, 2000), 65.

12. Kirsch, *The Electric Vehicle and the Burden of History*, 73.

13. Kirsch, *The Electric Vehicle and the Burden of History*, 75.

14. Kirsch, *The Electric Vehicle and the Burden of History*, 82.

15. James J. Flink, *Automobile Age* (Cambridge, Mass.: MIT Press, 1990), 11.

16. Flink, *Automobile Age*, 19.

17. Black, *Internal Combustion*, 64.

18. Black, *Internal Combustion*, 65.

19. Black, *Internal Combustion*, 84.

20. Black, *Internal Combustion*, 99.

21. Douglas Brinkley, *Wheels for the World: Henry Ford, His Company, and a Century of Progress* (New York: Viking, 2003), 83–87.

22. Black, *Internal Combustion*, 105.

23. Black, *Internal Combustion*, 107–8.

24. Tom McCarthy, *Auto Mania: Cars, Consumers, and the Environment* (New Haven, Conn.: Yale University Press, 2007), 34. "Of the first million Model Ts that Ford sold, 64 percent went to the farm and small town market" (37).

25. McCarthy, *Auto Mania*, 38–39.

26. Daniel Yergin, *The Prize: The Epic Quest for Oil, Money, and Power* (New York: Free Press, 1993), 80.

27. Jane Holtz Kay, *Asphalt Nation: How the Automobile Took Over America and How We Can Take It Back* (Berkeley: University of California Press, 1997), 154–58.

28. Black, *Internal Combustion*, 105.

29. Thomas P. Hughes, *American Genesis: A Century of Invention and Technological Enthusiasm* (New York: Penguin, 1989), 33–36.

30. Kirsch, *The Electric Vehicle and the Burden of History*, 148.

31. Kirsch, *The Electric Vehicle and the Burden of History*, 134.

32. Black, *Internal Combustion*, 130.

33. Black, *Internal Combustion*, 131.

34. Black, *Internal Combustion*, 136.

35. Black, *Internal Combustion*, 140.

36. Black, *Internal Combustion*, 148.

37. *Wall Street Journal,* May 27, 1914, from Black, *Internal Combustion*, 156.

38. Flink, *Automobile Age*, 25.

39. Volti, *Cars and Culture*, 30.

40. Volti, *Cars and Culture*, 30.

41. Jan Whitaker, *Tea at the Blue Lantern Inn: A Social History of the Tea Room Craze in America* (New York: St. Martin's Press, 2002), 18.

42. McCarthy, *Auto Mania*, 47.

CHAPTER 5. MARCHING FOR PETROLEUM: SUPPLY AND WEAPONS

1. Heniz Guderian, *Blitzkrieg: In Their Own Words* (St Paul, Minn.: Zenith Books, 2005), 76–77.
2. Guderian, *Blitzkrieg: In Their Own Words*, 138.
3. Guderian, *Blitzkrieg: In Their Own Words*, 171–73.
4. Rudi Volti, *Cars and Culture: The Life Story of a Technology* (Baltimore: Johns Hopkins University Press, 2004), 44.
5. David A. Kirsch, *The Electric Vehicle and the Burden of History* (New Brunswick, N.J.: Rutgers University Press, 2000), 162–64.
6. Volti, *Cars and Culture*, 46.
7. Kirsch, *The Electric Vehicle and the Burden of History*, 165.
8. Daniel Yergin, *The Prize: The Epic Quest for Oil, Money, and Power* (New York: Free Press, 1993), 104–8; Ron Chernow, *Titan: The Life of John D. Rockefeller, Sr.* (New York: Random House, 1998), 168.
9. Yergin, *The Prize*, 170–72.
10. Yergin, *The Prize*, 172.
11. Yergin, *The Prize*, 177.
12. Alfred E. Eckes Jr., *The United States and the Global Struggle for Minerals* (Austin: University of Texas Press, 1979), 10–11.
13. Yergin, *The Prize*, 207–8.
14. David S. Painter, *Oil and the American Century* (Baltimore: Johns Hopkins University Press, 1986), 183.
15. Yergin, *The Prize*, 182.
16. Painter, *Oil and the American Century*, 183.
17. Painter writes: "Red Line Agreement was to ensure that the development of the region's oil took place in a cooperative, rather than a competitive manner." The organization changed its name in 1929 to the Iraq Petroleum Company. Each organization was a British corporation and its legal provisions enforceable in British courts. Painter, *Oil and the American Century*, 5.
18. Eckes, *The United States and the Global Struggle for Minerals*, 58.
19. Painter, *Oil and the American Century*, 9.
20. Painter, *Oil and the American Century*, 9.
21. Yergin, *The Prize*, 380.
22. Yergin, *The Prize*, 382.
23. Yergin, *The Prize*, 343.
24. Yergin, *The Prize*, 382.
25. Painter, *Oil and the American Century*, 34.
26. Yergin, *The Prize*, 387.
27. Grace, *Russian Oil Supply*, 280.
28. Grace, *Russian Oil Supply*, 281.
29. Painter, *Oil and the American Century*, 11.

30. Yergin, *The Prize*, 395.

31. Yergin, *The Prize*, 401.

32. Painter, *Oil and the American Century*, 17.

33. Painter, *Oil and the American Century*, 35.

34. Yergin, *The Prize*, 423.

35. Painter, *Oil and the American Century*, 46–47.

36. Yergin, *The Prize*, 427–28.

37. Grace, *Russian Oil Supply*, 287.

38. Todor Balabanov and Raimund Dietz, "Eastern and East West Energy Prospects," in *Dismantling the Command Economy in Eastern Europe*, ed. Peter Havlik (Boulder, Colo.: Westview Press, 1991), 125, 137.

39. Yergin, *The Prize*, 430.

CHAPTER 6. CONSUMING CULTURES

1. William Bogard, *The Bhopal Tragedy: Language, Logic, and Politics in the Production of a Hazard* (Boulder, Colo.: Westview Press, 1989), ix.

2. E. L. Doctorow, *World's Fair* (New York: Random House, 1985), 252–53.

3. Shane Hamilton, *Trucking Country: The Road to America's Wal-Mart Economy* (Princeton, N.J.: Princeton University Press, 2008), 100–101.

4. Hamilton, *Trucking Country*, 115.

5. For more information, see U.S. Centennial of Flight Commission, "Air Travel: Its Impact on the Way We Live and the Way We See Ourselves," at www.centennial offlight.gov/essay/Social/impact/SH3.htm.

6. Christian Anton Smedshaug, *Feeding the World in the 21st Century: A Historical Analysis of Agriculture and Society* (London: Anthem Press, 2010), 49–50.

7. Smedshaug, *Feeding the World*, 180–81.

8. See, for instance, Richard Tucker, *Insatiable Appetite: The United States and the Ecological Degradation of the Tropical World* (New York: Rowman and Littlefield, 2007).

9. See Donald Worster, *Dust Bowl: The Southern Plains in the 1930s* (New York: Oxford University Press, 2010), and David R. Montgomery, *Dirt: The Erosion of Civilizations* (Berkeley: University of California Press, 2007), 150–52.

10. Smedshaug, *Feeding the World*, 221.

11. Michael Pollan, *Omnivore's Dilemma: A Natural History of Four Meals* (New York: Penguin, 2006), 44.

12. Pollan, *Omnivore's Dilemma*, 45.

13. James McCann, *Maize and Grace: Africa's Encounter with a New World Crop, 1500–2000* (Cambridge: Harvard University Press, 2007).

14. Smedshaug, *Feeding the World*, 221.

15. Montgomery, *Dirt*, 197.

16. Evan D. G. Fraser and Andrew Rimas, *Empires of Food: Feast, Famine, and the Rise and Fall of Civilizations* (New York: Free Press, 2010), 248–49.

17. Montgomery, *Dirt*, 199–200.

18. Jeff Meikle, *American Plastic: A Cultural History* (New Brunswick, N.J.: Rutgers University Press, 1995), 78.

19. Devra Davis, *When Smoke Ran Like Water: Tales of Environmental Deception and the Battle against Pollution* (New York: Basic Books, 2002), 250.

20. J. Benach et al., "The Geography of the Highest Mortality Areas in Spain: A Striking Cluster in the Southwestern Region of the Country," *Occupational and Environmental Medicine* 61 (2004): 280–81.

21. Information from Environmental Safety Group, "CEPSA Oil and Health in the Campo de Gibraltar," at www.esg-gib.net/cepsa-oil-and-health-in-the-campo-de -gibraltar/.

22. Information from Environmental Safety Group, "CEPSA Oil and Health in the Campo de Gibraltar," at www.esg-gib.net/cepsa-oil-and-health-in-the-campo-de -gibraltar/.

23. Ike Sriskandarajah, "Human Rights in 'Cancer Alley,'" Public Radio International, April 26, 2010, at www.pri.org/science/environment/human-rights-in-cancer -alley1965.html.

24. Sergei Blagov, "Russia Wary of Trans-border Pollution from China," Ohmy News, May 6, 2006, at english.ohmynews.com/articleview/article_view.asp?at_ code=328776.

25. Peter Maass, *Crude World: The Violent Twilight of Oil* (New York: Vintage Books, 2009), 93–98.

26. Duncan Clarke, *Crude Continent: The Struggle for Africa's Oil Prize* (London: Profile Books, 2008), 524–27. Also Rajen Harshe, "Politics of Giant Oil Firms," *Economic and Political Weekly* 38, no. 2 (January 11–17, 2003): 113–17.

27. Ike Okonta and Oronto Douglas, *Where Vultures Feast: Shell, Human Rights and Oil* (San Francisco: Sierra Club Books, 2001), 157–60.

28. Field Reports, "Knee Deep in Crude," Environmental Rights Action, www .eraction.org/.

29. Field Reports, "Knee Deep in Crude."

30. Edward Harris, "Sorrows Still Spring from Nigeria's First Oil Well," *Seattle Times*, July 6, 2008.

31. Maass, *Crude World*, 58–60.

32. Quoted from Roger M. Olien and Diana Davids Olien, *Oil and Ideology: The Cultural Creation of the American Petroleum Industry* (Chapel Hill: University of North Carolina Press, 1999), 172.

33. Donovan Hohn, *Moby-Duck* (New York: Viking, 2011), 10.

34. Hohn, *Moby-Duck*, 215.

35. Jeremy Rifken, *The Hydrogen Economy* (New York: Penguin, 2002), 23.

36. Giles Slade, *Made to Break* (Cambridge: Harvard University Press, 2006), 3–4. "Planned obsolescence is the catch-all phrase used to describe the assortment of techniques used to artificially limit the durability of a manufactured good in order to stimulate repetitive consumption."

CHAPTER 7. TO HAVE AND HAVE NOT

1. Michael Klare, *Blood and Oil: The Dangers and Consequences of America's Growing Dependency on Imported Petroleum* (New York: Metropolitan Books, 2004), 9.

2. Mary Kaldor, Terry Lynn Karl, and Yahia Said, eds., *Oil Wars* (London: Pluto Press, 2007), 2–4.

3. Peter Maass, *Crude World: The Violent Twilight of Oil* (New York: Vintage Books, 2009), 3.

4. Anthony Garavente, "U.S. Companies Race to Take Advantage of Iraqi Oil Bonanza," *New York Times*, January 14, 2010.

5. Christian Anton Smedshaug, *Feeding the World in the 21st Century: A Historical Analysis of Agriculture and Society* (London: Anthem Press, 2010), 35.

6. Daniel Yergin, *The Prize: The Epic Quest for Oil, Money, and Power* (New York: Free Press, 1993), 612.

7. Although Mexico wrestled control of its oil industry from foreigners in 1938, it quickly receded from the lucrative international market due to insufficient capital for investment. Other nations also attempted to set up their own arrangements for oil development, including Venezuela, which in 1943 signed the first "fifty-fifty principle" agreement that provided oil producers with a lump sum royalty plus a fifty-fifty split of profits, and Iran, which passed a law demanding the termination of previous agreements with Anglo-Iran (referred to as Anglo-Persian prior to 1935 and British Petroleum after 1954) and then nationalized its oil operations in May 1951 when such an agreement failed to occur. (A new British-Iranian agreement was signed the following year. The newly restored Shah of Iran became a pillar of American Middle East policy until the Iranian Revolution in 1979.)

8. See Fiona Venn, *The Oil Crisis* (London: Longman, 2002), and Raymond Vernon, ed., *The Oil Crisis* (New York: W. W. Norton, 1976).

9. Ibid.

10. *New York Times*, February 5, 1974.

11. *New York Times*, January 21, 1974. See Karen R. Merrill's collection, *The Oil Crisis of 1973–1974: A Brief History with Documents* (Boston: Bedford/St. Martin's, 2007).

12. Andrew Scott Cooper, *Oil Kings: How the U.S., Iran, and Saudi Arabia Changed the Balance of Power in the Middle East* (New York: Simon and Schuster, 2011), 163.

13. Amory Lovins, *Soft Energy Paths: Towards a Durable Peace* (New York: Friends of the Eath International, 1977), 121–22.

14. Daniel Horowitz, *Jimmy Carter and the Energy Crisis of the 1970s* (Boston: Bedford Books, 2005), 20–25.

15. Horowitz, *Jimmy Carter and the Energy Crisis of the 1970s*, 43–46.

16. For more information about SPR, see Bruce Beaubouef, *The Strategic Petroleum Reserve: U.S. Energy Security and Oil Politics, 1975–2005* (College Station: Texas A&M University Press, 2007).

17. Justin Blum, "Chavez Pushes Petro-Diplomacy," *Washington Post*, November 22, 2005.

18. John D. Grace, *Russian Oil Supply: Performance and Prospects* (London: Oxford University Press, 2005), 105.

19. Grace, *Russian Oil Supply*, 107.

20. Grace, *Russian Oil Supply*, 110–12.

21. Maass, *Crude World*, 29–31.

22. Maass, *Crude World*, 40–42.

23. Maass, *Crude World*, 49–50.

24. Kaldor et al., *Oil Wars*, 6–8.

25. Nancy Birdsall and Arvind Subramanian, "Saving Iraq from Its Oil," *Foreign Affairs* 83, no. 4 (July–August 2004): 77.

26. See, for instance, Jim Krane, *City of Gold: Dubai and the Dream of Capitalism* (New York: St. Martin's, 2009).

CHAPTER 8. "PEAK OIL," CLIMATE CHANGE, AND PETROLEUM UNDER SIEGE

1. William Cronon, *Changes in the Land* (New York: Hill and Wang, 1991), 183.

2. Kenneth Deffeyes, *Hubbert's Peak: The Impending World Oil Shortage* (Princeton, N.J.: Princeton University Press, 2001), 4.

3. See, for instance, Jack Doyle, *Taken for a Ride: Detroit's Big Three and the Politics of Air Pollution* (New York: Four Walls Eight Windows, 2000).

4. Ross Gelbspan, *The Heat is On* (Reading, Mass.: Perseus Books, 1995), 9–13.

5. Paul Crutzen, "Geology of Mankind," *Nature* 415, no. 23 (January 3, 2002).

6. Brian Black and Gary Weisel, *Global Warming* (New York: Greenwood/ABC-Clio, 2010), 67–70.

7. Black and Weisel, *Global Warming*, 150.

8. Black and Weisel, *Global Warming*, 145.

9. Jim Motavalli, *Electric Car* (San Francisco: Sierra Club Books, 2001), 40.

10. David A. Kirsch, *The Electric Vehicle and the Burden of History* (New Brunswick, N.J.: Rutgers University Press, 2000), 205.

11. Bill Vlasic, "As Market Shifts, Ford Sees Profits Fleeing," *New York Times*, May 23, 2008, www.nytimes.com/2008/05/23/business/23ford.html.

12. David Kiley, "Ford to Build Small Fiestas in Mexico: Hatchback Coming," *Business Week*, May 30, 2008, www.businessweek.com/autos/autobeat/archives/2008/05/ford_to_build_s.html.

13. Information drawn from "GM, Ford, and Chrysler Lose to Imports in July," FQuick, August 1, 2007, www.fquick.com/blog/sort.php?keyword=honda&page=3.

14. Information drawn from Joel K. Bourne Jr., "Green Dreams: Making Fuel from Crops Could Be Good for the Planet—after a Breakthrough or Two," *National Geographic*, November 2007, at ngm.natiaonalgeographic.com/2007/10/biofuels/biofuels-text.

15. Jad Mouwad, "More Saudi Oil Goes to China than to U.S.," *New York Times*, March 20, 2010.

16. Quoted in Dadi Zhou, "The Process of Sustainable Energy Development in China," Carnegie Endowment for International Peace, August 7, 2009, www.carnegieendowment.org/publications/index.cfm?fa=view&id=23482.

17. Zhou, "Process of Sustainable Energy Development in China."

18. Paul Gregan et al. "GM's Hummer China Deal Collapses," *Financial Times*, February 23, 2010.

19. Brian Black and Richard Flarend, *Alternative Energy* (New York: Greenwood/ABC-Clio, 2010).

20. Thomas Friedman, "Making America Stupid," *New York Times*, September 14, 2008.

21. Michael Wines, "Cars Multiply, but Chinese Still Can't Find a Fast Lane," *New York Times*, December 23, 2010.

EPILOGUE: RESOURCE CURSE: TIME FOR AN OIL CHANGE?

1. Peter Maass, *Crude World: The Violent Twilight of Oil* (New York: Vintage Books, 2009), 169.

2. Maass, *Crude World*, 222.

3. Terry Lynn Karl, *Paradox of Plenty: Oil Booms and Petro-States* (Berkeley: University of California Press, 1997), 241.

4. Karl, *Paradox*, 242.

5. Information from Steve LeVine, "The Oily Subtext of South Sudanese Independence," *Foreign Policy*, January 11, 2011, at oilandglory.foreignpolicy.com/posts/2011/01/11/the_oily_subtext_of_south_sudanese_independence.

6. Tyler Priest and others, special issue *Journal of American History*, "Oil in American Life," Spring 2012.

Index

Note: Page numbers of figures (tables, charts, etc.) are *italicized.*

About the Author

Brian C. Black, professor of history and environmental studies at Penn State Altoona, is the author or editor of several books, including the award-winning *Petrolia: The Landscape of America's First Oil Boom*. His articles appear in *OnEarth* magazine, *USA Today*, *Junior Scholastic*, and the *Christian Science Monitor*, as well as scholarly journals. A specialist in the environmental history of North America, Black specifically studies humans' changing ideas of energy. Residing in the energy landscape of central Pennsylvania, Black has seen the ridge and valley section gutted for coal, capped with wind turbines, and now fracked for natural gas. Petroleum, though, makes for the most compelling story of all.